Lois Hole's

Northern Flower Gardening

Bedding Plants

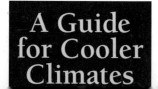

A Guide
for Cooler
Climates

Northern Flower Gardening
Bedding Plants

By Lois Hole
with Jill Fallis

Photography by Akemi Matsubuchi

Best Wishes
Lois H.

LONE
PINE

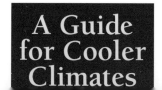
A Guide
for Cooler
Climates

The Publisher

Lone Pine Publishing	Lone Pine Publishing	Lone Pine Publishing
206, 10426–81 Avenue	202A–1110 Seymour Street	16149 Redmond Way, #108
Edmonton, Alberta	Vancouver, British Columbia	Redmond, Washington 98052
Canada T6E 1X5	Canada V6B 3N3	USA

Canadian Cataloguing in Publication Data
Hole, Lois, 1933–
    Lois Hole's northern flower gardening

(Lois Hole's gardening guides)
Includes index.
ISBN 1-55105-039-0

    1. Flower gardening—Canada.   2. Bedding plants—Canada.
I. Fallis, Jill, 1960–   II. Matsubuchi, Akemi.   III. Title.
IV. Title: Northern flower gardening.   V. Series: Hole, Lois,
1933–   Lois Hole's gardening guides.

SB422.H64 1994   635.9'312'0971   C94-910330-6

Editor-in-chief: Glenn Rollans
Design and layout, cover design: Carol S. McKellar
Proof: Jennifer Keane
Photography, including cover: Akemi Matsubuchi
Additional photography:
Jill Fallis   12, 13a, 18, 19a, 47a, 61, 63b, 73b, 87a, 89, 95a, 97b, 122,
        128, 137, 144, 147a, 149a, 161, 175a, 181b, 196b, 223b, 225, 253a.
Derek Fell   85a, 163, 173, 185.   Christopher Lemay   49b.
Steve Makris   5.   Mastertag   84, 85c, 184.
Pan American Seed   242.   Park Seed   139, 189.

The publisher gratefully acknowledges the assistance of Alberta
Community Development and the Department of Canadian Heritage, and
the financial support provided by the Alberta Foundation for the Arts.

This book is written for the customers who visit our greenhouses, for the guests at my gardening talks, for the readers of my columns, for novice and master gardeners and for anyone who derives pleasure from setting plants into the soil and watching them grow.

Finally, my deep appreciation goes to the skilled plant breeders who develop new varieties of flowers and make the world a more beautiful place in which to live.

DEDICATION

Putting together a book takes an immense amount of work, and it requires the involvement of many people. I have the hands-on knowledge of growing the plants, what their needs and uses are and which plants to recommend for certain situations, but that on its own is not enough to create a book. I rely on my family and the staff to provide their expertise in different areas.

Special thanks to Wayne McNamara, John Jordan and all the gardeners who invited us into their yards.

Janelle Grice, our resident expert on dried flowers, shared her knowledge on everlasting flowers and created some of the splendid bouquets that you will see in our photographs. Many of our staff grow the plants featured in this book in their own gardens at home.

The combined efforts of all these people (and the guidance of our publishers at Lone Pine) are required to create the final product. Although it is my name that appears on the cover, these are the people who deserve much of the credit.

ACKNOWLEDGEMENTS

Many of our employees contributed to this book by growing and caring for the plants that we photographed, and by sharing their knowledge of gardening.

Table of Contents

Bedding Plants

Northern Flower Gardening: Bedding Plants is your guide to growing the best of the best annual bedding plants. We have selected 92 plants that have proven their performance in northern gardens year after year, and for each we describe:

- available flower colours
- height range
- planting directions, including how and when to transplant or plant from seed, and frost tolerance
- growing needs, including recommended light levels and watering directions
- tips for growing and using the flowers.

We will show you glorious gardens, ideas for growing, strategies to make gardening easy and enjoyable, and ways to extend your garden into your home.

Northern Flower Gardening: Bedding Plants is designed to help you find success and avoid frustration in the garden. Many people have contributed their knowledge: my family, our employees, our customers, our friends, guests at my gardening talks and readers of our gardening columns. This book compiles years of experience, and it shares with you all that we have discovered about the needs of annual plants.

The Annual Flower Garden

Many splendid flower gardens contain a mixture of plant types—annuals, roses, bulbs and perennials. The wide range of plants to choose from can make it difficult to decide what to include in your garden.

We had the same difficulty deciding what to include in this book. Because there are so many choices, it would require an immense volume to properly address each one. After much discussion, the most sensible choice seemed to be to divide our advice on the flower garden into volumes by plant types. And so, in this first volume of *Northern Flower Gardening*, we discuss only annual bedding plants.

Annuals are one of my favourite categories of plants. They can almost instantly transform a

Opposite: Nigella, stocks, dahlias and mealy cup sage (Salvia farinacea) add summer splendour to a mixed flowerbed.

bare patch of soil into a glorious garden, they provide colour and beauty all summer long, and they are easy to grow.

WHAT IS AN ANNUAL BEDDING PLANT?

By strict definition, an 'annual' is a plant that completes its life cycle—from seed to bloom and back to seed—in a single season. We use 'bedding plants' as a rough synonym for 'annuals' because, especially in northern gardens, most annuals perform best if they are given a head start indoors and then transplanted to the garden once the outdoor growing season begins.

We think of annuals as plants that provide flexibility and allow you to change your landscaping ideas every year, or even in midsummer. If you paint your house, for example, or simply want a new look, you can immediately bed out annual flowers of different colours to complement or contrast.

A vivid display of colour is created by this mix of schizanthus, calendula, alyssum, kochia and annual phlox.

You can grow annuals in their own beds, or you can mix and match them with perennials, ornamental grasses and shrubbery. Some air-dry easily for everlasting arrangements, and you can bring others indoors in containers in the fall to extend the beauty of the summer garden into year-round pleasure. Most annuals can be cut by the armload for bouquets throughout the season, and many provide heady fragrances.

LEARNING THE HARD WAY

To this day, the subtle scent of a snapdragon takes me back to my mother's garden, where I spent some of the best days of my childhood summers. I remember picking snapdragons for bouquets and sneaking a few blooms from the bottoms of the stems, where they were not likely to be noticed, so that I could play with them, making each flower 'talk' by squeezing the back of the bloom so that its 'mouth' would open and shut.

My passion for growing began there, as a child in my mother's garden. That passion continues in my own family, and we have had the good fortune to transform the love of growing into a successful, family-run greenhouse business that allows us all to be involved every day in something we truly enjoy. Growing flowers is now a mainstay of our business; in a single season, we sell over 4 million annual bedding plants, perennials, shrubs and house plants.

My husband Ted and I started out as growers of fresh vegetables for farm-gate sales. Ted had a university degree in agriculture, but neither of us had a background in farming. We built our first greenhouse to grow vegetable seedlings for our own gardens, intending to gain an earlier harvest. The greenhouse was visible from the road, and people driving by began to stop to ask if they could buy these young plants.

Then and now: our first greenhouse (above) was a fairly simple affair that has grown (below) into a year-'round operation.

One year Ted started a few types of flowers—petunias, snapdragons, marigolds, pansies and dahlias—in the greenhouse, just to give our flower gardens an earlier start. We were extremely fortunate in that almost every seed germinated. There were more flowers than we could use, so we gave some away when customers bought the vegetables. The next year, people came back for the flowers, so we decided to extend our business to growing these bedding plants. We ran a small advertisement in the local newspaper and quickly sold the lot of them.

One spring, when our operation was still fairly new, the young son of a customer, a boy about four years old, tried to be especially helpful. He brought me a handful of plant tags—all carefully pulled from our packs of petunias—which labelled the flowers pink, red and white. We could no longer tell what colour the flowers would be, and we had to wait until the blooms opened or else sell them to the few customers who were not particular about colour. Luckily, petunias are one of the bedding plants that bloom early in the packs.

As with anything new, there were many times that we learned the right way to do something the hard way—by first doing it wrong.

Some annuals are less tolerant of the cool temperatures characteristic of northern gardens than others. For example, we discovered that marigolds fall into this category of tender plants after we lost a whole lot of them to an early spring frost. In the years since our marigold disaster, the whole family has spent many spring evenings outside in the dark, covering flat after flat of bedding plants. The solution to spending as few of your evenings like this as possible, which we pass on in this book, is to learn which plants are most hardy, and which need be protected when there is a risk of frost.

We hope that, with the advice in *Northern Flowering Gardening: Bedding Plants*, some of our readers will be able to avoid the hard lessons.

Coordinating the flower colours in pots and beds provides a pleasing show at Marlene Jubenville's home in Edmonton, Alberta.

Flowers enhance the everyday activities of summer life. A backyard barbecue, for example, is more pleasurable when guests can relax surrounded by the sight and scent of pretty flowers. A dinner party—for which the hostess had made an otherwise simple table glorious with a shallow bowl overflowing with fragrant, dark-purple petunias from her garden—stays in my memory as the epitome of bringing the enjoyment of a flower garden indoors.

My young grandchildren love to bring in bunches of flowers they have picked themselves, and my mother still grows a splendid garden at 87 years of age. Regardless of how simple or elaborate, any garden is a success if it brings you joy.

FLOWER GARDENING IS FOR EVERYONE

When people suggest that growing annual flowers is an expensive proposition, I often compare the amount spent on dinner at a good restaurant to the cost of planting a garden with bedding plants. Both are pleasurable experiences. A nice meal, however, lasts only a single evening while a garden is full of fragrance, colour and beauty for several months and can be enjoyed by family, friends and passers-by alike; both are about the same price.

13

This simple planting (top) provides a cheerful display of colour for months yet contains only six plants that would cost less than $20 to purchase. Matching pots of Red Madness petunias (left) set on a mulch of white rock were the innovative solution for the Hincheys of Edmonton, Alberta, who created a garden low in both maintenance and cost.

Choosing Which Annuals to Plant

What I like best about annuals is their versatility. Most can be grown in patio containers or in a variety of garden settings. Virtually all annual flowers bloom non-stop throughout the summer, which makes it unnecessary to coordinate successive blooming periods.

One of the keys to success with annuals is deciding what you want from them, and choosing the best plants for those purposes.

EXPERIMENTING WITH NEW VARIETIES

Plant breeders work constantly to make improvements on existing varieties, and seed companies introduce new developments every year. Be willing to experiment in your own garden; it will add fun to gardening and likely improve your rate of success.

We test new plant varieties each year in our show gardens.

Every year we test many new plant varieties in our own show gardens and trial beds, to ensure they will perform well in our customers' gardens. Throughout the season, in all types of weather, we grade the plants on their performance: for the number, quality and size of flowers, for their ability to ward off pests, for their performance in various weather and microclimates, and for other factors. Customers and staff alike walk among the flowers, examining the plants and making notes for their next year's gardens. Through this process, we constantly update and change our list of recommended plants and varieties.

Refer to the next section, 'Where to Plant Annual Bedding Plants,' and to the appendices on pp. 257–64 to make it easier for you to select which plants are best for your garden.

Every garden has its own microclimates— definite areas that are distinctly different from the surrounding areas. Fences, trees and tall plants can provide shelter from the wind and trap heat; low-lying areas are more often subject to early frosts than are hill-top gardens. Through experimenting in your own garden, you will discover the best locations for each plant. For example, impatiens that does not prosper in a certain area may flourish when planted only a few feet farther over in the same bed, because conditions there are just that much more to its liking.

Put bedding plants where they'll perform best. Grow plants that like heat and need little moisture in hot, dry areas, and grow plants that prefer wet conditions in low-lying, boggy parts of the garden. Refer to the plant descriptions and appendices later in this book before deciding what to plant where.

Under similar conditions of care, plants grown in shade tend to be taller and less bushy and they tend to produce fewer flowers than the same plants grown in the sun. Most shady annuals will grow reasonably well in sunny locations, but they will require more water than when planted in the shade.

Where to Plant Annual Bedding Plants

15

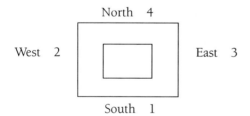 Tuck a few annual flowers into potted herb gardens or window boxes, or at the base of tomatoes, peppers or other vegetables that are growing in containers. Bright marigolds, trailing lobelia and fragrant yellow pansies add splashes of colour. The tiny faces of violas peeking out between your favourite herbs provide charm. Sweetly-scented alyssum in a hanging basket of strawberries is a nice touch, and French marigolds decorating pots of vegetables transform an otherwise utilitarian planting into a handsome display.

```
           North   4
        ┌──────────────┐
West  2 │   ┌──────┐   │  East   3
        │   │      │   │
        │   └──────┘   │
        └──────────────┘
           South   1
```

The areas are numbered 1 to 4 from sunniest to shadiest. Southern exposures receive the most sun. Shade is intensified by obstruction such as decks, fences, tall plants, trees and shrubs, which may also reduce the amount of moisture received from rainfalls. Microclimates in your yard affect how well plants grow in each location.

PLANTS FOR SHADY SPOTS

These are the plants we have found grow well in shady areas. Plants marked '*' are the best choices for very shady areas.

Rose Perron of St. Albert, Alberta, solved the problem of a shady, east-facing garden with this planting of nicotiana and fibrous begonias, along with planters of impatiens and lobelia.

*Asparagus Fern
*Begonia
Black-Eyed Susan Vine
Browallia
Coleus
*Dracaena
Dusty Miller
Fuchsia
Geranium (ivy and zonal types only)
Impatiens
*Ivy
Lobelia
Four O' Clock
Nasturtium
Nemesia
Nemophila
Nicotiana
Nierembergia
Nolana
Pansy
Petunia (double-flowering types can take more shade than others)
Salpiglossis
Salvia (*S. splendens* only; the other types need sun)
Scaevola
Schizanthus
*Spider Plant
Torenia
Viola

PLANTS FOR WET SPOTS

Low-lying, wet areas are often the most frustrating parts of the garden. In these areas, we have had success growing only three annuals: four o'clock, nolana and the pretty marsh plants known as meadow foam. Four o'clock and nolana prosper in sun or shade, but meadow foam prospers only in sun.

Some areas of the garden are extremely warm, such as those near heat-radiating brick walls or those on the sunny side of reflective surfaces, such as white stucco walls.

For these areas, choose only plants with excellent heat tolerance, such as:

Amaranthus	Ice Plant
Castor Bean	Kochia
Celosia	Lantana
Clarkia	Marigold
Cleome	Moon Vine
Cosmos	Portulaca
Datura	Statice
Dracaena	Strawflower
Gazania	Tagetes
Heliotrope	Verbena

If a sunny area of the garden is also very dry, choose plants with excellent drought tolerance. Remember that young plants must be well-watered until their root systems have developed to the point where they can sustain the plants through periods of drought. After the plants are established, you need water them only occasionally. The following plants, once established, do well in dry areas:

African Daisy	Lantana
Castor Bean	Nolana
Celosia	Poppy
Clarkia	Portulaca
Cosmos	Salvia (*S. farinacea*
Gazania	and *S. horminum*,
Gomphrena	not *S. splendens*)
Ice Plant	Scaevola
	Verbena

Hanging Baskets for Windy Locations

Many apartment dwellers face the challenge of a windy balcony added to the already challenging restrictions of limited light and space for growing.

Remember: Planters in windy areas need to be watered more often, because evaporation rates are higher. Check moisture levels once or even twice a day, especially during heat waves. Fasten each basket securely to its hook.

The following plants in hanging baskets result in splendid displays of flowers in full sun to partial shade:

Fibrous Begonia

Ivy (English, Nepeta and Vinca ivies are best)

French Marigold

Nolana

Petunia (the variety Madness because of its superior weather tolerance)

Portulaca

Scaevola

Tagetes

A Little Gardening Terminology

These fibrous begonias have been used as accent plants, to highlight a cedar.

Gardening terminology is sometimes confusing. The term 'border,' for example, may mean a bed that runs along the edge of something, such as a lawn, driveway or pathway.

At the front of this border (meaning 'flowerbed') may be a border (meaning 'edge') formed by a row of 'border plants.'

A 'border plant' is usually fairly low growing and quick spreading.

The same confusion arises with the term 'feature.' A 'feature planting' is a garden that is the focal point of a yard, while a 'feature plant' is the focus of a particular bed.

Alyssum is one of the most popular border plants. This nicotiana has been grown as a background plant.

These sweet peas have been used to create a screen.

A mixed border (flower-bed) of snapdragons and petunias with a border (edging) of alyssum.

How to Plant Annuals

Northern gardeners who live in areas with relatively short growing seasons face a challenge: few annuals grow quickly enough from seed to flower to accommodate even an early spring sowing. There are two main ways to overcome this challenge: buy bedding plants from growers who sell seedlings that are ready to bed out, or you can start your own plants indoors.

THREE WAYS TO GET STARTED

1. Start plants from seed indoors.

- This approach may save money in the long run, and it can supply you with a wide range of plants.

- This can be one of the most rewarding ways to grow when you meet with success, and one of the most frustrating when you do not.

- Most homes do not have ideal conditions for growing seedlings; some plants are so challenging to raise to the seedling stage that many retail greenhouses purchase their young plants from specialist growers.

- Starting plants from seed requires a lot of time.

2. Sow seeds directly into the garden.

- This is the cheapest way to get started.

- You need only to prepare the soil for sowing, ensure that it does not dry out while seeds are germinating and then thin the emerging seedlings.

In order to grow top-quality plants from seed indoors, you will need: seeds, potting soil, seedling trays, fertilizer, grow lights, vermiculite, fungicide and a mist bottle for watering.

- It takes longer for plants to bloom from seed than from bedding plants, and you may run out of summer before your flowers bloom.

- Your choice of plants that will grow successfully from seed in northern gardens is limited.

3. Buy established bedding plants.

- This is the simplest way to start your garden, and it provides immediate results.

- Bedding plants are convenient and relatively inexpensive, but they are more costly than seed.

- This approach usually offers the widest selection of plants; professional growers often have access to varieties which are not available as seed through retail outlets.

My mother used to start her petunias from seed indoors every year. At that time there was no other choice; the small town where we lived had no greenhouses to supply bedding plants. She grew her seedlings without all the supplies that we now recommend, so she often had low germination rates or seedlings that died before reaching maturity.

Nowadays, it is easier to meet with success in growing your own seedlings indoors, because the necessary supplies can be found almost anywhere. Here's what you need to do:

- Fill a seedling flat to within a half-inch (1 cm) of the top edge with a good quality seedling mixture (a potting soil with a high percentage of peat moss and perlite). Avoid using garden soil, because it tends to become hard and inhibits proper rooting of seedlings, and it may contain insects and disease.

- As a general rule, plant seeds no deeper than the thickness of the seed. For most plants, use three seeds per cell in the flat. Plants with very small seeds, such as alyssum and lobelia, should be planted at the rate of eight to ten seeds per cell.

- Cover the seeds with a thin layer of vermiculite to prevent drying.

- Water just enough to moisten the soil. Use a misting bottle with a very fine spray when watering, to avoid dislodging the seeds.

When buying seeds or bedding plants, keep in mind that not all mixtures are created equal. A 'formula mix' represents the packager's or grower's optimum combination, with guaranteed percentages of each colour. For example, if red is considered a favourite shade, there may be five red flowers to every white one. A 'hybrid mix,' on the other hand, is an entirely random mixture of different colours.

- For the best possible results, use a fungicide shortly after planting to prevent 'damping off' (rotting of seedlings).

- Tag each container with the date planted and the variety of seed.

- Cover the flat with a sheet of plastic wrap or a plastic dome to improve humidity (remove once seedling have fully emerged). Use grow lights to enhance germination and growth.

- Place the flat on a heated table, heat register or the top of a refrigerator. This warms the soil and promotes rapid germination. Check progress twice daily, in the morning and again at night. It is extremely important to remove flats from heat as soon as seedlings begin to emerge.

- When seedlings produce their second set of leaves, fertilize with a plant-starter fertilizer, such as 10-52-10, at one-quarter strength, once a week.

- Never allow the seedling mix to become dry. Germinating seeds are very intolerant of dry soil and will often die even if the soil becomes dry for a short time.

Annuals vary greatly in the time they take from seeding to maturity. See the descriptions of individual plants later in this book to determine how long to allow from seeding to transplanting into the garden. These descriptions also contain information on storing begonia tubers, and starting geraniums and fuchsias from cuttings.

DIRECT-SEEDING THE GARDEN

Most of the flowers I recall seeing in the gardens of the small town where I was raised are ones that were direct-seeded. Every yard had masses of poppies, rows of sunflowers and beautiful sweet peas. Back then, people had fewer options, but even now, with a wide selection of plants available, many of these flowers still rank among my favourites.

I often ask Ted to include a row or two of these flowers when he seeds our vegetable garden, especially a long row of zinnias that I

To make sowing seedling flats easier, Ted, my husband, used to shape a piece of cardboard into a funnel and tape it onto an electric razor. This simple and effective 'seeder' evenly distributes the seed and eliminates problems with handling tiny seeds.

As a general rule, small seeds are planted early and large seeds are planted late, because they sprout more quickly.

can cut by the armload for fresh bouquets throughout the summer, without disturbing the show in the flower garden.

This is our list of annuals that can be grown from seed in the garden. Some can be seeded late in the season, for mid-summer flowers. Others are tolerant of cool soil and can be sown into the garden before the last frost in spring. Refer to individual listings for details.

African Daisy

Baby's Breath

Bachelor's Button

Calendula

Canary Bird Vine

Castor Bean

Clarkia

Cosmos

Four O'Clock

Larkspur

Lavatera

Malva

Morning Glory

Nasturtium

Queen Anne's Lace

Poppy

Sunflower

Sweet Pea

Zinnia

Shirley poppies can be sown into the garden as soon as the ground is workable in spring.

One of the most exciting times in my mother's life came when we moved to Edmonton, where her choices in garden flowers suddenly increased dramatically through the availability of a wide selection of bedding plants in several greenhouses.

When shopping for bedding plants, look for those that are healthy, bushy and neither too small nor too tall. Tiny plants are difficult to handle and often do not survive being transplanted. Too much height indicates that the plants are 'overgrown' in their cells, which, curiously enough, usually means the plants will be stunted in their growth after being transplanted.

BUYING BEDDING PLANTS

When buying tall plants—those that reach a mature height of two feet (60 cm) or greater—as bedding plants, look for ones that are short and stocky. Those that are 'stretched' or already flowering are likely to suffer transplant shock and may never achieve strong, uniform growth in the garden.

Some growers do successive seedings in the greenhouse (several sowings of the same plant at different times over a period of weeks). Even if you are planting in June, you should still look for top-quality plants of an ideal age for transplanting.

BEFORE YOU PLANT

Before planting anything in the garden, you should do a couple of things to greatly improve the floral show. The first is to ensure that there is an adequate amount of topsoil. Flower beds need a minimum eight to 12 inches (20 to 30 cm) of good quality soil.

The second is to mix in some granular fertilizer or bonemeal, and also some organic matter. We get our best results by adding lots of compost mixed with peat moss to the garden each year. Organic matter acts like a sponge, improving the ability of the soil to retain water and nutrients, and resulting in impressive plant growth and vigour. Well-rotted manure is another good choice.

Before you begin planting, water the flats well and let the plants sit for five to ten minutes. Always use a plant-starter fertilizer such as 10-52-10 immediately after transplanting to help roots become established.

If you buy bedding plants and need to store them for two or three days—because it has rained and you can't get into the garden, or you were called away on business, or for whatever reason—keep them in a shaded area of the garden where they are unlikely to dry out. Soak them thoroughly before leaving them, and again when you are able to turn your attention to them. If you are worried about frosts, store the plants inside the house in the brightest possible location. Take them outdoors again as soon as you can, and treat them as you would when hardening off.

HARDENING OFF

Hardening off simply means to gradually acclimatize bedding plants from indoor to outdoor temperatures over a period of several days before planting. The result is a 'tougher,' more hardy plant in the garden. Plants that have been hardened off are usually sturdier, bushier and better able to withstand all types of weather, than are those that have not been through this process.

Some greenhouses sell plants that have already been hardened off. However, because this process involves a lot of labour and space, not every greenhouse or nursery carries it out.

To harden off your own seedlings, all you need to do is place the pots or packs outdoors in a sunny area at least a week prior to planting. Don't forget to water every day, because plants that dry out in the pack usually do not fully recover.

If there is a risk of frost, cover the flats or containers with an old sheet, towel or blanket, a roll of burlap, sheets of newspaper or a cardboard box. Never use plastic, because it has virtually no insulation value. If bringing the plants indoors overnight is more convenient, then do so, but remember to return them to their sunny location outdoors the next morning, after the temperature has risen above freezing.

The Mysterious G.P.S.
A funny thing happens every spring. Customers bring in languishing plants that suffer from a mysterious ailment. Most often, we can diagnose this as G.P.S.—the Garage Plant Syndrome. Never, ever store plants in the garage any longer than a single night or day! There is simply not enough light to support them. This is one of the surest ways to kill plants, or at the very least, to severely weaken them. Weakened plants are more prone to pests, they are usually stretched and spindly and their blooming is often delayed.

25

This guide often specifies recommended spacing as a range. Here are some factors to consider when determining how far apart to plant:

- *Close spacings result in a better show in groupings and borders; larger spacings allow the plants to produce more flowers for cutting.*
- *Plants in shady areas spread less quickly than do those in sunny areas.*
- *If you are planting late in the spring, space plants more closely together than you would when planting earlier in the season.*

How to
TRANSPLANT BEDDING PLANTS FROM A CELL-PACK INTO THE GARDEN

1.

Time required to transplant a single plant: under 1 minute

2.

1) *Stephanie Adams prepares to plant a flat of Total Madness petunias.*
2) *Pinching the bottom of each cell in the plastic pack makes it easier to get the plants out.*
3) *Gently break up the rootball of each plant to enable the roots to spread into the soil as the plants grow.*
4) *Firm the soil around the plant after transplanting.*

3.

4.

After seven to ten days of this treatment, the plants will have hardened off and are ready to be planted into the garden.

CONTAINER GARDENS

I love container gardens of all descriptions: patio pots, window boxes, hanging baskets and moss planters. Container gardens allow you to plant flowers where it would otherwise be difficult or impossible. What I like best is that containers permit earlier planting than does an open garden, because the soil is warm and it is easy to cover the pots or move them indoors if there is a risk of frost.

Container gardens also provide flexibility, because you can move them. Flowering pots can transform a lawn for an outdoor wedding or a garden party. Restaurant patios or backyard decks become more inviting places for guests with bright baskets of flowers.

When Scott Ryton of St. Albert, Alberta, grew tired of the maintenance required to keep up his traditional garden, he paved over the soil areas and switched to container gardening.

Almost any annual bedding plant can be grown in a container. Simply decide what feature is most important to you: flowers for fragrance or cutting, climbing vines to create privacy screens or just a pretty pot.

One of the tricks to creating a spectacular show is to use more plants than you would when planting in an open garden. Experiment with different combinations. Unconventional mixtures can be surprisingly pleasing. I particularly remember a former employee who enthusiastically produced planters with combinations of plants that I would never have thought to include—and customers loved them.

Almost anything can be used as a container, as long as it has adequate drainage. The bigger the container the better, because small pots dry out too quickly. To reduce the amount of soil needed to fill large containers, put a layer of small stones in the bottom.

Certain annuals can be brought indoors in the fall as houseplants. To prevent bringing in bugs, spray any plants you bring into the house with an insecticidal soap. Also consider isolating these plants from other houseplants for a short while to ensure that the spray has taken effect and to reduce the possibility of infesting other plants.

I always use a good-quality potting soil in containers. Potting soil packages sometimes refer to 'soil-less mix,' because they actually contain no soil at all. We use a combination of perlite, peat moss, horticultural lime and slow-release fertilizer in our greenhouses. Although at first I was horrified to imagine plants growing without any soil, I have never been happier with the results. The plants just grow better, and watering is much easier than in ordinary garden soil, which has a tendency to become so hard in containers that it is often difficult for air, roots and moisture to penetrate. Some people are tempted to try creating their own potting soil, but because it is difficult to get a consistent mix at home, this is not something I recommend.

KEYS TO SUCCESS WITH CONTAINER GARDENS

1. Water often and thoroughly.

2. Remember to 'deadhead'—that is, to remove the finished flowers—to promote further blooming.

3. Fertilize regularly, because the original soil nutrients are soon used up by the large number of plants in a small space. I recommend adding a generous pinch of 20-20-20 fertilizer to the watering can each time you water.

By following these three simple steps on a regular basis, you are guaranteed a glorious display throughout the season.

HOW TO PLANT A UFO

Number of plants required: 10

Price of container: less than $10

Time required to plant: 15–20 minutes

1) *The creators of this deceptively stark-looking hanging planter gave it the trade name 'UFO' ('Unidentified Flowering Object').*
2) *It is important to firmly pack the soil to prevent the plants from falling out when watered.*
3) *Gently poke a plant into each planting hole. 'Teeth' help to hold the plants in place.*
4) *Add 5 plants to the open soil surface on top. Impatiens is the best choice for this type of planter, because these plants form a solid mass of flowers.*
5) *Within 3 or 4 weeks after planting, the UFO becomes a flowering ball. In another week or two, not even the bottom of the pot will be visible. To keep your UFO looking its best, water daily and fertilize weekly.*

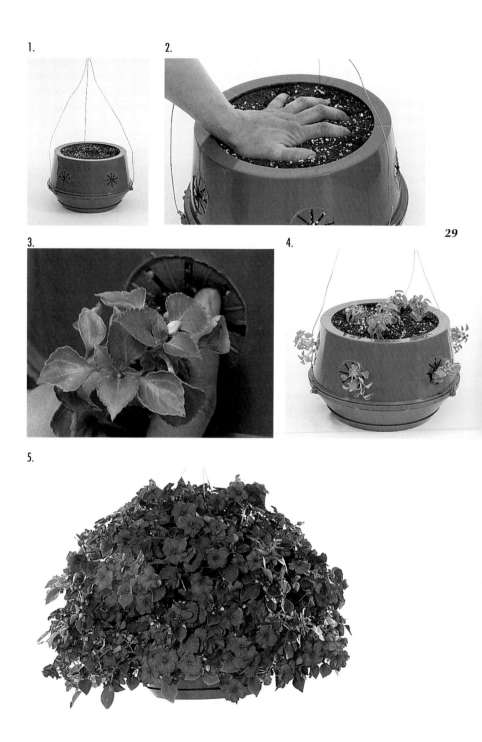

How to create a moss planter

Number of plants required: 52

Price of container (with liner): approximately $100

Time required for planting: ¹/₂–1 hour

1) For moss planters, choose a sturdy, wrought-iron frame and a wire liner that will last for years.
2) Line the basket with sphagnum moss. Use one hand to support the moss underneath the liner and to tuck in any stray pieces.
3) Cap the top edges with moss for a more attractive finish and to create a lip that will hold the soil in place.
4) Fill the moss-lined basket with a good-quality potting mix. A high percentage of perlite and peat moss is important for moisture retention. Moss planters dry out more quickly than other types, since they are exposed to air on all sides.
5) A dracaena planted in the centre adds height and texture.
6) A wooden dowel makes it easy to poke planting holes in the moss.

30

2.

3.

4.

5.

6.

7.

8.

9.

7) Plant in even rows just below the wire rims of the basket.

8) Poke ivy around the bottom of the basket and, last, fill the open soil on top with plants. This basket has impatiens around the sides and tuberous begonias on top. Water the finished planter until the top fills with water and let it soak through to the bottom.

9) Within 3 or 4 weeks after planting, the moss planter is transformed into a solid ball of flowers. To keep it looking its best, water until moisture runs out the bottom. Do this at least every second day, and fertilize once a week with 20-20-20.

Northern Flower Gardening

How to plant a strawberry barrel

Number of plants required: 22

Price of container: about $35

Time required to plant: 30 minutes

1) Any wooden planter with planting holes can be referred to as a strawberry planter. The model shown here has a flat back and can be mounted onto a wall.
2) Gently poke a plant into each hole.
3) Carefully line each hole with sphagnum moss, to prevent the plants from becoming dislodged when watered.
4) Add 4 plants to the open soil area at the top of the planter.

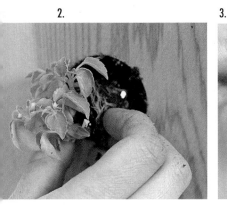

5.

6.

7.

5) The built-in watering tube distributes water throughout the planter.

6) Impatiens is the best choice for this type of planter, because the plants spread quickly into a solid mass of flowers.

7) After 3 or 4 weeks, the strawberry planter will be encased in blooms. Look after your planter by always keeping the watering tube filled to the top, and fertilize once a week with 20-20-20.

When to Plant

Many annuals can be planted outside early without any danger of damage from frost or snow. Plants that are set into the garden early—as long as it's not too early—generally become 'tougher' and perform better throughout the season than those planted later. As an added bonus, they flower earlier and longer than those planted later in spring.

The standard advice to gardeners is to plant in spring once the danger of frost has passed. Check with your local weather office for the date of the average last spring frost in your area. In general, once leaves are out on native trees, it means the area is safe from hard frosts until fall.

As with anything in life, there are no guarantees: no one can guarantee a 'safe-planting date.' Many gardeners in our region, for example, wait until the long weekend around the 24th of May to plant their gardens. In many years, however, the weather allows planting earlier: in 1993, for example, Edmonton's last spring frost was April 21—two full weeks before the average date and a month before the traditional 'safe' date!

For an early garden, use annuals that can withstand light frosts. Pansies and snapdragons, for example, are very frost-hardy and can withstand temperatures below freezing without harm, so we usually plant them into our gardens in early April.

I like to take a chance on getting an earlier and longer show of flowers by planting early in the spring. There may be a frost or two, which means the plants must be covered, but in our area, we are never completely without risk, and many annuals are not harmed by light frosts. More often than not, when I gamble on planting early, my garden will be in full colour while others are just starting out.

In general, annuals that can be direct-seeded can be planted earlier than most of those that are transplanted as bedding plants. Container gardens can always be started early, because they are so easy to cover or to move indoors overnight. Shade-loving plants like impatiens and fuchsia are exceptions, because they are

EXAMPLES OF APPROXIMATE FROST-FREE PERIODS IN SOME SELECTED COMMUNITIES

Area	Last Spring Frost	First Fall Frost	Frost-free Period (# of Days)
British Columbia			
Vancouver	March 31	November 3	216
Prince George	June 6	August 31	85
Alberta			
Calgary	May 25	September 15	112
Edmonton	May 6	September 24	140
Saskatchewan			
Regina	May 24	September 11	109
Manitoba			
Churchill	June 24	September 9	76
Winnipeg	May 23	September 22	121
Ontario			
Toronto	April 20	October 29	191
Quebec			
Montreal	May 3	October 8	157
New Brunswick			
Fredericton	May 19	September 23	126
Nova Scotia			
Halifax	April 30	October 19	171
Prince Edward Island			
Charlottetown	May 16	October 15	151
Newfoundland			
St. John's	June 1	October 11	131
Yukon			
Whitehorse	June 8	August 30	82
Northwest Territories			
Yellowknife	May 27	September 16	111
Alaska			
Anchorage	June 7	August 23	75
Washington			
Seattle	March 24	November 11	232
North Dakota			
Bismarck	May 14	September 20	129
Michigan			
Detroit	April 28	October 20	175
New York			
Buffalo	May 8	October 11	155
Vermont			
Montpelier	May 18	September 23	128

Source: Environment Canada, U.S. National Climatic Data Centre.
For more information about your area, contact your local government weather office.

fussy about temperatures and will not grow when nights remain very cool.

See individual plant descriptions for more information on when plants can safely be planted in the spring.

PROTECTING PLANTS FROM FROST

Protecting plants from frost is, unfortunately, a fact of life for northern gardeners. It is a necessity in both spring and fall, and occasionally even in midsummer. Fortunately, however, in most gardens it is a relatively easy task.

I cover plants with old sheets, towels or blankets, burlap sheeting or cardboard boxes—whatever is handy. Do not use plastic, because it is useless as insulation. Light snow in the spring or fall usually does little harm to plants, but instead acts as an insulator, as a blanket would. However, wet snow can break some plants.

In our early days of growing, we used potato sacks to cover the flats of bedding plants. Each sack would cover only three flats, and it took the entire family working for hours to cover all the plants. Now, huge rolls of burlap are available, and we can easily cover ten times the amount of plants in less time with just two people helping out.

On cool, cloudy days, clearing skies late in the afternoon or evening increase the risk of frost overnight. If the local weather office provides a frost warning but the evening sky remains cloudy, you may still want to cover your plants in case it clears and freezes later in the night.

We have rated the frost tolerance of each plant described in this guide as excellent, moderate or poor. Excellent frost tolerance means the plant continues to grow after several degrees of frost, moderate frost tolerance means it survives light frosts and poor frost tolerance means it cannot tolerate any frost at all, and may suffer even in temperatures a few degrees above freezing. As a general rule, most plants are more frost-hardy when mature in the fall than they are in the spring.

How to Care for Annuals with a Minimum of Effort

Overall, caring for annuals is relatively easy. Aside from pulling weeds, there are three tasks you should not overlook: watering, fertilizing and deadheading. There are ways to lessen maintenance even further.

Annuals grown in containers need almost no weeding.

Choosing plants suited to a particular area will lower the amount of attention they require. For example, I grow portulaca in a sandy, dry corner of my garden because it needs little water. This is easier than struggling with moisture-loving plants that never seem to grow properly in that area no matter what I do.

Drought-tolerant plants are a sensible alternative for people who are often away, as long as the garden location suits the plants' needs. I talk to many people who are great gardeners but spend a lot of time travelling during the summer, and as a result, have problems with plants that simply dry out and die. It makes a lot more sense to grow drought-tolerant plants in your hot spots than to return from vacation to find a bunch of dead bedding plants.

Refer above to 'Plants for Dry Spots' on page 17 for a list of drought-tolerant plants.

FERTILIZING

Plants need consistent nourishment. Fertilizers provide the nutrition that enables plants to grow properly and remain healthy. Regular fertilizing will encourage and increase flower production, bushiness and sometimes height. Plants which are properly nourished are more able, like people, to resist diseases and other stresses.

The addition of organic matter to your garden increases the number of beneficial microorganisms in the soil that, in turn, improve the soil's nutrient levels. All soils benefit from regular additions of organic matter, such as peat moss or compost. Organic matter opens clay soil, making it easier for air and roots to penetrate, and it binds sandy soil so that it dries out less quickly.

Most garden soils contain all of the nutrients essential for plant growth, but these nutrients are often available in insufficient amounts. Complete fertilizers, such as 20-20-20, make up for this shortfall.

The numbers that you see on fertilizer containers are percentages of the three major plant nutrient groups by weight. '20-20-20' means that the mixture is 20 per cent nitrogen, 20 per cent phosphate (phosphorous compounds) and 20 per cent potash (potassium compounds). Nitrogen (N) promotes leafy plant growth and lush leaves. Phosphorus (P) promotes root development and flower production. Potassium (K) promotes flower quality and disease resistance.

RECOMMENDED FERTILIZERS

The simplest type of fertilizer to use is a granular product which is added in a single application by mixing it into the soil before the plants are set in. This most often eliminates the need for weekly feedings throughout the season. I have found that granular fertilizers are excellent for many bedding plants; however, with rapidly growing or large plants, granular fertilizers cannot keep up with the demand for nutrients. To solve this problem, I recommend an occasional supplementary feeding with a water-soluble fertilizer.

Immediately after planting any bedding plant, use a solution of plant-starter fertilizer such as 10-52-10 to aid root development and help plants become established. Apply the fertilizer once per week for the first three weeks after planting.

Cutting flowers for bouquets on a regular basis lessens the need to deadhead. The rule of thumb for annual flowers is the more you cut the more they bloom. You can cut enough flowers for fresh bouquets every week, while still having blooms in the garden and plants that flourish quite happily.

Throughout the season, I use an all-purpose 20-20-20 fertilizer, either as a supplement to granular fertilizer, or on its own. The lower-analysis fertilizers, such as 1-2-1, work well, but they do not promote as much lush green growth and wonderful flowers.

Several years ago, I visited the home of a long-time customer who had the most lovely patio pots that I had ever seen, with masses of flowers simply bursting from their containers.

Her secret? She fertilized the plants every single time she watered, with just a pinch of 20-20-20 added to her watering can.

A good alternative is to feed plants once a week. Attaching a fertilizer dispenser to your hose makes this chore a snap, because the fertilizer is always at hand. Choose a set time, such as Saturday morning, to make it a habit you are less likely to skip. Your plants will thank you with a profusion of healthy blooms throughout the season.

Deadheading simply means removing dead flowers. An annual plant completes its life cycle when seed is set. By deadheading, you extend the flowering life of the plant by removing the dead blooms, thus preventing the plant from going to seed. The plant responds by producing many more flowers over a longer period of time.

Deadheading also keeps the garden looking neat and attractive. Towards the end of the season, you may want to allow certain plants to go to seed—those that produce attractive seed pods for drying, such as nigella and poppies, and those that are in the habit of self-sowing, such as bachelor's buttons, pansies and violas.

You can use shears or scissors to deadhead larger plants, such as geraniums and snap-dragons, but I usually just bend the finished flowerheads down to break the stems. Pinch off smaller flowers with your fingers.

Pinching, or removing the central growing tip of the plant, causes growth of side shoots further down the stem, resulting in a bushier plant that produces more flowers throughout the season.

Deadhead geraniums by breaking the stem just below the finished flowerheads. This is preferable to breaking the stem lower down, because it prevents the plant's main stem from being damaged. The empty flower stem will eventually turn brown and fall off on its own.

Often, as I chat with customers who have just purchased bedding plants or hanging baskets, I prune their plants—pinching off the flowers and pruning anything that looks a bit 'leggy.' Many people are initially horrified at this treatment, thinking that the plants are ruined. However, after I explain to them that this type of pruning encourages the plants to bush out and produce a greater number of flowers, and then send them home with some fertilizer, many come back a few weeks later to tell me how splendid the plants look.

To pinch back a stem, grasp the growing tip (the point of the stem above the top pair of mature leaves) between your thumb and forefinger, and remove it. Seedlings can be first pinched when they have three or four sets of leaves. Bedding plants can be pinched back as soon as you plant them in the ground, and again about three weeks after transplanting to encourage them to become even bushier. Right after pinching is an excellent time to fertilize.

With annuals that flower on many small stems, such as lobelia, deadheading flower by flower is impractical, so it is easier to shear. Shearing simply means to cut back the entire plant by one-quarter to one-third, and it requires no fancy tools—sharp household scissors will do nicely.

Shearing is usually recommended about mid-season, after a period of rapid growth, or whenever the plants slow down and begin producing fewer flowers. Shearing back at this point allows plants to renew fresh growth. They will soon be blooming again. Check individual plant descriptions later in this guide to determine whether a certain plant will benefit from this treatment.

Immediately following deadheading or shearing is an excellent time to fertilize.

WATERING

Proper watering requires patience. A once-over watering is seldom enough. Instead, you should soak the area thoroughly, wait a few minutes for the water to penetrate and then water again. You should thoroughly drench hanging baskets and patio pots.

It is best to water open gardens heavily at least once a week (except for plantings of drought-tolerant plants, which can get along on less). Container gardens should be watered once or twice a day during hot weather. Thorough, regular watering is preferable to frequent, light sprinkling; thorough watering uses less water and can lessen the chances of disease. I add compost or peat moss to the garden each year, to help retain moisture and loosen the soil.

I love watering plants; to me, it is one of the most relaxing aspects of gardening. To make watering easier and more efficient, I use a soft-rain nozzle on a water-wand. It's much easier to reach into flower beds and it has a gentle spray and a shut-off valve which eliminates the need to run back and forth from the main faucet to turn water on and off. I prefer this method to constantly filling a watering can.

I firmly believe that hand watering will never be completely replaced, but I also believe that, for those who have neither the time nor inclination to water everything by hand, there are many options. Ask staff at a garden centre for their recommendations on a watering system if you're determined to avoid your watering can.

Nearly half the water employed for domestic use ends up on lawns and gardens, and a considerable portion of that is wasted through evaporation and improper watering techniques. Learning how to water wisely will immediately reduce your water bill.

- Incorporate as much organic matter as possible before planting. Organic matter acts like a sponge: peat moss, for example, holds up to 20 times its own weight in water. Compost, peat moss and well-rotted manure are all recommended.

- When practical, group plants according to their water requirements. Keep those that need to soak up more water to their own beds rather than scattering them throughout

Try to get in the habit of pinching off a few faded flowers and any seed pods that have formed each time you water, or whenever you are admiring your plants. While deadheading is a task that needs to be done throughout the season, it actually requires little time and effort. For example, it takes only three to four minutes to prune a hanging basket, and the result of this effort is that the plants continue to flower beautifully throughout the summer.

EASY WAYS TO REDUCE YOUR WATER BILL

the landscape. This avoids wasting water on plants that do not really need it.

• Consider mixing relatively water-thirsty ornamentals with vegetables such as tomatoes, lettuce, peppers and eggplants for an attractive display with practical pay-offs.

• As long as you find them satisfying, choose plants suited to hot, dry areas that thrive on a minimum of water.

• Water early in the morning (ideally), on calm, cool evenings or when there is a light misting of rain. Moisture loss through evaporation is much less at these times.

• Trap rain water in barrels for use in the garden.

• Avoid oscillating sprinklers, because they lose through evaporation as much as 50 per cent of what they disperse, and they often waste water by spraying over paved areas.

Children love helping in the garden. My grandson Michael is so keen that he often cannot wait to get dressed before picking up the hose.

• Consider connecting a timer to the hose. This allows watering at off-peak hours—or while you are away, asleep or otherwise occupied— for a pre-set period.

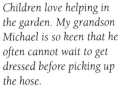

• For container gardens, use pots that hold water the longest. Porous clay and pressed paper dry out most quickly; plastic and glazed ceramic retain water longer. Deep pots need less watering than shallow pots. Light-coloured containers need to be watered less often than dark containers. Keep a saucer under pots to collect and hold run-off water.

A friend or neighbour who can come in to care for your plants while you are away is the best scenario. You can thank them for their attentions with something from the garden, such as a bouquet of fresh flowers on your return or a dried arrangement in the fall.

If you cannot manage to find someone to come in, here are some tips that can hold your plants for up to two weeks:

- Take hanging baskets down, water very thoroughly and place them in a shaded area of your garden. Absolutely soak containers and if possible move them out of the sun.

- Some plants, such as petunias and impatiens, can be cut back by up to one-third. Pinch off flowering shoots on snapdragons and pansies; this will keep them from going to seed.

- If possible, add to hot locations of the garden a layer of organic mulch, such as peat moss, to help retain the soil moisture.

- Fertilize everything before you go and water very thoroughly. When you return home from vacation, your garden will greet you with a fresh flush of flowers.

A cedar wheelbarrow makes a handsome home for geraniums, pansies and dracaena.

African Daisy

cream, yellow, bronze, orange

Dimorphotheca sinuata
Cape Marigold, Star of the Veld

Height: 8–12 inches (20–30 cm)

A wide swath of African daisies swaying in a gentle summer breeze is, to me, one of the most splendid sights in the garden. These bright, daisy-like flowers open each morning and close up each night and on cloudy days. African daisies are tidy, sun-worshipping plants that thrive in dry locations and bloom brilliantly on sunny days throughout the summer until frost, producing a profusion of neat, single flowers up to 3 inches (8 cm) across.

PLANTING

Seeding: Indoors, 3 weeks before transplanting. Outdoors from 1–2 weeks before the average last spring frost until the middle of May.

Transplanting: 1 week after the average last spring frost. Space 4–6 inches (10–15 cm) apart.

Frost Tolerance: Poor.

African daisies are among the most attractive daisy-type annuals, and they are perfect for hot, dry gardens. They are naturally drought-tolerant and can go quite a while without moisture.

GROWING

Full sun.

Mass plantings, rock gardens, on their own in large pots.

Water when dry.

RECOMMENDED VARIETIES

Aurantiaca Mixture • a pretty mixture of cream, yellow, bronze and orange flowers.

African daisies thrive in a garden in Whitehorse, Yukon, on the opposite side of the globe from their native home.

TIPS

If you want carefree plants for the garden at your weekend cottage, sow a large patch of African daisies for masses of bright, sunny colour all season long.

Cut African daisies in bunches and set them in vases near sunny windows. The flowers will probably close up at night.

I recall one gardener, an Englishwoman, telling me that she had been searching everywhere for these plants. She used to grow them in her garden in England, just loved the flowers and now wanted to bring the colours of Africa to her northern garden.

African daises are prettiest planted en masse on their own, rather than intermingled with other flowers. The larger the grouping, the better the overall show, and the sunnier the location, the greater the number of flowers. I find that spacing these plants fairly closely together results in a more spectacular show of colour and lets the plants keep each other upright.

Ageratum

mid-blue, deep purple-blue, white

Ageratum houstonianum
Blue Puffs, Floss Flower

Height: 6 inches (15 cm)

I rarely plant formal borders in my garden, but ageratum is the one plant that could persuade me to make an exception. The intense, rich colours of its feathery flowers offer a sharp contrast, especially against the bright hues of orange or yellow marigolds, red salvia or silver dusty miller. Ageratum is an early bloomer, with clusters of tiny, feathery flowers that almost completely cover its small leaves.

PLANTING

Seeding: Indoors 8–10 weeks before transplanting.

Transplanting: 3 weeks after the average last spring frost. Space 6 inches (15 cm) apart.

Frost Tolerance: Poor.

GROWING

Full sun to light shade.

Borders, edgings along walkways, in rock gardens, formal plantings, for impact in mixed beds with brightly coloured annuals, in patio containers.

Water regularly. Do not allow plants to dry out.

Ageratum has the most even growth habit of all the annual border plants.

RECOMMENDED VARIETIES

Hawaii Series • available in mid-blue, deep blue and white (the best white ageratum!).

TIPS

Purchase bedding plants not yet in bloom.

Choose mid-blue ageratum for an extremely attractive display with salmon or pink geraniums.

*Gardeners love ageratum for its low maintenance requirements, even growth and bright flower colours. Above, formal design at the Legislature Grounds in Edmonton, Alberta.
At left, ageratum border yellow French marigolds.*

Alyssum

Alyssum is prized as much for its sweet perfume as it is for its beauty. It grows quickly and spreads into a lacy carpet of dainty flowers that create lovely borders in flower beds or billow into soft cushions that spill charmingly over the sides of containers. Alyssum begins blooming when the plants are very small and continues nonstop until frost.

deep pink, violet, rose, lavender, white

Lobularia maritima
Carpet Flower, Sweet Alyssum

Height: 4 inches (10 cm)

Alyssum is one of the most fragrant flowers, with a glorious honey-sweet scent. White-flowered varieties have the strongest fragrance.

PLANTING

Seeding: Indoors 6 weeks before transplanting.

Transplanting: 1 week after the average last spring frost. Space 6–8 inches (15–20 cm) apart.

Frost tolerance: Poor.

GROWING

Full sun to light shade.

Borders, planters, windowboxes, pots, hanging baskets, rock gardens.

Keep evenly moist. Alyssum goes to seed when it dries out, but it also dislikes being water-logged.

RECOMMENDED VARIETIES

Easter Bonnet • gentle scent; vivid colours do not fade; available individually in dark pink, violet and as a mixture of purple, rose, lavender and white.

New Carpet of Snow • pure white flowers with a lovely, strong fragrance.

TIPS

Purchase bedding plants that are less than 3 inches (8 cm) high: these spread more quickly and perform better after transplanting than do taller plants.

Plant alyssum near a doorway or along walkways so that its honey-sweet scent will greet you as you pass.

Tuck a few plants into a hanging basket of strawberries or an herb planter for an ornamental and fragrant display.

A capricious display of alyssum (above) adds fragrance and charm to the garden. Plant Easter Bonnet (left) varieties en masse in pots or windowboxes, or as a border around patio areas for a gently scented, glowing carpet of colour.

I remember a gardener who planted 3 or 4 different colours of alyssum inside a hollowed-out log. The effective was stunning, with the plants billowing over the sides in a beautiful, cushion-like mound.

Alyssum is easy to grow and needs no dead-heading. It quickly spreads into a solid mass of flowers.

Amaranthus

dark red

Amaranthus caudatus
Love Lies Bleeding, Tassel
Flower, Chenille Plant

Height: 36 inches (90 cm)

The exotic flowers of amaranthus look like plush, dark-red ropes trailing from the end of its stems. These sturdy plants are usually grown as a garden curiosity to contrast with more common flowers. I love to watch children examining this plant. They find its drooping tassels fascinating; my grandson tells me that they are like the bushy tails of animals.

PLANTING

Seeding: Indoors 8 weeks before transplanting.

Transplanting: 1 week after the average last spring frost. Space 18 inches (45 cm) apart.

Frost Tolerance: Poor.

GROWING

Sunny location.

Background or feature plant, in flower beds, herb or vegetable gardens or large containers.

Keep evenly moist.

Fertilize plants in containers regularly.

Amaranthus has excellent heat tolerance, and it grows well in hot areas of the garden as long as the plants are kept well watered. The name 'amaranthus' means 'unfading,' and it refers to the unfading colour of the long, drooping tassels.

Amaranthus, petunias and dinner-plate dahlias are delightful companions in my mother's garden.

51

Amaranthus is easy to grow. It needs very little care, other than watering.

RECOMMENDED VARIETIES

Usually available only under one of the names listed above.

TIPS

The tassels of amaranthus add interest to bouquets and everlasting arrangements. To dry the flowers, simply hang the stalks by the bend where the stem meets the tassel.

The plants sometimes need to be staked to keep them upright. We use a tomato cage to support amaranthus growing in a wooden half-barrel planter.

Asparagus Fern

green

Asparagus sprengeri

Height: Trails 12–18 inches
(30–45 cm)

If you want a light, airy look for your patio planters and hanging baskets, choose asparagus fern in place of ivy. Its fresh, bright-green foliage arches out in lush sprays and trails down the sides of containers. Asparagus fern is usually considered a houseplant, but I have found that these plants absolutely thrive outdoors in shady locations.

Asparagus ferns serve double duty: outdoors, they add airy grace to patio planters throughout the summer; indoors, they grow well as houseplants year 'round.

PLANTING

Seeding: Not recommended—it takes too long to produce sizable plants.

Transplanting: About a week after the average last spring frost. Space 6–8 inches (15–20 cm) apart.

Frost Tolerance: Poor.

GROWING

Full to partial shade.

Hanging baskets, containers of all types, as edging in raised beds.

Keep plants moist. The foliage turns yellow and sheds if the roots dry out.

Unlike many house-plants grown outdoors, asparagus fern has tough foliage that does not turn brown or tear in the wind.

RECOMMENDED VARIETIES

Usually available only under the names listed above.

TIPS

Asparagus fern can be trimmed and used as greenery to decorate fresh bouquets. This plant is gaining favour with florists, who use its lush, tumbling foliage to create a fresh, informal, garden look in wedding arrangements and bridal bouquets.

Asparagus fern with yellow and white tuberous begonias and English ivy makes a simple and pretty combination in planters.

A pot of pink geraniums and asparagus fern thrives on a partially shaded patio.

Aster

scarlet, rose, pink, peach, purple, blue, white

Callistephus chinensis
China Aster, Daisy Mum

Height: 6–36 inches
 (15–90 cm)

Asters bloom about midsummer, later than many annuals, but these splendid flowers are worth the wait and remain at their prime well into autumn. The flowers vary from daisy-like, with a single layer of petals, to curious, spider-like quills with a striking elegance, to fluffy powder-puff forms similar to chrysanthemums. All make wonderful, long-lasting cutflowers.

54

Asters are prized in floral arrangements because they last for weeks. They are among the best annuals for cutting, and one of the easiest cutflowers to grow. For years, we grew asters beside the house to sell in gorgeous bouquets.

PLANTING

Seeding: Indoors 6–8 weeks before transplanting.

Transplanting: 1–2 weeks after the average last spring frost. Space dwarf varieties 6–10 inches (15–25 cm) apart. Allow 8–12 inches (20–30 cm) between the taller varieties.

Frost Tolerance: Moderate.

GROWING

Full sun to light shade.

Grouped in mixed beds, cutting gardens or containers. Shorter varieties for uniform borders; tall varieties for backgrounds.

Aster flowers vary greatly in looks: (left to right) Single Rainbow, Powder Puff, Milady, Massagno.

Recommended Varieties

Pot 'n' Patio Mixture
- 6 inches (15 cm) tall; uniform borders; mix of white, pink, blue and scarlet.

Starlight Series • 6–8 inches (15–20 cm) tall; has the quilled blooms usually found only on taller varieties; individually in deep blue, medium blue and rose.

Milady Series • 8–10 inches (20–25 cm) tall; great for taller borders; short-stemmed cutflowers; individually in scarlet, rose, blue, white and also as a mixture.

Massagno Mixture • up to 20 inches (50 cm) tall; unique, quilled, spider-type flowers on sturdy stems; excellent wind resistance; wide range of colours.

Single Rainbow Mixture • up to 30 inches (75 cm) tall; giant blooms 3 inches (8 cm) across that resemble daisies with contrasting centres; mixture includes solids and bicolours in vivid hues.

Powderpuffs Mixture • up to 36 inches (90 cm) tall; double flowers, 2 inches (5 cm) across with yellow centres that disappear when flowers are mature; white, shell-pink, rose, peach, crimson, azure and mid-blue.

Tips

If you are hosting a late summer wedding or other celebration, plant a row or two of asters in your vegetable garden to provide splendid flowers for decorating.

You can chop off an entire plant of the variety Powderpuffs and simply drop it into a vase for a stunning bouquet.

Asters will last 2–3 weeks in bouquets, provided the water is changed regularly.

Some flowers have a dedicated following of gardeners who plant them year after year. Asters are one of these flowers. Many veteran gardeners tell me they would never have a flower bed without asters, because they are as beautiful in the garden as they are in bouquets.

55

Milady asters (top) highlight my mother's garden. Massagno asters (above) make a glorious bouquet.

'Aster' means 'star' in Greek. The botanical name is Greek for 'beautiful crown' and refers to the shape of the flowers.

Baby's Breath

white

Gypsophila elegans
Annual Baby's Breath

Height: Up to 20 inches (50 cm)

Annual baby's breath has large, showy flowers. It is one of the first annuals that can be planted in the spring.

Airy masses of delicate, single flowers in profuse sprays make the annual baby's breath a favourite for summer weddings. Because it looks so splendid in bouquets, this type of baby's breath is most often added to the garden as a source of flowers for cutting. Annual baby's breath blooms quickly and is easy to grow.

PLANTING

Seeding: Indoors 4–6 weeks before trans-planting. Outdoors a week before the average last spring frost.

Transplanting: A week after the average last spring frost. Space 12 inches (30 cm) apart.

Frost Tolerance: Moderate.

GROWING

Sunny location.

Cutflower gardens, open beds.

May require staking.

Recommended Varieties

Covenant Garden • a world-famous variety; large, pure-white flowers with strong stems.

Snow Fountain • a selection of the above variety, with 20% more blooms.

Tips

Annual baby's breath blooms quickly, about 6–8 weeks after sowing, but the flowers last only a few weeks in the garden. For a continuous supply of flowers throughout the summer, sow 2 or 3 times, about 2 weeks apart.

Consider planting baby's breath in a corner of the garden, where the gap left when the plants are finished is not really noticeable.

Although I have often read that annual baby's breath is difficult to transplant, we have never had a problem. We have met with great success using bedding plants over the last several years. For best results, purchase cell-packs that contain short, stocky, young plants.

Annual baby's breath differs in appearance from the more common perennial favoured by florists. The annual flowers are larger, single-petalled and more showy. The flowers of perennial baby's breath are better for drying than those of annual varieties.

Blue nigella combined with annual baby's breath makes an elegant and long-lasting bouquet. Annual baby's breath also looks stunning alone in a simple glass vase.

Bachelor's Button

red, rose, pink, purple, lilac, blue, white, yellow

Centaurea cyanus
Bluebottle, Cornflower, French Pink, Ragged Sailor

Height: 12–36 inches
(30–90 cm)

For early-blooming, long-lasting flowers that can be sown directly into the garden, few annuals can match bachelor's buttons. Bachelor's buttons are best known for their bright-blue blooms that provide a beautiful contrast to the orange of poppies, calendula and marigolds. New varieties, however, provide a wider range of colours. Most are unscented, except the variety Sweet Sultan, which has a gentle perfume.

One of the most striking yet practical uses of bachelor's buttons I have seen was on an acreage, where the gardener had sown a small meadow of bachelor's buttons near a row of trees for a burst of colour in the landscape. This idea works best in a sunny location, because in the shade the plants get too tall and tend to flop over.

PLANTING

Seeding: Indoors 4–6 weeks before transplanting. Outdoors from 2 weeks before the average last spring frost until mid-June.

Transplanting: 1 week after the average frost-free date. Space 6–8 inches (15–20 cm) apart.

Frost Tolerance: Moderate.

GROWING

Sunny location.

Backgrounds, cutting gardens, mixed beds and meadow gardens.

The variety Sweet Sultan prefers a dry location.

Bachelor's buttons provide flowers for bouquets early in the season, and they are one of the easiest annuals to grow.

RECOMMENDED VARIETIES

Frosted Queen Mixture • up to 36 inches (90 cm) tall; unusual flowers in combinations of red and pink, violet and pale blue, lilac and dark blue, and pure white.

Finest Series • up to 30 inches (75 cm) tall; blue, pink, red, rose-pink, white; also as a mixture.

Sweet Sultan Mix • up to 30 inches (75 cm) tall; sweetly scented; unique, large, quilled blooms; white, pink, lilac and yellow.

I prefer tall varieties of bachelor's buttons, because they are better for cutting. The sunnier the location in the garden, the more blooms are produced.

TIPS

For a meadow of flowers for bouquets, mix bachelor's buttons seeds with those of poppies, cosmos and Queen Anne's lace. Scatter the seeds in a 1-foot-wide (30 cm) band.

A bouquet of bachelor's buttons and snapdragons lasts well over a week.

These flowers always remind me of the blue-and-white kitchen in our old farmhouse. The wooden table was covered with a blue-and-white cloth, and I used to place a bouquet of bright-blue bachelor's buttons in the centre. This cheery combination always drew exclamations from friends and relatives.

Balsam

orange, rose, pink, white

Impatiens balsamina
Lady Slipper, Rose Impatiens

Height: 15 inches (30 cm)

Balsam is the perfect plant for the gardener who wants something different that does not require a lot of extra work. Balsam is related to impatiens, and it is just as easy to grow. This old-fashioned flower is popular in Europe and is often found tucked into cottage gardens. The rose-like flowers of balsam are borne between its leaves on tall, sturdy stalks, from June until frost.

PLANTING

Seeding: Indoors 8–10 weeks before transplanting.

Transplanting: 2 weeks after the average last spring frost. Space 8 inches (20 cm) apart.

Frost Tolerance: Poor.

GROWING

Partial shade to full sun.

Borders, mixed flower beds, cottage gardens, in windowboxes, patio pots, planters.

Water regularly to keep soil moist.

Balsam is an old-fashioned flower that has a nostalgic appeal for people who remember seeing it in their grandmothers' gardens, and who now grow it year after year in their own gardens.

Balsam is an uncommon plant with distinctive beauty, and it often inspires visitors to ask for its name.

Recommended Varieties

Colour Parade Mixture • miniature rose-type flowers in pastel shades of orange, rose, pink and white.

Tips

In an unseasonably cool spring, delay planting until shady areas have had a chance to warm.

Group several plants together in the garden for the best display.

This pretty pot of balsam and pansies was growing outside a summer cabin at a lake near our city. The plants prosper on minimal care during weekend visits.

Balsam is a reliable plant that always does quite well, but it likes warmth. These plants flourished in a pot set under a large tree, which sheltered them from cool winds and filtered the sunlight.

Begonia

red, coral, pink, white, orange, salmon, apricot, yellow

Begonia x semperflorens 'cultorum'
Fibrous Begonia, Wax Begonia

Begonia x tuberhybrida
Tuberous Begonia

Height:
Fibrous: 5–8 inches
(13–20 cm)
Tuberous: 8–14 inches
(20–28 cm)

Begonias come in two distinctly different types: fibrous and tuberous. Fibrous or wax begonias are short, compact plants with small flowers, and they are absolutely outstanding for fully shaded areas. Tuberous begonias are showy, large-flowered plants—and one of my favourites. These are the flowers I find people most often like to boast about, for the size of the blooms.

PLANTING

Seeding: Tuberous begonias are slow to root. Start from tubers 12–14 weeks before planting outdoors. Fibrous begonias are difficult to grow from seed, but if you want to try, allow 10–12 weeks before transplanting.

Transplanting: 3 weeks after the average last spring frost. Space fibrous begonias 8 inches (20 cm) apart, and tuberous varieties 10–12 inches (25–30 cm) apart.

Frost Tolerance: Poor.

This array of begonias includes: pink fibrous; white, trailing-type tuberous; the unique picotee flowers of the tuberous variety Pin-Up; and Non-Stop tuberous in yellow and red.

GROWING

Fibrous types in full shade to partial sun. Tuberous types in full to partial shade.

Fibrous for uniform borders, in planters, hanging baskets or moss baskets. Tuberous in almost any setting: tall borders, feature plants, mass plantings, hanging baskets, moss planters, containers of all types.

Keep well-watered. Begonias like cool, moist soil.

Fibrous begonias (above) are the very best annual for growing in fully shaded areas, whether in planters, hanging baskets, mass displays or borders. Tuberous begonias bloom in a rainbow of colours. Insects rarely bother either type.

Fibrous begonias (left) are tidy plants and one of the lowest-maintenance annual flowers. To tidy them up, simply brush your hand across the tops of the flowers.

American Hybrid varieties of tuberous begonias produce the largest flowers. A single bloom entirely covers the palm of a hand.

Tuberous begonias often bear two types of flowers: the showy double blooms (female) and a lesser number of single blooms (male). Pinching off the single flowers results in larger double blooms.

RECOMMENDED VARIETIES

Fibrous

Prelude • 5–6 inches (13–15 cm) tall; very early blooming; green leaves; performs well through both heat and rain; picotee coral with white edge, pink, rose, scarlet and mixtures.

Tuberous

American Hybrid • 12–14 inches (25–28 cm) tall; the largest flowers up to 5 inches (12 cm) across; unique colour combinations; 2 very showy types of flowers, with either ruffled edges or resembling roses; over 30 colours available.

Pin-Up • 10 inches (25 cm) tall; award-winning variety; beautiful, single-petalled, picotee flowers are 3^1/2 inches (9 cm) across; stunning pure white or pink with bold rose margins set off by yellow centres.

Nonstop • 8–10 inches (20–25 cm) tall; many double flowers borne on top of the plants; apricot, scarlet, orange, pink, rose, salmon, white and yellow.

TIPS

I often float the flowers of tuberous begonias in a shallow bowl of water for a lovely display on indoor tables.

Icy-white begonias are perfect for brightening a shaded area.

Begonias can be brought indoors in the fall as houseplants, if you have a bright, sunny place to put them. They will probably look pretty for only a short while, because light levels inside a house are usually too low to support these plants. After the blooming has finished, trim the plants back and store tuberous varieties as directed below.

To overwinter tuberous begonias, dig up and bring the tubers indoors after a light frost has killed the tops—but before a heavy frost freezes the tubers. Dig up the tubers, allowing some soil to cling to them. Dry thoroughly for a couple of weeks. At this point, the remaining soil on the tubers should easily break away. Store them at temperatures of 40–50° F (4–10° C) in peat moss, perlite or vermiculite. The tubers must be started indoors in late January or early February to produce summer blooms. The varieties Nonstop and Pin-up seldom produce tubers large enough to overwinter and are therefore not recommended for storage.

Every year, we hang fibrous begonias in moss baskets outside our front door. Our entranceway faces north and receives very little sun, and begonias are one of the few annuals that can be relied upon to flower profusely in this kind of situation.

65

Tuberous begonias are one of the best flowers for moss planters. Here, they combine with impatiens, dracaena and lobelia.

Bells of Ireland

green

Moluccella laevis
Moluccella

Height: 24 inches (60 cm)

Bells of Ireland add unusual grace to gardens, bouquets and dried arrangements. The long spires of apple-green bells provide dramatic contrast to colourful flowers. One of the most beautiful bouquets I have ever seen was one that my daughter-in-law, Valerie, created from her garden, combining bells of Ireland with pink lavatera, white Queen Anne's lace and blue Salvia horminum.

PLANTING

Seeding: Indoors 8–10 weeks before transplanting.

Transplanting: 1–2 weeks after the average last spring frost. Space 6–8 inches (15–20 cm) apart.

Frost Tolerance: Moderate.

GROWING

Sun to light shade.

Mass plantings, cutting gardens, as accent plants or backgrounds.

Water moderately.

RECOMMENDED VARIETIES

No specific varieties developed to date; usually available only under one of the names listed above.

Although I have read that bells of Ireland are difficult to transplant, we have never had a problem. We have met with great success using bedding plants over the last several years.

Tips

If you want perfectly straight, long stems, stake the plants, because they sometimes flop over if left unsupported in the garden. Or just let them grow: I find that twisted and curved stems add interest to my arrangements.

Florists like to use these tall stems to add a dramatic flare to arrangements. Some recommend removing the protruding leaves from stalks for a tidier display.

Bells of Ireland are easy to dry. Simply place the stems in a container with only an inch (2.5 cm) or so of water. As the water evaporates, the stems dry slowly and usually retain their green colour, although some stems may turn to brown.

Technically, the flowers of bells of Ireland are the tiny white blooms inside the bells, which would often go unnoticed if not for their subtle, fresh fragrance.

These unusual green stems provide striking accents to bouquets and dried arrangements.

Bells of Ireland are like many annual flowers in that the more you cut them, the more stems they produce.

Black-eyed Susan Vine

yellow, orange, white

Thunbergia alata

Height: Climbs or trails to
36 inches (90 cm)

One of the prettiest flowering annual vines is the black-eyed susan vine. It is smaller than most annual flowering vines, so it is well-suited to growing in hanging baskets and garden pots. The black-eyed susan vine blooms as it climbs, with open flowers and heart-shaped leaves all the way up the length of each stem.

PLANTING

Seeding: Indoors 6–8 weeks before transplanting.

Transplanting: 3–4 weeks after the average last spring frost. Space 6–8 inches (15–20 cm) apart.

Frost Tolerance: Poor.

GROWING

Partial shade to partial sun. A warm, sheltered spot is perfect.

Hanging baskets, in pots or window-boxes, trailing over edges or climbing on a small lattice, against a fence or trellis, trailing over walls.

Keep soil wet. Plants that dry out will likely die.

The black-eyed susan vine climbs by twining stems. In a hanging basket, it has the pleasing habit of climbing up and covering the hanger with blooms as well as trailing over the sides.

RECOMMENDED VARIETIES

Susie Mix • 1½-inch orange, yellow and white flowers, with and without black centres.

TIPS

In an unseasonably cool spring, delay planting until shady areas have had a chance to warm.

I find that this plant really prospers from regular fertilizing twice a week throughout the growing season.

I like to mix black-eyed susan vine in a container or hanging basket with trailing blue lobelia for the splendid contrast in floral colours.

Plant black-eyed susan vine inside a tomato cage or peony ring. It will quickly climb to become a 3–4 foot high (90–120 cm) pyramid of flowers.

Black-eyed susan vine prefers a sheltered location (top) with filtered sunlight. We find that hanging a basket from the branch of a tree in the backyard (above) provides a lovely view from our kitchen window.

🌿 *Black-eyed susan vine is one of the fastest-growing annual vines. It climbs extra-ordinarily quickly and produces masses of pretty flowers.*

Brachycome

blue, purple, pink

Brachycome iberidifolia
Swan River Daisy

Height: 8–12 inches
(20–30 cm)

When brachycome is blooming in hanging baskets inside the greenhouse, it is the flower that we are asked about more than any other. Brachycome's flowers look like unusual black- or golden-eyed trailing daisies. The delicate blooms are beautiful in mixed hanging baskets and containers as well as in the garden.

PLANTING

Seeding: Indoors 8 weeks before transplanting. Outdoors from 4 weeks before the average last spring frost until the beginning of June.

Transplanting: 1 week after the average last spring frost. Space 6–8 inches (15–20 cm) apart.

Frost Tolerance: Moderate.

GROWING

Partial to full sun.

Hanging baskets, planters, windowboxes, pots, as edging, in rock gardens.

Keep soil moist, particularly in containers. Brachycome will die if allowed to dry out.

Fertilize regularly.

RECOMMENDED VARIETIES

Blue Star • 8–12 inches (20–30 cm) tall; sweetly scented, 1-inch (2.5 cm) blooms; unique petals are rolled-up instead of flat; blue flowers.

Pink Swirl • 8–12 inches (20–30 cm) tall; pink flowers with yellow centres.

Purple Splendour • 9 inches (23 cm) tall; purple-blue flowers with yellow or black centres.

TIPS

Snip off a few flower stems to add variety to mixed fresh bouquets.

We plant brachycome with different combinations of plants. In hanging baskets, it is often combined with Dahlberg daisies for a delicate effect with contrasting colours.

Gardeners who love purple flowers are thrilled with a mixture of lavender-flowered ivy geraniums, lobelia and brachycome. I favour this flower in combination with white ivy geraniums, which have a striking lavender eye that is set off by brachycome's purple petals.

Brachycome looks delightful trailing from hanging baskets and springing forth from containers. The varieties Pink Swirl and Purple Splendour (above, right) combine well with tuberous begonias in a dragon pot.

Browallia

violet

Browallia speciosa major
Bush Violet

Height: 10–12 inches
    (25–30 cm)

Browallia is not often found in northern gardens, probably because not many people know about it. Browallia grows into a striking, rounded bush, liberally sprinkled with bluebell-like flowers 1¼ inches (3 cm) across that cascade evenly from all sides.

PLANTING

Seeding: Indoors 12–14 weeks before transplanting.

Transplanting: 3–4 weeks after the average last spring frost. Space 4–6 inches (10–15 cm) apart.

Frost Tolerance: Poor.

GROWING

Partial to full shade.

Hanging baskets, containers, borders, flower beds.

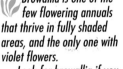 Browallia is one of the few flowering annuals that thrive in fully shaded areas, and the only one with violet flowers.
    Look for browallia if you want an uncommon plant for shaded areas of your garden.

RECOMMENDED VARIETIES

Blue Bells Improved • violet-blue, 1¼-inch (3 cm) flowers.

Tips

Keep soil moist. Browallia wilts quickly when it dries out but is somewhat forgiving if this doesn't happen too often. It also dislikes being waterlogged, so avoid planting in areas that are low-lying or have poor drainage.

In an unseasonably cool spring, delay planting until shady areas have had a chance to warm. Browallia is not at all frost-hardy and does not like cool temperatures.

Browallia does not need a large container to produce good-sized specimens. Five small plants growing in a 10-inch (20 cm) pot resulted in this impressive show.

Browallia likes a sheltered location. This plant thrives in a protected corner underneath an overhang, in a site that receives morning sun. Placing the pot on top of a stand raises it to a level visible from the street.

Calendula

yellow, orange, red-orange, apricot, gold

Calendula officinalis
English Marigold, Pot Marigold

Height: 16–18 inches
(40–45 cm)

Calendula is a flower that, until fairly recently, looked just as it did hundreds of years ago in England. In the last few years, however, plant breeders have developed new varieties that are shorter and more compact, with blooms more closely resembling chrysanthemums than the traditional daisy-like flowers. The range of colours has been expanded slightly, and some varieties have attractive petals tipped in dark red.

74

Calendula is an exceptionally easy flower to grow as long as it has lots of sun and is kept well-watered. It is quite frost-hardy and can be seeded directly into the garden in early spring, or in late spring, because it blooms so quickly. Calendula will continue to bloom after light frosts.

PLANTING

Seeding: Indoors 6–8 weeks before transplanting. Outdoors from a week before the average last spring frost until the middle of June.

Transplanting: 1 week after the average last spring frost. Space 8 inches (20 cm) apart.

Frost Tolerance: Moderate.

GROWING

Full sun to very light shade.

Tall borders, cutting gardens, containers, in herb and vegetable gardens.

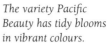
The variety Pacific Beauty has tidy blooms in vibrant colours.

RECOMMENDED VARIETIES

Pacific Beauty • very uniform growth; apricot, gold, lemon, orange and a mixture.

TIPS

Newer varieties are sometimes difficult to find in seed packets, so it may be necessary to purchase bedding plants. Professional growers often have access to varieties that cannot be found on retail shelves.

Calendula is sometimes considered to be a flowering herb. It has edible greens that are tasty when boiled. The flowers are also edible, and the petals can be used to dye food a saffron-yellow colour.

Calendula is one of the earliest-blooming annuals. Its cheerful flowers have long, strong stems and will stay fresh for up to 2 weeks after cutting. The flowers in this bouquet are Touch of Red Mix, grown from seed, and Pacific Beauty.

Canary Bird Vine

yellow

Tropaeolum peregrinum
Canary Bird Flower,
Canary Creeper

Height: Up to 12 feet (3.6 m)

A family friend grows canary bird vine along her chain link fence to enclose a sunny patio area in the backyard where her young children play. This beautiful vine climbs quickly to almost completely cover her 8-foot fence with masses of tiny, yellow flowers. The fence provides perches for birds who like to hide among the foliage and feed on the seeds of the finished flowers.

PLANTING

Seeding: Indoors 4–6 weeks before transplanting. Outdoors from a week before the average last spring frost until the first week in June.

Transplanting: One week after the average last spring frost. Space 12 inches (30 cm) apart to produce a screen.

Frost Tolerance: Poor.

GROWING

Sunny locations.

Screens, against a house, trellises, fences or archways, on trellises in large containers, in hanging baskets.

To allow this vine to reach its maximum height, keep it well-watered and fertilize regularly throughout the season.

Canary bird vine needs no other maintenance.

Canary bird vine is an amazingly fast-growing vine that reaches up to 12 feet (3.6 m) in a single season and produces masses of tiny flowers.

Recommended Varieties

Usually available only under one of the names listed above.

Tips

Canary bird vine can be grown in a patio garden or on a balcony if given a large container, such as an oak barrel, with a support on which to entwine itself.

Experiment by growing canary bird vine in a hanging basket.

Canary bird vine self-seeds readily. We often discover volunteer plants sprouting in our compost mix from seeds dropped by the previous year's plants. One of these volunteers recently appeared in a pot of pepper plants. Rather than pulling it out, we gave it a bamboo stake to climb on, and it provided a pretty backdrop for the peppers.

One of the most splendid plantings of canary bird vine I have seen was the front of a south-facing house. The canary bird vine furnished privacy as well as shade when the owner was sitting on his front deck, and, from the street, it provided a stunning display of flowers that passersby often asked about.

We found another impressive idea in a garden where canary bird vine transformed a tall, dead tree stump into an object of beauty.

Canary bird vine (top) is related to the nasturtium, but its open-faced blooms more closely resemble tiny orchids. It is the largest and most reliable of the annual vines (above).

Candytuft

rose, pink, carmine, purple, mauve

Iberis umbellata
Annual Candytuft,
Globe Candytuft

Height: 8–15 inches
(20–38 cm)

Annual candytuft blooms throughout the season in tidy mounds of colour, providing a refreshingly different look. It is rather unusual to find this type of candytuft in northern gardens, simply because it is unfamiliar to many gardeners. It is, however, easy to grow and can be seeded directly into the garden in spring.

PLANTING

Seeding: Indoors 6 weeks before transplanting.

Transplanting: 1 week after the average last spring frost. Space 6–8 inches (15–20 cm) apart.

Frost Tolerance: Moderate.

Candytuft planted en masse in the garden provides a charming display of brilliant colour.

GROWING

Sunny location.

Borders, rock gardens, mass plantings, in patio containers on its own or mixed with other plants.

Water when dry but not parched.

RECOMMENDED VARIETIES

Flash Mixture • 8–10 inches (20–25 cm) tall; umbrella-shaped flowers in a mixture of rose, pale pink, carmine, purple and mauve shades.

Giant White Hyacinth • 12–15 inches (30–38 cm) tall; fragrant white flowers; excellent cutflower.

Candytuft produces a bright display in this garden in Whitehorse, Yukon.

TIPS

When buying candytuft as bedding plants, be sure to choose young plants that are not yet in bloom. Plants that are overgrown or are older than 6 weeks have a tendency to become stunted and do poorly after being transplanted into the garden.

Candytuft makes a wonderful short-stemmed cutflower.

Candytuft will flower from June until frost, provided the fresh flowers are cut regularly or the spent flowers are removed.

Years ago, a gardener told me that she grew candytuft to create the bouquets and floral arrangements for her daughter's wedding. The results were beautiful, and impressive for originality as well as the vibrant colours.

Carnation

red, pink, orange, white, yellow

Dianthus caryophyllus
Annual Carnation

Height: 6–18 inches
(15–45 cm)

Carnations are one of the most popular cutflowers because of their long-lasting, elegant blooms and their great variety of eye-catching colours. Many varieties are also graced with a delicious sugar-and-spice scent. Both my sons remember these flowers from their childhood because of the strong, cinnamon-sweet fragrance that drifted into the house through the screen door on warm summer evenings.

PLANTING

Seeding: Indoors 10–12 weeks before transplanting.

Transplanting: 1 week after the average last spring frost. Space 8–10 inches (20–25 cm) apart.

Frost Tolerance: Excellent.

GROWING

Sunny locations.

Flower beds, cutting gardens, containers.

Tall varieties may need staking.

Annual carnations provide a continuous display of blooms throughout the season, and a constant supply of long-lasting, elegant flowers for fresh bouquets.

Carnations can be one of the most fragrant annual flowers, but only certain varieties are scented.

RECOMMENDED VARIETIES

Enfant de Nice • 14 inches (40 cm) tall; highly fragrant; nice mix of colours.

Floral Essence • 6–8 inches (15–20 cm) tall; very spicy scent; great for containers; red, white, pink, yellow and bicolours.

Knight Series • 12 inches (30 cm) tall; large, double blooms; stiff, strong flower stems that do not need staking; rose, scarlet, crimson, picotee white and red, orange, yellow, white and a mixture.

TIPS

Carnations often produce multiple blooms per stem. To produce larger flowers, prune off the side buds, leaving only the top central bud on each stem.

If you are growing carnations specifically for cutting, you may wish to stake the plants to ensure perfectly straight stems. Carnations sometimes drag their heavy heads in the soil, particularly after a rainfall.

To have enough carnations on hand for a specific summer occasion, such as a wedding or anniversary party, consider planting a long row of a tall variety in your vegetable garden. Remember to deadhead the plants to make sure they continue blooming.

Plant fragrant varieties near a screen door or window that is often open, so you can enjoy their scent from inside the house as well as in the garden.

Handle carnations with care when picking or arranging the flowers. The stems and buds can be crisp and break easily, particulary if conditions are moist just before they are harvested.

To dry carnation flowers, simply tie about 5 stems in a bunch and hang them upside down. For best results, stagger the flower-heads up the length of the bunch.

The best time to pick flowers for bouquets or for drying is mid-morning, after the dew has dried from the plants (top). Flowers that are half-open are best. Carnations last up to 3 weeks after cutting (above).

My son Jim recalls being sidetracked on his way to the vegetable garden, as a small boy, by the scent of carnations. He says that carnations were the one flower that he could not resist stopping to smell, and he often picked a bloom or two to bring along with him.

Castor Bean

green

Ricinus communis
Castor Oil Plant

Height: 10 feet (3 m)

The castor bean is an extremely fast-growing plant that is often grown for the exotic appearance of its huge, serrated leaves. Landscapers favour it for contrast in the garden. I have often seen it growing in Vancouver's Stanley Park, near the rose garden, and alongside the Butterdome at the University of Alberta in Edmonton. Around the home, it can also be used as a screen to hide unattractive areas.

PLANTING

Seeding: Indoors 8–10 weeks before transplanting.

Transplanting: 1 week after the average last spring frost. Space apart 2–3 feet (60–90 cm) to form a screen.

Frost Tolerance: Poor.

GROWING

Sunny locations.

Background plantings, as a feature plant, screens, annual bush, in large containers.

Castor bean is one of the fastest-growing annuals and spreads extremely quickly into a massive-leaved bush.

This low-maintenance plant needs relatively little water and thrives in hot, dry locations.

RECOMMENDED VARIETIES

Zanzibariensis • very fast-growing; huge, green, deeply lobed leaves.

Sanguineus • fast-growing; large, reddish-green leaves.

TIPS

Although castor bean is sometimes found on lists of poisonous plants, this need not be a major concern in northern gardens, where it rarely produces its toxic seeds because our growing season is so short. Its leaves are also somewhat toxic, but they are unlikely to be eaten by children or pets in a sufficient quantity to cause poisoning because they taste bad.

Castor bean is said to repel gophers and moles.

The final size of a castor bean plant is limited by the size of its container. Once this plant becomes root-bound, it will stop growing, as shown by these 2 specimens (above), which were planted at the same time. If you are growing castor bean in a container, choose the largest pot possible. The leaves of Sanguineus (left) have a striking reddish tinge.

Celosia

red, salmon, orange, pink, bronze, yellow, cream

Celosia cristata
Cockscomb Celosia,
Crested Celosia

Celosia plumosa
Feather Celosia, Plumed Celosia,
Prince of Wales Feather

84 *Celosia spicata*
Wheat Celosia, Pink Tassels

Height: 5–28 inches
(13–70 cm)

Celosia flowers are among the most bizarre and spectacular of all annuals. There are 3 distinctly different types: crested celosia, with intricate, convoluted flowerheads that resemble brain coral or rooster's combs; feather celosia, with soft, plume-like spires; and wheat celosia, with stiff, tassel-like flowers similar to heads of wheat. All combine spectacularly with other flowers in the garden. They make excellent cutflowers and dry well for permanent arrangements.

PLANTING

Seeding: Indoors 8–10 weeks before transplanting.

Transplanting: 2 weeks after the average last spring frost. Space 6–8 inches (15–20 cm) apart.

Frost Tolerance: Poor.

GROWING

Full sun.

Borders, mixed beds, mass plantings, containers. Feather and wheat celosia in cutting gardens, as well.

Celosia provides unsurpassed colour and unusual flowers for hot, dry areas of the garden. It will thrive in hard-to-plant areas such as parched beds near heat-radiating brick walls.

RECOMMENDED VARIETIES

Crested Celosia

Jewel Box Mixture •
  5 inches (13 cm)
  tall; compact plants;
  large blooms in a
  colourful mix of
  yellow, pink,
  orange, red, salmon,
  cream and bronze.

Feather Celosia

Castle Series •
  14 inches (36 cm)
  tall; 8-inch (20 cm)
  plumes; pink,
  yellow and scarlet.

Century Mixture •
  28 inches (70 cm)
  tall; bushy, 13-inch
  (33 cm) plumes;
  mixture of cream,
  orange, red, rose
  and yellow shades.

Wheat Celosia

Spicata Pink Tassels •
  28 inches (70 cm)
  tall; 2–3-inch
  (5–8 cm) long tassels; pale silvery-pink.

TIPS

All types of celosia are wonderful in bouquets. Pick the flowers when they are fully developed. They generally last slightly over a week after cutting. Change the water frequently to extend their life in a vase.

To dry celosia, hang small bunches upside-down for about a week. Stagger the flowerheads up the length of each bunch for best results.

Feather celosia (top) does best in regions where summers—even if short—are hot and dry. The papery petals of wheat celosia (above, left) are usually pink, but new varieties have purple flowerheads. Crested celosia's bizarre flowers (above) glow in jewel-like colours.

Citrosa

green

Pelargonium citrosum
'Van Leenenii'
Citrosa Plant,
Mosquito Repellent Plant

Height: Up to 5 feet (150 cm);
spreads to an equal size.

Citrosa is often mistakenly referred to as 'citron-ella,' and it is popular for its mosquito-repellent qualities. Many people have raved to us about how well it worked in their gardens. Citrosa is an attractive plant that is similar in appearance to a scented geranium. Its thick foliage has a pleasant, lemony fragrance that repels mosquitoes within 10 feet (3 m) of the plant.

Citrosa was developed in the Netherlands by horticulturist Dirk Van Leenen. Professional growers tell us this plant is genetically engineered from lemon-scented geranium and a plant called the grass of China (Cymbopogon nardus), which contains oil of citronella, a common ingredient in insect repellents. The geranium genes give the plant to ability to spread its lemony scent, which is what keeps mosquitoes away.

PLANTING

Seeding: This plant is propagated from cuttings.

Transplanting: 1 week after the average last spring frost. Only a single plant per pot. In the garden, space 6–8 inches (15–20 cm) apart.

Frost Tolerance: Poor to moderate.

GROWING

Partial to full sun; the sunnier the location, the better.

Best in pots around patios, balconies, decks or outdoor sitting areas.

Trim foliage occasionally to increase bushiness.

RECOMMENDED VARIETIES

There is only one type.

TIPS

Plant in large containers. The larger the container, the bigger the plants will grow.

Citrosa really responds to regular watering and fertilizing, which support its rapid, vigorous growth. By watering containers daily and fertilizing once a week, you will be rewarded with huge, bushy plants by the end of the season.

Use the foliage of citrosa instead of a mosquito repellent. Simply crush a leaf between your fingers and rub it over exposed areas of your body. Citrosa repels many biting insects.

In the fall, bring citrosa indoors until the following spring. Place the plants in a bright, sunny room. A strong scent will be released by the plant when it is moved, but this soon diminishes once the plant is stationary.

Citrosa can also be overwintered in the same manner as a geranium. Refer to the 'Geranium' section for directions.

87

My co-author's son, Morgan Fallis, loves his 'mosquito plant' and often uses the rough-textured foliage to ease the itch of mosquito bites. By doing so, he spreads the repellent fragrance onto his skin and prevents further bites.

Citrosa is the only effective horticultural mosquito repellent in the world, as far as we know. Citrosa is environmentally friendly, hypo-allergenic and safe for children.

Citrosa occasionally produces tiny, lavender flowers similar to those of a scented geranium.

Clarkia

salmon, pink, mauve, red, white

Clarkia unguiculata
  (C. elegans)
Garland Flower,
Rocky Mountain Garland

Height: Up to 24 inches (60 cm)

Clarkia is another relatively uncommon plant in northern gardens. It is, however, easy to grow, and has pretty puffs of flowers that resemble little roses all up the length of its tall stems. I like to see clarkia planted in groups, rather than singly or in lines, because the plants hold each other upright and produce a striking show of colour.

PLANTING

Seeding: Indoors 6 weeks before transplanting. Outdoors around the date of the average last spring frost.

Transplanting: 2 weeks after the average last spring frost. Space 6–8 inches (15–20 cm) apart.

Frost Tolerance: Excellent.

GROWING

Partial shade to partial sun.

Mass plantings, backs of borders, feature plant.

Pinch out growing points of seedlings to induce bushiness.

Water only when soil is dry.

This flower is named after Captain William Clark of the Lewis and Clark expeditions.

RECOMMENDED VARIETIES

Usually available only under one of the names listed above.

TIPS

Add spikes of clarkia to bouquets. Cut when only a few flowers on the spikes are open—the others open almost immediately after the spike is placed in water. The flowers generally last just over a week after cutting.

Clarkia is a hardy annual that makes a splendid display in mass plantings and thrives with very little maintenance. It blooms all summer, from the uppermost stem tips right down to the ground. Crowding the plants together tends to encourage more blooms.

Clarkia is easy to grow. It is hardy, can be seeded into the garden early in spring, and thrives in hot, dry areas of the garden.

Cleome

red, pink, purple, white

Cleome hasslerana
Spider Flower

Height: 36–48 inches
(90–120 cm)

We grew cleome years ago, but few people wanted to buy this distinctive flower. Suddenly, it has been rediscovered as a must-have plant for the garden. Cleome's trumpet flowers are arranged in crown-like clusters with long, curving stamens that give the flowerhead a distinctly spidery appearance. Their gentle scent is most noticeable when you are working near the plants.

PLANTING

Seeding: Indoors 8–10 weeks before transplanting.

Transplanting: 2 weeks after the average last spring frost. Space 12–15 inches (30–40 cm) apart.

Frost Tolerance: Moderate.

GROWING

Hot, sunny locations.

Background or feature plant, in large containers.

Cleome blooms all summer long, withstands hot conditions and is among the easiest annuals to grow.

RECOMMENDED VARIETIES

Queen Series • large flowers; cherry-red, lilac, rose-pink and white.

TIPS

Plant several together in groups for the best display.

Avoid planting in windy locations, or provide stakes to support the plants.

Cleome does well in hot areas of the garden, such as flowerbeds near heat-radiating walls.

Cleome is favoured by florists for large, dramatic arrangements. I like to see these flowers displayed on their own, in a simple glass vase or pitcher.

Several cleome plants together (above, left) make the best display in the garden. White flowers (above) provide a cool elegance.

Cobaea

purple

Cobaea scandens
Cathedral Bells, Cup and Saucer
Vine, Mexican Ivy, Monastery
Bells, Purple Climber

Height: 10 feet (3 m)

The common names for cobaea suggest the beauty of this vine, which grows at an impressively quick rate, with lush foliage, curling tendrils and 2-inch (5 cm), cup-shaped, velvety flowers. Cobaea can be used as a screen to shelter exposed patios, since it does not mind the wind. It provides a pretty backdrop for outdoor seating areas.

PLANTING

Seeding: Indoors 4–6 weeks before transplanting.

Transplanting: 2 weeks after the average last spring frost. Space 12 inches (30 cm) apart to produce a screen.

Frost Tolerance: Moderate.

GROWING

Sunny locations.

Screens and trellises, in large containers with supports to climb upon.

RECOMMENDED VARIETIES

No specific varieties developed to date; usually available only under one of the names listed above.

Cobaea is a fast-growing annual vine with beautiful, purple, cup-shaped flowers, each with a saucer- like calyx.

Tips

Cobaea climbs by pretty curling tendrils that will cling to almost anything. One gardener grew it near her entranceway against a support pillar, which it completely covered by clinging to the brickwork.

Cobaea grows well in a large container if its tendrils can cling to something. We potted 6 small plants, 3 on each side of a trellis that was placed in the middle of an oak-barrel planter. The plants quickly encased the 3- by 5-foot (90 x 150 cm) wide trellis with lush foliage, and they produced a splendid show of flowers.

This vine usually flowers in mid to late summer, but if summer temperatures are cool, the blooming period may be delayed.

Although waiting for cobaea's flowers is an exercise in suspense, I find the progression fascinating (above, left). The buds remain tightly closed for several days before they balloon out and finally open, one after the other, to pale-green flowers. Over the next few days, the flowers gradually turn lilac and finally (above) to their full, intense hue.

Coleus

gold, lime green, red, rose,
cream, orange

Coleus x hybridous
Flame Nettle

Height: 12 inches (30 cm)

Breeding developments in coleus in recent years have resulted in a rainbow of vivid colours in striking combinations—a far cry from the rather insipid colours that were available when we first started growing this plant many years ago.

Coleus has its own place amongst annuals, because it is the only one that has multicoloured leaves. The colours can be mixed or matched—last summer we grew coleus in a series of oak-barrel planters along the boulevard park in front of our greenhouses. Some barrels had strong contrasts (vivid lime-green coleus with bright-orange tuberous begonias) while others had almost perfectly matched hues (dark-orange coleus with orange-flowered geraniums and pansies). The effect was splendid.

PLANTING

Seeding: Indoors 8–10 weeks before transplanting.

Transplanting: 4 or 5 weeks after the average last spring frost. Space 6–8 inches (15–20 cm) apart.

Frost Tolerance: Poor.

GROWING

Partial shade to partial sun.

As an accent plant in containers, hanging
baskets, borders, rock gardens.

Keep soil moist.

To maintain bright foliage colour, remove the
tiny lilac flowers as they appear.

RECOMMENDED VARIETIES

Wizard • superb colour combinations; does not
need to be pinched; golden, pineapple, red,
rose, sunset and a mixture.

TIPS

Faded foliage indicates too
much sun.

Try mixing various colours
of coleus in the garden to
create a spectacular patchwork.

*Coleus brightens shady
areas in a planter with
tuberous begonias,
nasturtiums and nicotiana
(above, left). Grown en
masse in the garden
(above), coleus produces a
dramatic sheet of colour.
Pinch out central leaves to
encourage plants to bush
out (below).*

🌿 *Coleus is the only annual with
vivid, multicoloured foliage. Few
annuals are as easy to grow outdoors,
and it can also be grown indoors as a
houseplant.*

Cosmos

orange, yellow, pink, red, white, cream

Cosmos bipinnatus
Common Cosmos,
Garden Cosmos

Cosmos sulphureus
Mexican Aster

Height: 10–36 inches
(25–90 cm)

Cosmos is one of the loveliest garden flowers. There are 2 distinctly different types: the more common garden cosmos, and the less common Mexican asters. Garden cosmos is a tall, elegant plant with feathery foliage and daisy-like flowers in shades of pink, red and white. Mexican aster is a shorter plant that makes excellent borders, with smaller, double flowers in orange and yellow.

PLANTING

Seeding: Indoors 4–6 weeks before transplanting. Outdoors from 1 week after the average last spring frost until mid-June.

Transplanting: 2 weeks after the average last spring frost. Space short varieties 6–8 inches (15–20 cm) apart, and tall varieties 10–12 inches (20–30 cm) apart.

Frost Tolerance: Moderate.

GROWING

Sun; does well in hot, dry locations.

Borders, mass plantings, meadow gardens, cutting gardens, in containers, as feature plants or sprinkled among other flowers.

Water when dry.

Cosmos grows well in poor soil.

Cosmos is among the easiest annuals to grow. It grows quickly from seed scattered in the garden, does well in poor soil, needs little supplementary watering and requires only occasional deadheading.

The name of these flowers is from the Greek kosmos, meaning 'beautiful.'

Recommended Varieties

Mexican Aster

Ladybird • 10–12 inches (25–30 cm) tall; 1¹/₂-inch (4 cm) flowers; award-winning variety; orange, yellow and a mixture.

Garden Cosmos

Daydream • up to 36 inches (90 cm) tall; large, single, pale pink flowers with distinct rose centres.

Dazzler • up to 36 inches (90 cm) tall; giant, single, crimson flowers.

Pinkie • up to 36 inches (90 cm) tall; giant, single, rose-pink flowers.

Picotee • up to 36 inches (90 cm) tall; giant, single, bicoloured flowers; some rosy-red with white centres and some pure white with rosy-red centres.

Seashells Mix • up to 36 inches (90 cm) tall; distinctive flowers with unique petals that form fluted seashells around yellow button-like centres; creamy white, satin or shell pink, and 2-toned with crimson and pink interiors.

Sonata • up to 24 inches (60 cm) tall; giant, single flowers; more flowers than most varieties, held on top of mounded plants; available in white and a mixture including pink, rose, red and white.

Tips

The flowers of cosmos are wonderful in bouquets. They can be mixed with other flowers, or gathered alone in bunches. Their feathery, fern-like foliage eliminates the need to add greenery to a bouquet. Pick when flowers are open, but the petals are not yet lying flat. Cosmos lasts slightly longer than a week after cutting.

Seashells cosmos is particularly coveted for bouquets, because of its unique flowers. Each petal is tubular and flares at the tip into a trumpet. White Seashells mixed with pink helipterum is one of my favourite summer bouquets.

Garden cosmos is fast-growing and does well even in the short summers of the Yukon Territories (top). Mexican asters, shirley poppies and mealy cup sage (Salvia farinacea) create a meadow of flowers for bouquets (above).

Dahlberg Daisy

yellow

Dyssodia tenuiloba
  (syn. *Thymophylla
  tenuiloba*)

Height: 4 inches (10 cm);
  trails to 12 inches
  (30 cm)

My daughter-in-law Valerie discovered the Dahlberg daisy while flipping through an American seed catalogue many years ago. We brought a few plants in on a trial basis, planted them into hanging baskets, and fell in love with the results. Dahlberg daisy sprays upwards and out from containers in a gentle curve. It has fragrant, feathery foliage and myriad bright-yellow daisies that provide a cheery mix in hanging baskets and containers.

PLANTING

Seeding: Indoors 6–8 weeks before transplanting.

Transplanting: 2 weeks after the average last spring frost. Space 4–6 inches (10–15 cm) apart.

Frost Tolerance: Moderate.

GROWING

Sun.

Trailing in hanging baskets, windowboxes and planters, for low borders, edging, and in rock gardens.

RECOMMENDED VARIETIES

Golden Fleece • single, daisy-type, golden yellow, 1-inch (2.5 cm) flowers.

Tips

Dahlberg daisies do not need deadheading, because the finished flowers look tidy and the plants will continue to bloom throughout the season.

A customer recently sent in a photograph of her beautiful window-box, in which she had planted Dahlberg daisy with yellow and cream gazanias and lobelia in red and pale blue. The effect was charming.

I like to combine the bright yellow of Dahlberg daisies with flowers that provide a colour contrast. Ivy geraniums in fiery red or bright rose are great partners in hanging baskets, because they also curve up and away from the container.

Dahlberg daisies look splendid spilling onto a garden path, where the fragrance may be released when passersby brush against the plants.

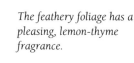

The feathery foliage has a pleasing, lemon-thyme fragrance.

Dahlberg daisy can be used with geraniums for variety in sunny container gardens.

Dahlia

red, rose, orange, gold, yellow, white

Dahlia pinnata

Height: 14–36 inches
     (35–90 cm)

Dahlias make marvellous cutflowers. A bunch of dahlias in a vase makes a splendid bouquet, all on its own. The variety Octopus (opposite, lower) is particularly striking for the size and unusual look of its flowers.

The year we started our first greenhouse we grew a lot of dahlias, and just a few other types of flowers. One of the reasons I chose to include dahlias in this book is my memory of seeing their splendid show in my mother's garden every summer. Nostalgia tempts many gardeners to grow particular plants, but there are other good reasons to grow dahlias. They are rich, aristocratic flowers that come in many sizes and types, and in a wide spectrum of unsurpassed colours.

PLANTING

Seeding: Indoors 8–10 weeks before transplanting.

Transplanting: Bedding plants or tubers 2 weeks after the average last spring frost. Space bedding plants 10–12 inches (20–30·cm) apart.

Frost Tolerance: Poor.

GROWING

Sun to light shade.

Borders, backgrounds, feature plants, containers, mass displays, cutting gardens.

Recommended Varieties

Figaro Mixture • 14–16 inches (35–40 cm) tall; masses of 3-inch (8 cm) flowers; yellow, gold, orange, scarlet, crimson, white.

Harlequin Mixture • 14–16 inches (35–40 cm) tall; early-blooming; intriguing flowers with matching or contrasting inner petals; combinations of white, yellow, red and pink.

Sunny Series • 14–16 inches (35–40 cm) tall; 3-inch (8 cm) double flowers in red, rose and yellow.

Octopus Mixture • 24–36 inches (60–90 cm) tall; huge flowers up to 6 inches (15 cm) across; unusual petals that twist and curl; strong stems and many flowers in a full range of colours.

Tips

Dahlias bloom about midsummer, later than many annuals, but these splendid flowers are worth the wait and remain at their prime well into autumn.

Octopus Mixture dahlias grow large enough for the plants to act as a screen to cover unattractive areas in a yard.

Dahlias are my mother's favourite flower. She has grown them every year since I was a little girl. The variety Harlequin (top) has handsome flowers with matching or contrasting inner petals.

All of the above recommended varieties are grown from seed, and they usually do not produce tubers of a size suitable for storage. I prefer dahlias from seed because they are generally easier to grow. Dahlias from tubers often have larger flowers, but they tend to be slower to bloom and more likely to need staking, and they require constant watering and fertilizing to stay in flower.

For information on storing tubers, refer to the instructions under 'Begonia.'

Daisy

white, yellow

*Chrysanthemum
paludosum*
Annual Daisy,
Annual Marguerite

*Chrysanthemum
multicaule*
Annual Daisy, Butter Daisy

Height: 7–10 inches
(18–25 cm)

There is something particularly appealing about the daisy's simple flowers—they look fresh and clean, and people just love them. Annual daisies bloom as bedding plants in cell-packs before being planted into the garden, and in early spring, they produce a solid carpet of refreshing colour on the greenhouse tables. These daisies produce an equally fine show in both the garden and containers.

PLANTING

Seeding: Indoors 8–10 weeks before transplanting.

Transplanting: On or about the date of the average last spring frost. Space 6–8 inches (15–20 cm) apart.

Frost Tolerance: Moderate.

Annual daisies have charming flowers and the plants are extremely tolerant of drought.

GROWING

Partial to full sun.

Borders, edging, planters, annual groundcovers, rock gardens, combined with other plants in windowboxes, patio pots and hanging baskets.

Recommended Varieties

Snowland • 10 inches (25 cm) tall; white flowers with yellow centres.

Yellow Buttons • 7–8 inches (18–20 cm) tall; round-petalled, bright yellow flowers.

Tips

Deadheading keeps these plants tidy, although it is not essential. Annual daisies will continue to bloom whether or not the spent flowers are removed.

Annual daisies are splendid as accent plants in containers, where they provide bright bursts of colour that contrast with larger-flowered feature plants such as geraniums. We have used daisies in various combinations in patio pots and huge moss planters for several years.

The 2 types of annual daisies work well together as a mixed border in the garden (above), with a row of the taller white daisies (opposite) planted behind the shorter yellow daisies (top).

Datura

white, yellow, lilac

Datura inoxia, D. metel
Angel's Trumpet, Hindu Datura,
Horn of Plenty, Indian Apple,
Thorn Apple, Trumpet Flower

Brugmansia arborea,
  B. x candida,
  B. suaveolens
  (syn. *Datura*)
Angel's Trumpet, Brugmansia

Height: 3–5 feet (90–150 cm)

Everyone agrees that datura is a showy, exotic plant in the garden, but not everyone in botanical circles agrees on what to call them. We refer individually to the plant with upright, white, lilac or yellow trumpet flowers as datura, to the plant with dangling, yellow or white bell flowers as brugmansia, and to both collectively as datura. Each is an impressive plant with large, showy, musky-scented flowers.

PLANTING

Seeding: Not recommended, because it takes too long to grow from seed.

Transplanting: 3 weeks after the average last spring frost. Space 12–24 inches (30–60 cm) apart in the garden.

Frost Tolerance: Poor.

Datura is, without a doubt, one of the most attention-grabbing plants in the garden.

GROWING

Heat and sun.

Background or feature plant; in large containers.

Water heavily.

Datura is sometimes called 'thorn apple,' for its habit of producing round, spiky seedpods. The flowers last only a single day, but by midsummer they are produced in a continuous sequence until fall frosts. Brugmansia is often categorized as a conservatory plant. If you have this type of sunroom in your house, bring the plant indoors at the end of the season—it may eventually reach a height of up to 10 feet (3 m).

Recommended Varieties

Usually available only under one of the names listed above.

Here are what we find to be the differences in the various types:

B. arborea • over 5 feet (150 cm) tall; dangling, yellow or white, 8-inch (20 cm) bell flowers.

B. x candida • 3–4 feet (90–120 cm) tall; dangling, 8-inch (20 cm) bell flowers; usually white, but sometimes available in pink; single and double-flowered forms available.

B. suaveolens • up to 5 feet (150 cm) tall; the old favourite; dangling, 7-inch (18 cm) trumpet flowers; usually white, but sometimes yellow or lilac.

D. inoxia • 3 feet (90 cm) tall; upright, pink or lavender trumpet flowers.

D. metel • 2–5 feet (60–150 cm) tall; upright, trumpet flowers; usually white, but sometimes yellow or purple; single and double-flowered forms available.

Tips

Plant datura in the largest container available to allow it to grow to its full size. The plants grow quickly and can double in size within a week of being repotted, but they will stop growing once their roots fill the container. For best results, use only a single plant per pot.

The leaves and seeds of datura are poisonous. Do not plant in areas where small children play.

Brugmansia is a tropical-looking plant (above) that can grow to an immense size, with a showy display of huge flowers (top).

Dianthus

red, pink, purple, white

Dianthus chinensis
Annual Pink, China Rainbow
Pink, Chinese Pink

Height: 4–10 inches
(10–25 cm)

Dianthus is a charming flower with fringed petals and bright colours. It fits into almost any garden setting. We often mix it with other flowers in containers for bright splashes of colour. Some varieties have a spicy fragrance, similar to that of carnations. Fragrant varieties should be planted around a patio, or in pots where their perfume can be fully appreciated.

PLANTING

Seeding: Indoors 8–10 weeks before transplanting.

Transplanting: As soon as the ground is workable in spring, regardless of when you expect the last spring frost. Space 6 inches (15 cm) apart.

Frost Tolerance: Excellent.

GROWING

Sunny locations.

Borders, containers, edgings, mass plantings, rock gardens, cottage gardens.

Do not allow plants to dry out.

Many gardeners tell me they find dianthus a nostalgic flower. It reminds them of the perennial sweet william that grew in their parents' or grandparents' gardens. The annual dianthus has the benefit of blooming non-stop throughout the summer.

Dianthus can be one of the longest-blooming annuals, provided the plants are deadheaded. It blooms early and will continue to flower through the first fall frosts.

Recommended Varieties

Parfait Series • 4–6 inches (10–15 cm) tall; award-winning variety; early-flowering; even growth habit; 2-inch (5 cm) flowers accented with distinct eyes; crimson and scarlet, each with a distinct dark eye.

Telstar Series • 8–10 inches (20–25 cm) tall; award-winning variety; blooms early and continues with a profusion of flowers all summer; excellent heat tolerance; 1½-inch (4 cm) flowers; pink, purple, scarlet, white, picotee and a mixture.

Tips

Dianthus is generally disease-free and untroubled by insects.

Plant dianthus in a pot or windowbox in early spring to brighten your doorstep or apartment balcony. It looks pretty on its own or mixed with bright pansies, which are even more tolerant of frost than is dianthus.

Dianthus is related to the carnation, and it too is a long-lasting cutflower.

Parfait dianthus (above) demonstrates the changes plant breeders aim to create. The flowers are larger and more prolific, and they are borne close to the leaves. Parfait plants are compact and rounded, so they produce a mound of solid colour in pots and make an even, uniform border. The plant shown here is Strawberry Parfait. Its mate is Raspberry Parfait, which has similar flowers in crimson shades.

Telstar dianthus (left) blooms non-stop through the heat of the summer. Hot temperatures often cause older varieties to stop flowering.

Dracaena

green

Cordyline indivisa
Spike Grass, Spikes

Height: 36 inches (90 cm)

The tall spikes of dracaena are most often seen in the centre of patio pots and in windowboxes, where they provide height and contrast. Dracaena as a feature plant greatly enhances formal gardens with its smooth, sword-shaped leaves, and several plants staggered in a row between other annuals make a dignified, orderly border.

PLANTING

Seeding: Not recommended, because it takes far too long.

Transplanting: Around the date of the average last spring frost. Space as required to attain the desired effect, from 8 inches (20 cm) apart.

Frost Tolerance: Excellent.

GROWING

Full shade to full sun.

In the centre of containers and windowboxes, as an accent plant for borders and flower beds.

Dracaena needs no maintenance other than occasional watering, and it is relatively untroubled by insects and plant diseases.

RECOMMENDED VARIETIES

Usually available only under one of the names listed above.

Dracaena is one of the hardiest annuals. It can withstand several frosts and a fair bit of snow without noticeable effects. One gardener told me that she left a plant in her garden, where it remained green and healthy throughout the fall. On December 1st, she finally took pity on it, and brought it indoors as a houseplant.

Tips

Dracaena with bright-red geraniums and dark-blue trailing lobelia make a strikingly simple, classic combination in planters.

Experiment with the variegated houseplant types of dracaena to add variety and accent colour to planters. These types of dracaena are more tender and must be given a fairly shaded, sheltered location.

Dracaena is technically not an annual, but we treat it as one because it does not survive most northern winters. In milder climates, it can grow into a huge plant. Many people manage to keep their plants year after year: some bring dracaena indoors in the fall and treat it as a houseplant, others dig up the entire plant and overwinter it in much the same manner as geraniums and fuchsias.

A long row of dracaena with Tango geraniums and nepeta ivy makes a dignified display.

Dracaena is the only annual that does well in both full shade and full sun.

Leave the raising of dracaena seedlings to professional growers! Seed is slow to germinate, and dracaena has a high rate of non-viable seeds. It takes 18 months from seeding to produce plants of the size we are accustomed to seeing for sale in retail greenhouses.

Dusty Miller

silver

Centaurea cineraria
   (Senecio cineraria)
Silver Dust

Tanacetum ptarmiciflorum
   (syn. Chrysanthemum
   ptarmiciflorum)
Silver Lace

Height: 8–14 inches
   (20–35 cm)

Although they are actually 2 entirely separate species of plants, the 2 types of dusty miller serve the same purpose in the garden, differing mainly in the look of their leaves. Silver Lace has fine, lacy, greenish-silver leaves while Silver Dust has deeply lobed, fern-like, silvery-white leaves. Both these foliage plants make a striking display when mixed with brightly coloured flowering annuals, such as geraniums, salvia and marigolds.

PLANTING

Seeding: Indoors 10–12 weeks before transplanting.

Transplanting: Around the date of the average last spring frost. Space 8 inches (20 cm) apart.

Frost Tolerance: Excellent.

GROWING

Partial shade to partial sun.

Borders, edgings, accent plants, containers, to create patterns in formal garden designs.

Prune plants as required to maintain their low, bushy shape.

Silver Dust plants that have been left in the garden through the winter often look as if they were alive. They are not, but they have been perfectly preserved in a way similar to freeze-drying.

Recommended Varieties

Silver Dust •
8–12 inches
(20–30 cm) tall;
deeply lobed,
silvery-white leaves.

Silver Lace •
12–14 inches
(30–35 cm) tall;
fine, lacy, silvery-
green foliage.

Tips

For a soft, subtle effect, grow dusty miller
with only white-flowered plants. We added
dusty miller to a whiskey-barrel planter filled
with white geraniums, petunias, lobelia and
alyssum. We especially appreciate an all-white
combination around a patio where we often sit
outdoors on late summer evenings. White petals
reflect light and appear to glow in the semi-
darkness of the night.

*The two types of dusty
miller differ in their size,
leaf shape and colour.*

*A combination of silver dust,
pansies, geraniums, ageratum and
dracaena creates a striking border.*

Dusty miller has beautiful silvery
foliage unlike that of any other
annual. It provides a fine companion to
almost any flower.
  Dusty miller, like most annuals that
are grown for their foliage, is a low-
maintenance plant. It needs little more
than to be watered. Dusty miller is
relatively untroubled by plant diseases
and is of little interest to bothersome
insects.

ing Scented Stock

a bicornis
Evening Stock, Night Scent,
Night Scented Stock

Height: 14–16 inches
(36–40 cm)

The heavenly, cocoa-butter, sweet scent of these modest flowers is addictive—if you plant them once, you will probably want them in your garden every year. Put the plants near a doorway, around an outdoor sitting area, under an open window—wherever you can enjoy their powerful fragrance.

PLANTING

Seeding: Indoors 5–6 weeks before transplanting. Outdoors very soon after the average last spring frost.

Transplanting: Around the date of the average last spring frost. Space 6 inches (15 cm) apart.

Frost Tolerance: Moderate.

Evening scented stocks really sparked my love for fragrant annuals the year we planted them beside the back porch. On warm summer evenings, their powerful scent would drift into the house through open windows and fill every room with sweet perfume.

GROWING

Sunny location.

Mixed flower beds, windowboxes, planters, patio pots.

RECOMMENDED VARIETIES

Usually available only under one of the names listed above.

Evening scented stocks are among the most fragrant of annuals; as the name implies, their divine perfume is strongest in the evening.

Tips

If you are sowing these plants directly into your garden, seed thickly and thin by picking out only a few seedlings. Create a miniature meadow of fragrance by scattering seed in a 1-foot-wide (30 cm) band.

Many gardening advisors recommend planting evening scented stocks among other, more attractive annuals, because their flowers are not particularly showy and they are sometimes rather straggly plants with a tendency to flop over. However, I find that planting a dense patch provides a pretty show of flowers, with plants that hold each other upright.

Some people have told me that they like to snip off a few flower stems to poke into a bouquet for fragrance.

Evening scented stocks prefer cool weather, so they do well in northern climates.

Flowering Cabbage and Kale

burgundy, red, pink, white, green

Brassica oleracea
Ornamental Cabbage,
Ornamental Kale

Height: 6–12 inches
(15–30 cm)

These unusual and decorative plants provide striking accents in the garden with their attractive, colourful foliage. Flowering cabbage and kale are large, frost-hardy rosettes of deeply cut and frilled leaves that appear flower-like. Both prefer cooler weather, and their colour actually intensifies as temperatures drop in the fall.

PLANTING

Seeding: Indoors 6–8 weeks before transplanting.

Transplanting: As soon as the ground is workable in the spring. Space 12–18 inches (30–45 cm) apart.

Frost Tolerance: Excellent.

GROWING

Sun but not heat.

Ornamental borders, mass plantings, accent plants, as edging, in small groups or as a single feature plant in the centre of flower beds and containers.

Flowering cabbage and kale are low-maintenance plants that provide a very long season of colour. Because they are highly tolerant of frosts, they can be planted out in the very early spring and left in the ground until late fall; in milder areas, they can be planted in the fall for colour throughout the winter.

Flowering cabbage and kale are among the hardiest of annuals. They can withstand temperatures to 20° F (-7° C), and the foliage colour actually intensifies in cooler temperatures.

Recommended Varieties

Dynasty Series • flowering cabbage; 12 inches (30 cm) tall; colourful, semi-waved, open rosettes of green leaves with colourful centres; tight, compact heads; pink, red, white and a mixture.

Kamome Series • flowering kale; 6–8 inches (15–20 cm) tall; early-colouring, dwarf plants with fringed leaves and finely ruffled edges; red and white.

Tips

When buying bedding plants from a green-house, choose small plants. Seedlings which have been growing in a container for more than 6 weeks will not produce full heads.

Ornamental cabbage and kale are edible, but eating them is not recommended—the leaves are very bitter.

For early spring or fall colour, plant a long row of ornamental cabbage or kale in a window-box, or as a small group in a large container, such as a whiskey barrel.

Ornamental cabbage resembles a gigantic, ruffled rose (above). Ornamental cabbage and kale are favoured in commercial plantings because the plants are larger than many annuals and extremely uniform. Their bright colours and consistent shapes create splendid patterns en masse in flower beds (below, left).

115

For an unusual, long-lasting cutflower or a table centrepiece, cut a plant off at its base and place it in water (above).

Four O'Clock

red, pink, violet, yellow, white

Mirabilis jalapa
Beauty of the Night,
Marvel of Peru

Height: 24 inches (60 cm)

Four o'clock's trumpet-shaped flowers usually open around the hour suggested by the plant's name, but they will remain open throughout the day when skies are overcast. Flowers that open in the late afternoon or early evening and close up the following morning, such as four o'clocks, daturas and moon vine, make interesting combinations with flowers such as morning glories, which open afresh each morning.

PLANTING

Seeding: Indoors 4–6 weeks before transplanting. Outdoors 2 weeks after the average last spring frost.

Transplanting: 1 week after the average last spring frost. Space 12–18 inches (30–45 cm) apart.

Frost Tolerance: Poor.

Four o'clocks are most remarkable plants that habitually open their flowers in the late afternoon and release a wonderful, rich fragrance on warm evenings.

GROWING

Sunny locations; does well in hot sites.

Back of borders, in large containers, as an annual hedge, screen, annual shrub, in cottage gardens.

Can be planted in poor soil.

Recommended Varieties

Usually available only under one of the names listed above.

Tips

We grew four o'clocks in a whiskey barrel planter, with a tomato cage to support the plants.

Four o'clocks are slow to mature and usually do not bloom until midsummer, but the floral show is worth the wait. At first, the flowers open in ones and twos, and then by the dozens.

A single cut stalk of four o'clock fills an entire room with a heady, rose-jasmine perfume.

Four o'clock is so named because of its remarkably punctual habit of opening its flowers in the late afternoon. The word Mirabilis means 'miraculous,' for its ability to sometimes produce flowers of several different colours on a single stalk. Four o'clocks are technically not annuals, but they are treated as such because they do not survive our winters. In warmer climates, the plants grow as perennials and produce deep, tuberous roots that can weigh more than 40 pounds (18 kg)!

Fuchsia

red, orange, purple, mauve,
pink, white

Fuchsia x hybrida
Lady's Eardrop

Height: Trailing 12–24 inches
(30–60 cm)

Fuchsias are elegant, exotic-looking flowers in a range of colours and flower types. They are most often planted alone in hanging baskets, but they look equally stunning when combined with other plants in any type of planter. The showy flowers range from the size of a thumbnail to the size of the palm of your hand.

PLANTING

Seeding: Sowing is not recommended. Fuchsias are generally propagated from cuttings 8–12 weeks before transplanting.

Transplanting: 2 weeks after the average last spring frost. Space bush varieties 6–8 inches (15–20 cm) apart in the garden.

Frost Tolerance: Poor.

GROWING

Partial shade to partial sun, in a site sheltered from wind.

Hanging baskets, windowboxes, patio planters.

Pinch shoots to encourage bushiness.

Fuchsias are elegant plants that provide a showy display throughout the summer. In early May, I love to walk through the greenhouses under hanging baskets of fuchsias in full bloom. The effect is like having a ceiling of solid flowers.

The largest flowers are those of Pink Marshmallow, more than twice as big as the average-sized fuchsia. 'Corolla' is the term used to describe the outer petals, and 'corona' is the term for the inner petals.

Recommended Varieties

Most fuchsias are 2-toned, with 1 colour on the corona (inner petals), and another on the corolla (outer petals).

Double-Flowered Varieties

Blue Eyes • mauve corona, rosy-red corolla

Bicentennial • deep coral corona, soft coral corolla

Dark Eyes • purple corona, red corolla

Hawaii Night • white corona, purple corolla

Personality • reddish-purple corona, red corolla

Pink Marshmallow • huge, single-coloured, blush-pink flowers.

Rosy Ruffles • rose-coloured, ruffled corona, pink-white corolla

White Eyes • white corona, red corolla

Winston Churchill • purple-blue corona, rose-pink corolla

There are thousands of varieties of fuchsias, and new ones are constantly being introduced by plant breeders. Gardeners who love these plants find the constantly changing selection exciting. Many of our regular customers wait impatiently each spring for our greenhouse to open, so they can see what new colour combinations have become available.

Many gardeners purchase fuchsias early in the spring, to ensure that they receive their preferred varieties at a good price. This means, however, that they must keep the plants indoors until the weather warms enough to permit planting outdoors. In order to keep the plants healthy indoors during the early spring, place them in the sunniest possible location in your house—preferably in a south or west window. Allow the soil to dry slightly between waterings. Fertilize weekly with a balanced fertilizer such as 20-20-20.

On warm days when the temperature is above 60° F (15°C), put the plants outside in a sunny spot. This helps to acclimatize the plants to the outdoors. Don't forget to bring them in at night. Remember, due to the lower light levels in your home, blooms and buds may drop and the plants may stop blooming periodically. This condition is temporary and your plants will bloom again once they are outside in a sunny location. (Geraniums can be treated in the same manner.)

Single-Flowered Varieties

Black Prince • miniature; violet-black corona, pink corolla

Little Beauty • miniature; lavender corona, rose corolla

Marinka • solid-red flowers

TIPS

To keep fuchsias blooming throughout the summer, simply remove the dark-purple, cherry-like seedpods after finished flowers drop. Because these plants bloom so prolifically, a weekly fertilizing program is strongly recommended.

Fuchsias can be brought into a bright, sunny location indoors in the fall to serve as houseplants. They will look pretty for only a short time, because light levels inside a house are generally too low to support vigorous growth. After the blooming has finished, trim the plants back and store as directed for geraniums.

Dark Eyes (above) is a double-flowered variety, with the typical profusion of flowers. Little Beauty (left) is a single-flowered miniature, with masses of tiny, half-inch (2 cm) flowers. In their native state in New Zealand, Tahiti, and from Mexico to Patagonia, fuchsias grow into impressive trees. This specimen (right), growing at our greenhouses, is about 30 years old.

Gazania

yellow, orange, bronze, pink,
white

Gazania splendens
Treasure Flower

Height: 8 inches (20 cm)

Gazanias have large, bright, daisy-like flowers with amazingly precise, dark patterns that vary ever so slightly from flower to flower. These plants do well in hot, dry locations and are a good choice for planters on windy balconies. The flowers are sun-worshippers, and they close up at night and on very cloudy days.

PLANTING

Seeding: Indoors 11–12 weeks before transplanting.

Transplanting: 1 week after the average last spring frost. Space 6–8 inches (15–20 cm) apart.

Frost Tolerance: Moderate.

The progressive opening of these flowers in the morning is fascinating. One day, about mid-morning, I stopped by a pot of gazanias to pinch out the dead flowers. On passing by again, only about an hour later, I discovered that the number of open flowers had almost doubled.

GROWING

Hot, sunny locations, the sunnier the better.

Edgings, borders, mass plantings, in groups among low-growing evergreen shrubs, at the front of a sunny flower garden, in containers.

Water only when dry.

Recommended Varieties

Daybreak Series •
bright orange, bright
yellow, bronze,
apricot and gold,
and a mixture.

Tips

Gazania's finished
flowers and unopened
buds look somewhat
similar. Be careful when
deadheading that you
do not mistakenly
pinch out the buds.
The finished flowers
appear slightly messy.

*Gazanias have thick leaves with soft, silvery undersides,
and sunny flowers in glowing colours (above). The tiny,
purple cupflowers in the foreground are nierembergia.
Gazanias are native to South Africa.*

*Gazanias are strikingly
beautiful flowers that
thrive in hot, dry areas of the
garden.*

Geranium

red, orange, coral, salmon,
pink, violet, lavender, white

Pelargonium x hortorum
Zonal Geranium,
Double-Flowered Geranium

Pelargonium peltatum
Ivy Geranium,
Hanging Geranium

124

Pelargonium x domesticum
Pansy Geranium,
Martha Washington Geranium,
Lady Washington Geranium,
Regal Geranium

Pelargonium x hortorum
 'hybrid'
Hybrid Geranium,
Seed Geranium,
Single-Flowered Geranium

Height: 10–18 inches
         (25–45 cm)

Geraniums are one of the most popular bedding plants in the world. Their array of flower colours and growth habits allows them to be planted into almost any garden.

Geraniums will always be one of my most-loved flowers. Over the past 25 years, we have tried well over 100 different varieties in our greenhouses. It has been hard to drop some of our favourites, but the new varieties that replace them have marked improvements in colour intensity, flower size, leaf colour and uniformity of growth.

Zonal geraniums are the most common type, with large, double flowerheads. These plants are propagated from cuttings, and they do well in almost any garden setting. Ivy geraniums have medium-sized double and semi-double flowerheads and are best in hanging baskets, windowboxes and patio planters. Pansy geraniums have spectacular, large flowers with dark blotches and serrated, fragrant leaves; they make great accent plants. Hybrid geraniums have medium-sized, single-petalled flowerheads; they are ideal for windowboxes and mass plantings.

PLANTING

Seeding: Sowing is not recommended. Geraniums are generally propagated from cuttings 8–12 weeks before transplanting.

Transplanting: 1 week after the average last spring frost. Space hybrid and ivy types 8 inches (20 cm) apart, and zonal and pansy types 10–12 inches (25–30 cm) apart.

Frost Tolerance: Moderate.

GROWING

Sunny location best; all varieties tolerate light shade. Ivy geraniums grow best in partial sun to partial shade.

Mass plantings, in containers of all types, as accent or feature plants, in flower beds.

Pinching ivy geraniums results in bushier plants.

RECOMMENDED VARIETIES

Zonal Geraniums

Red-flowered • Disco (carmine with crimson eye on each petal); Tango (a blazing dark red—the most popular variety in the world)

Salmon-flowered • Schönehelena (large flowers, rosy-salmon); Sunbelt Coral (deep coral)

Pink-flowered • Blues (bright pink with white eye on each petal—our most popular pink geranium); Katie (rose-pink)

Purple-flowered • Fox (dark lavender); Precious (pastel mauve)

White-flowered • Alba (icy white)

Other colours • novelty varieties: Mrs. Cox (pink, white and green variegated leaves, small pink flowers); Mrs. Parker (greyish-green-and-white leaves, pastel-pink flowers)

Tango is the most popular variety of geranium in the entire world.

125

Red is by far the most popular colour in geraniums. In a recent study conducted by one of the world's largest producers of geraniums, red made up 42% of purchases, with salmon as the runner-up at 20%. Pink was the next most popular choice, at 14%, followed by purple at 8%, white at 4% and all other colours combined at 12%.

126

Pink Mini-Cascade is the type of ivy geranium commonly found throughout Europe. Alyssum adds fragrance to this windowbox display.

Ivy Geraniums

Red-flowered • Barock (dark red, semi-double); Bingo (intense red, double); Elizabeth (scarlet, double); Red Mini-Cascade (cherry-red, single-petalled flowers, European type); Nanette (coral-red, double)

Salmon-flowered • Judy (deep coral, double); Salmon Queen (brilliant deep salmon)

Pink-flowered • Belladonna (pink, rosebud-type flowers); Grace (light pink, double); Lulu (fuchsia with a hint of red, semi-double); Marilyn (bright pink, double); Monique (dark candy pink, semi-double); Narina (intense dark rose, semi-double); Nicole (candy-pink, double); Pink Mini-Cascade (soft-pink, single-petalled flowers, European type); Sybil Holmes (dark candy-pink, rosebud-type, a longtime favourite)

Purple-flowered • Butterfly (light purple, double); Lila Mini-Cascade (lavender, single-petalled flowers, European type)

White-flowered • Snow Queen (clear white petals with a small magenta marking in the centre, semi-double)

Other colours • Alpine Glow (white with lilac edges, single-petalled flowers); Mexicana (white with scarlet edges, single-petalled flowers); Picotee (white with pastel pink edges, single-petalled flowers); Pretty Girl (white with orange edges, single-petalled flowers); Rosie O'Day (white with rose edges, single-petalled flowers)

Pansy geraniums have spectacular, large flowers and serrated, fragrant leaves.

Pansy Geraniums

Usually available only under one of the names listed above, in a wide range of flower colours, most often with distinctive markings in contrasting hues.

Hybrid Geraniums
(all are single-petalled flowers)

Red-flowered • Lone Ranger (bright cardinal-red); Pinto Red (bright scarlet); Pinto Scarlet (bright scarlet)

Salmon-flowered • Cameo (deep salmon-coral); Pinto Blush (light salmon); Pinto Salmon (medium salmon)

Pink-flowered • Neon Rose (brilliant hot-pink); Picasso (electric violet-rose); Pinto Rose (dark candy-pink with a white eye on each petal)

Purple-flowered • Pinto Quicksilver (silvery lavender)

White-flowered • Pinto White (icy white)

Other colours • Orange Appeal (the first true orange geranium); Pinto Bicolour (red and white)

Some gardeners like to purchase large geraniums early in the spring, so that they can be sure to get the varieties they want. This means they must keep the plants indoors until the weather warms. For instructions on how to keep geraniums healthy during this period, refer to the information under 'Fuchsia.'

A single geranium plant makes a strong statement at the doorway of this home in Victoria, B.C.

Scented geraniums have tiny, insignificant flowers and are considered to be more of an herb than an ornamental plant. The leaves are often used to flavour teas, jellies and cakes, or to add fragrance to sachets and potpourris. Scented geraniums have a range of distinctive fragrances—including lemon, rose, apple, ginger, peppermint, coconut, apricot and lime—which are released from their leaves. I like these plants near outdoor seating areas, where their fragrance can be best appreciated.

Tips

Keep plants neat and encourage more blooming by removing finished flowerheads. You can use scissors to remove them, but I find it easier just to snap the flowerheads off with my fingers. Leaving a couple inches of stem prevents damaging the plant. The leaves will hide these stem ends until they turn brown and fall off.

Most geraniums (except hybrid types) can be brought indoors in the fall as houseplants in bright, sunny locations. They will look pretty for only a short while, however, because light levels inside a house are generally too low to support these plants. After the blooming has finished, trim the plants back and store as directed below.

How to Overwinter Geraniums

Geraniums can be brought indoors for the winter, but they do require some special attention so they will bloom again the following spring. Here are the steps to take:

1. When the plants cease blooming, cut away half of the growth with sharp scissors or small pruning shears. Store in a cool, dark spot at 45–50° F (7–10°C); cold rooms, heated garages and unfinished basements are ideal. Water only enough to keep the soil from becoming completely dry. All of the leaves of the plant will fall off and the stems will become woody.

2. In February, trim the stems to one-third of their original height, and bring the pots into a location with lots of direct sunlight. Temperatures higher than normal room temperature (ideally 70–75° F/21–23° C) encourage quicker growth—try placing the pots on top of the refrigerator or on a sunny windowsill. Water just enough to moisten the soil. Allow the top two-thirds of the soil to dry out between waterings. Fertilize with 20-20-20.

3. When the new growth appears, remove the plant from its pot and shake off the old soil. Repot using new potting soil into a pot just large enough to contain the roots. Fertilize every 2 weeks with 20-20-20.

4. Once shoots are 3–4 inches (8–10 cm) long, take cuttings from the old plants. At this point, we usually discard the original plants, because the cuttings result in geraniums that are fuller, greener and more vigorous. Cut new leaves off cleanly at the base with a sharp knife. Dip the cut end into a rooting compound, shake off the excess and plant in a good quality starter mix (a fine-textured potting medium that usually contains a mild fertilizer). Place plants in a sunny window and keep evenly moist. Fertilize every second week with 10-52-10 fertilizer at half-strength.

5. On warm, sunny days in the early spring, set the plants outside in a sheltered area, and bring them indoors before the cool of the evening. This treatment increases the amount of light they receive, resulting in more vigorous growth, and it also hardens off the plants.

These steps can also be used for fuchsia plants that have been overwintered. With fuchsias, however, you can allow the original plant to continue growing, and also take cuttings a total of 2 or 3 times. Each fuchsia plant usually produces 20–30 cuttings.

Godetia

red, pink, white

Clarkia amoena
(Godetia amoena)
Farewell-to-Spring, Satin Flower

Height: 12 inches (30 cm)

Godetia seems to be a flower of contradiction. Its petals have such rich colour and satiny sheen that you would expect this to be a plant that requires pampering, yet godetia does better in poor soil than in rich soil. One year we planted it in an area of the garden where the soil was entirely clay, and the plants thrived, producing a profusion of graceful blooms. Ever since, I have recommended godetia for poor soil areas.

PLANTING

Seeding: Indoors 6 weeks before transplanting. Outdoors on or about the date of the average last spring frost.

Transplanting: 1 week after the average last spring frost. Space 8–10 inches (20–25 cm) apart.

Frost Tolerance: Moderate.

GROWING

Partial shade to full sun.

Mixed flower beds, rock gardens, planters.

Godetia needs very little attention after planting.

RECOMMENDED VARIETIES

Dwarf Double Azalea Flowered Mixture •
mixture of silky flowers in shades of pink,
white and red.

Satin Series • dwarf plants ideal for rock
gardens; plants become smothered in silky
single flowers in shades of pink, white, red,
rose and salmon.

TIPS

Do not over-fertilize godetia. It is an exception to most plants in that an abundance of
nutrients will diminish rather than increase the
floral display. A general rule for this plant is to
fertilize it every second time you fertilize other
annuals.

Godetia produces its best show when planted
in groups.

Godetia will sometimes self-sow, if it finds a
spot to its liking. One gardener told us she had
planted godetia in her garden 4 years ago, and
that new plants have appeared in her garden
every spring since.

*Godetia is one of the
showiest annuals, with
vivid satiny flowers, yet it
will flourish in the poorest
of garden soils.*

Gomphrena

purple, rose, red

Gomphrena globosa
Globe Amaranth

Height: 12–24 inches
(30–60 cm)

Gomphrena is gaining popularity as a dried flower because it works well in mixed arrangements and provides variety with its clover-like blooms. Over the past few years in particular, plant breeders have been working to increase this plant's appeal by producing larger flowerheads in a wider range of colours. Pastel shades such as salmon and mauve are among the newest hues.

PLANTING

Seeding: Indoors 6–8 weeks before transplanting.

Transplanting: 2 weeks after the average last spring frost. Space 10–12 inches (25–30 cm) apart.

Frost Tolerance: Moderate.

GROWING

Warm, sunny locations best; does well in dry areas of the garden.

Backgrounds, cutting gardens, as tall borders, in pots or raised beds.

Water only when soil is dry; dislikes being waterlogged.

Gomphrena is a wonderful flower to add to fresh or dried floral arrangements. Its round flowers retain their colours when dried.

RECOMMENDED VARIETIES

Usually available only under one of the names listed above.

TIPS

Gomphrena's round flowers provide splendid accents in mixed bouquets. For best results, cut for bouquets when the flowers are nearly open, and slightly split the bottoms of the stems. The flowers last about 7–10 days after cutting.

To dry gomphrena's flowers, harvest when they are fully globe-shaped. We like to remove the foliage before hanging the stalks to dry. Tie about 5 stems in a bunch and hang upside down. For best results, stagger the flowerheads up the length of the bunch.

Dried flowerheads were glued onto a grape vine base to create this stunning wreath.

Heliotrope

deep purple

Heliotropium arborescens

Height: 14 inches (35 cm)

Heliotrope is an old-fashioned flower that is enjoying a resurgence in popularity as people rediscover its fragrance and intensely purple flowers, but it is often easier to grow than it is to find. Heliotrope is worth the search, however, because it is one of the most undemanding and highly perfumed of all annuals.

PLANTING

Seeding: Indoors 10–12 weeks before transplanting.

Transplanting: 3 weeks after the average last spring frost. Space 12 inches (30 cm) apart.

Frost Tolerance: Poor.

GROWING

Sunny location.

Patio pots, windowboxes, planters, tucked into hanging baskets for fragrance.

Water evenly; heliotrope does not like to dry out nor become waterlogged.

Heliotrope is one of the most fragrant annuals. Its deep purple flowers have a heavenly vanilla scent.

Recommended Varieties

Blue Wonder • large, deep purple flower-heads; bushy compact plants.

Tips

Heliotrope grows well in sunny, hot areas of the garden, as long as the plants are kept moist. My daughter-in-law Valerie grew heliotrope in window-boxes attached to her south-facing back porch, where the plants thrived.

Heliotrope's fragrance attracts hummingbirds and bees. A plant near the vegetable garden helps to ensure the pollination of cucumbers, melons, zucchini and squash.

Heliotrope is one of the most frost-sensitive plants. Cover whenever there is a risk of temperatures dropping to near freezing.

To fully appreciate heliotrope's fragrance, plant it near an outdoor seating area (above) or under a window that is often open.

The bright oranges and yellows of French marigolds (below) set off heliotrope's deep purple flowers splendidly.

Helipterum

carmine, rose, silvery white

Helipterum roseum
Acroclinium, Rhodanthe,
Sunray Everlasting

Height: 12 inches (30 cm)

One of the best plantings of everlasting flowers I have ever seen was in a tiered garden in the backyard of a west Edmonton home. Don Lubinski grew miniature meadows of several different everlasting flowers side by side: a square of helipterum next to xeranthemum, followed by rosy perennial baby's breath, annual statice and others. The flowers throve in their hot, sheltered location, and they provided a splendid patchwork of colours for creating dried arrangements long after the summer had passed.

PLANTING

Seeding: Indoors 6 weeks before transplanting.

Transplanting: 2–3 weeks after the average last spring frost. Space 8–10 inches (20–25 cm) apart.

Frost Tolerance: Poor.

Helipterum's pretty, daisy-like flowers have papery petals and bright-yellow centres, and they look as fresh in dried arrangements as they do in the garden.

GROWING

Full sun.

Backgrounds, cutting gardens, as tall borders, in pots or raised beds.

Dried helipterum flowers are almost indistinguishable from fresh flowers.

RECOMMENDED VARIETIES

Usually available only under one of the names listed above.

TIPS

Helipterum is wonderful in fresh bouquets. One of my favourite bouquets last summer was pink helipterum and white seashells cosmos together in a simple vase. For bouquets, pick the flowers when they are fully open. They last 7–10 days after cutting.

For best drying results, pick the flowers at the bud stage. The best time of day to collect them is mid-morning, after the dew has dried from the plants. Tie the flower stems in bunches and hang with the blossoms upside down, in a dry, shady, well-ventilated area. Stagger the flower-heads up the length of the bunch.

A sunny planting of helipterum creates a pretty, meadow-like effect. The smaller, rosy magenta flowers at the right in this photo are xeranthemum, another annual that is splendid for cutting and drying.

Hollyhock

white, rose, red, pink, yellow

Alcea rosea
  (Althea rosea)
Annual Hollyhock,
Garden Hollyhock

Height: 4–5 feet (1.2–1.5 m.)

There are hollyhocks and hollyhocks and holly-hocks: single and double-flowered, perennial, biennial and annual. Annual hollyhocks are the ones that complete their life cycle—from seed to flower to seed—in a single season. They can be somewhat difficult to distinguish from their longer-lived relatives at a glance from the untrained eye, but annual hollyhocks are generally shorter, with impressive, more rounded, fully double flowers that resemble those of a peony.

These plants are one of the tallest annuals, with splendid flowers that provide striking height in flower beds and look equally impressive in bouquets.

PLANTING

Seeding: Indoors 3–4 weeks before transplanting. Outdoors in the late fall or about a week before the average last spring frost.

Transplanting: 2 weeks after the average last spring frost. Space 24 inches (60 cm) apart.

Frost Tolerance: Moderate.

GROWING

Sunny locations best, but tolerates light shade.

Back of borders, excellent accent plant, in rows against a fence or wall, in perennial beds and cottage gardens.

Water heavily. These plants do not like to dry out.

Recommended Varieties

Powderpuffs Mixture • strong, sturdy stems; double blooms of white, rose, red, pink and yellow.

Tips

Pinch out the central growing tip when seedlings are about 4 inches (10 cm) tall, or immediately after transplanting. This results in multiple flower stalks on short, stocky plants that stand up well in windy locations.

The flowerstalks of hollyhocks provide dramatic height in bouquets. Hollyhocks have hollow stems, and florists often recommend filling the stems with water to maximize the life of the cut blooms. If you want to try this, simply turn them upside down, pour water into them until they are full and plug the ends with cotton balls. The flowers generally last 7–10 days after cutting.

For the showiest display of flowers, start with fresh seed or new plants every year. Powderpuffs is a hybrid variety, and seed from hybrid plants often cannot be relied upon to reproduce all the characteristics of the parent plant. Hollyhocks often self-seed, but the offspring of annual types are inferior plants without the truly magnificent double flowers of the parent.

Photo courtesy of Park Seed Co., Cokesbury Rd., Greenwood, SC 29647-0001

Hollyhocks generally bloom from late June or early July through August. They sometimes flower again in September.

Ice Plant

red, purple, pink, yellow

Mesembryanthemum crystallinum
Livingstone Daisy

Delosperma spp.
Sea Fig, Sea Marigold

Height: 3–6 inches (8–15 cm).

Livingstone daisy is a prostrate, creeping plant that can spread to 12 inches (30 cm) across. Ice plant from cuttings will trail to that length in a hanging basket.

Ice plant brightens hard-to-plant areas of the garden with its vivid, daisy-like flowers. These plants grow well in hot, dry areas and in poor soil.

The 2 species of ice plant are genetically unrelated, although their spidery-petalled flowers look remarkably similar. In the greenhouse, we usually differentiate between the two by referring to M. crystallinum as 'Livingstone daisy,' and to Delosperma as 'ice plant from cuttings.' The two differ in their foliage: Livingstone daisy has fleshy leaves, while ice plant from cuttings has succulent, needle-like foliage. Both have sun-worshipping, daisy-like flowers that close up at night and on cloudy days.

PLANTING

Seeding: Livingstone daisy indoors 6–8 weeks before transplanting. Ice plant is propagated from cuttings, because it takes too long to grow from seed.

Transplanting: 1 week after the average last spring frost. Space 8 inches (20 cm) apart.

Frost Tolerance: Moderate.

GROWING

Full sun.

Mixed borders, rock gardens, annual ground-covers, edgings, in flowerbeds against sunny walls, in containers (ice plant from cuttings is better for hanging baskets, because it trails).

After plants are established, keep them on the dry side. They dislike being overwatered.

RECOMMENDED VARIETIES

Livingstone Daisy
(Mesembryanthemum)

Lunette • a profusion of sparkling, bright yellow, single-petalled flowers with rosy-red centres.

Mixture • single-petalled flowers in a mixture of red, purple, pink and yellow.

Ice plant from cuttings
(Delosperma *spp.*)

No specific varieties developed to date; only available under 1 of these 2 names.

TIPS

A longtime family friend, Laura Henry, grew Livingstone daisies in a large container set in the middle of her backyard. The plants thrived in their hot location, with an absolutely beautiful display of flowers.

Another family friend once lived in a house with 2 built-in planters at the bottom of the front steps. The planters were rather shallow and dried out quickly in the hot sun of a southwestern exposure. They also received a lot of reflected heat from white-painted concrete walls. Finding plants to grow in that environment was a challenge, and although many plants were tried, ice plants (from cuttings) always did the best.

People who have travelled along the interstate highways in California often remark on the showy plants growing on the adjacent hillsides. These are ice plants (Delosperma). In warmer areas, they grow as perennials. In northern gardens, we often treat them as annuals simply because they usually do not survive our winters.

Livingstone daisies are also known as 'ice plants' because they produce droplets on their leaves that glisten in the sun like crystals of ice.

Impatiens

burgundy, red, purple, lavender,
orange, salmon, pink, white

Impatiens wallerana
Busy Lizzie, Garden Impatiens,
Lucy, Patience Plant

Impatiens wallerana
'double'
Double-Flowering Impatiens,
Rosebud Impatiens

Impatiens x 'New Guinea'
New Guinea Impatiens

Height: 8–12 inches
(20–30 cm)

Garden impatiens is one of the most popular bedding plants, because it serves so many purposes in the garden, needs little attention and produces a solid mass of bright flowers throughout the season. Double-flowering impatiens has pretty flowers that resemble rosebuds. New Guinea impatiens has colourful, showy leaves, and larger but fewer flowers than garden impatiens.

PLANTING

Seeding: Indoors 8–10 weeks before transplanting.

Transplanting: 2 weeks after the average last spring frost. Space 4–6 inches (10–15 cm) apart.

Frost Tolerance: Poor.

GROWING

Partial shade to sun (but not hot or dry).

Garden impatiens in mass plantings, borders, edgings, hanging baskets, containers of all types, in rock gardens.

Rosebud impatiens and New Guinea impatiens as feature or accent plants, in hanging baskets, containers of all types.

Recommended Varieties

Garden Impatiens

The following 3 varieties are all bushy, compact plants with excellent garden performance; together they provide an outstanding range of floral colours.

Accent • unusual colours include carmine and lilac.

Dazzler • unusual colours include apricot, hot cherry-red, and white with a burgundy eye.

Super Elfin • unusual colours include a rose-pink and colour picotee, and pale lilac with a lavender eye.

Rosebud Impatiens

Rosebud Series • lavender, orange, pink, red, rose, salmon or white.

New Guinea Impatiens

Paradise Series • large, well-formed flowers; leaves are either brilliantly variegated or dark bronze, contrasting with unique flower colours; very compact, early flowering and prolific bloomer; excellent garden performance; 13 colour combinations.

Impatiens is one of the best plants for shady areas, because it provides a solid carpet of flowers in a wide range of unsurpassed colours, including Super Elfin Swirl (above). Impatiens blooms from early June right through until the first fall frost and is among the least demanding of all annuals. New Guinea impatiens (below) has showy leaves and larger but fewer flowers than garden impatiens.

Matching pots of impatiens and geraniums guide visitors across this front lawn to a garden wedding in Edmonton, Alberta.

Impatiens is the most popular bedding plant in the United States. In our greenhouses, it ranks behind petunias, marigolds and lobelia. Because of its immense popularity, considerable money is invested in constantly improving existing varieties. New hybrids can now be grown in sunny areas, as long as the soil is cool and moist—historically impatiens was a plant that was restricted to the shade.

TIPS

In an unseasonably cool spring, delay planting until shady areas have had a chance to warm.

Water regularly. Allowing the plants to dry out will greatly diminish the number of flowers.

Keep New Guinea impatiens moist. When they become dry, the leaves and flowers turn brown and dry on the edges, and the flowers drop off. If this happens, pinch off the damaged leaves, and be more consistent with future watering. At the seedling stage, however, New Guinea impatiens cannot tolerate cool, wet conditions. Seedlings should not be fertilized until they are well-rooted.

Finished flowers fall cleanly from the plants, so no deadheading is required. To remove any dead petals, lightly brush your fingertips across the tops of leaves. Give hanging baskets a gentle shake.

If you are going away on holiday for a week or two, cut back impatiens plants by up to one-third before you leave. When you return home, the plants will greet you with a fresh flush of flowers.

Giant Himalayan impatiens (top) is a less common type that is quickly gaining popularity. Although these huge plants are technically annuals, they should be given a permanent location in the garden, because new plants grow quickly and reliably each spring from seed set the previous season. Impatiens blooms in such abundance that the flowers completely hide a strawberry barrel planter (above). Triple rows of impatiens (left) create a decorative border around a garden pond.

Ivy

green, cream, silver

Hedera helix
English Ivy

Senecio mikanioides
German Ivy, Green Wax Ivy, Heart Ivy, Parlour Ivy, Water Ivy

Cymbalaria muralis
Kenilworth Ivy

Lamiastrum galeobdolon variegatum
Lamiastrum, Silver Nettle Vine, Herman's Pride

Nepeta
Nepeta Ivy, Creeping Charlie

Vinca major variegata
Vinca Ivy

Senecio macroglossus variegatum
Wax Ivy, Wax Vine

Height: 12–36 inches (30–90 cm)

Any ivies we use to accent hanging baskets, window-boxes and patio planters are referred to as annuals, although some are actually perennial in milder regions. English ivy has the greatest range in leaf colours and shapes, while German and wax ivies are best for the most shaded locations. Lamiastrum, nepeta and vinca generally trail to the greatest lengths. Kenilworth ivy is a pretty plant with tiny leaves and small lilac flowers, and it is attractive enough to be grown on its own in a small pot. Vinca is my favourite type of ivy, with pretty variegated leaves on very long stems.

Ivies from top to bottom:
German
Nepeta
Lamiastrum
Kenilworth
English
Wax
Vinca

PLANTING

Seeding: Not recommended, because it takes too long.

Transplanting: 1 week after the average last spring frost. Space up to 4–6 inches (10–15 cm) apart.

Frost Tolerance: Moderate (most varieties) to poor (German, wax).

GROWING

English Ivy: Shade to partial sun.

German Ivy: Shade to partial shade.

Kenilworth Ivy: Full shade to partial sun.

Lamiastrum: Partial sun to partial shade.

Nepeta Ivy: Partial shade to full sun.

Vinca Ivy: Shade to sun.

Wax Ivy: Shade to partial sun.

Trailing in windowboxes, planters, patio pots and hanging baskets, trailing over walls, in rock gardens, as groundcover.

German ivy (above, left) has larger leaves than other types. Ivy adds the finishing touch to containers of all descriptions. Vinca ivy (above) trails to the ground from a mossball planter of tuberous begonias, impatiens and coleus.

RECOMMENDED VARIETIES

Usually available only under one of the names listed above.

English Ivy • deep-green foliage; many different leaf shapes and variegations.

German Ivy • large, deep-green, thick leaves; occasionally produces clusters of tiny, fragrant flowers.

Kenilworth Ivy • tiny, round, glossy green leaves; small lilac flowers; can be used in rock gardens as an annual groundcover.

Lamiastrum • striking foliage with distinct, silvery variegation; grows well as an annual groundcover or in a rock garden.

Nepeta Ivy • very fast-growing; round, green leaves, sometimes with white variegation; roots itself wherever the leaf base touches the soil.

Vinca Ivy • one of the longest trailers; bright green variegated foliage; often produces small lavender flowers.

Wax Ivy • thick waxy, solid green or variegated foliage.

Variegated types of English ivy (top) need a sunnier location than green varieties. The leaves of lamiastrum (left) have distinctive silvery markings.

TIPS

For apartment-dwellers with windy balconies, use nepeta, English or vinca ivies in containers or hanging baskets. These types do better than the others in exposed areas.

English, German, Kenilworth and wax ivies can be brought indoors in the fall as houseplants in sunny locations.

Nepeta sets off pots of red geraniums and pink New Guinea impatiens (above, left). Tropical houseplants add variety to a pot of wax ivy, impatiens and ivy geraniums (above, right). Kenilworth ivy (top) is stunning in a built-in window planter.

Kochia

green, purplish-red

*Kochia scoparia
trichophylla*
Burning Bush, Cypress Bush,
Fire Bush, Mexican Fire Bush,
Red Summer Cypress

Height: 24–36 inches
(60–90 cm)

*Kochia is a surprising annual that at first glance
appears to be a bushy evergreen shrub with great
symmetry. It is most often planted in groups or rows
to fill beds, where its soft, feathery foliage provides
a pleasing backdrop for flowering plants. A single
kochia plant can be used as a centrepiece in an open
flowerbed.*

PLANTING

Seeding: Indoors 6–8 weeks before transplanting. Outdoors about the date of the
average last spring frost.

Transplanting: 1 week after the average
last spring frost. Space 18–24 inches
(45–60 cm) apart. For hedges, space
from 12 inches (30 cm) apart.

Frost Tolerance: Moderate in
spring. Excellent in fall.

GROWING

Sunny locations.

Annual shrub, tall, uniform
borders, annual hedges,
background or feature plant.

*Kochia was the perfect plant for a
customer who came in looking for a
temporary solution for the bare yard of
his new home. He wanted something that
was quick-growing and fairly large, yet
inexpensive, as a stopgap measure until
he had time to plan a permanent
landscape. Six bedding plants produced a
12-foot (3.5 m) hedge, for a cost of just
a few dollars!*

RECOMMENDED VARIETIES

Usually available only under one of the names listed above. The cultivar *childsii* is very compact with uniform growth, but its foliage often remains green all season.

TIPS

Kochia is one of the fastest growing annuals. Many customers look at me in disbelief when I insist that, within a month-and-a-half, the plants will grow into bushes of up to 10 times their height when planted.

Kochia produces seed from flowers that most often go unnoticed on the plant. The seeds will often sprout in the garden the following spring. If you want to allow them to grow, thin the seedlings to the spacing recommended above to enable the plants to reach their full potential.

Kochia grows most quickly in hot areas of the garden (top). Cooler or shaded areas result in smaller plants. Kochia is a dense, fast-growing annual shrub with bright-green, feathery foliage that often turns purplish-red in the fall (above).

Lantana

red, orange, yellow

Lantana camara
Common Lantana,
Shrub Verbena

Height: 12–18 inches
(30–45 cm)

Lantana is a plant that we originally tried because it was reputed to thrive in hot, dry conditions. And it does; it is one of the very few annuals that will do well in those conditions and also grow well in a hanging basket. Lantana has pretty clusters of tiny flowers and fragrant foliage that gives off a lemony-sage scent when brushed.

PLANTING

Seeding: Not recommended, because it takes too long to grow from seed.

Transplanting: 2 weeks after the average last spring frost. Space 8–12 inches (20–30 cm) apart in the garden.

Frost Tolerance: Poor.

GROWING

Full sun.

Containers of all types including hanging baskets; as a feature plant in the garden.

Prune as necessary to shape plants and encourage bushiness.

RECOMMENDED VARIETIES

Usually available only under one of the names above.

TIPS

Lantana does well in hot, dry areas of the garden, such as flowerbeds that are near a heat-radiating brick wall or against a reflective surface, such as the side of a white, stucco house.

Because it is a shrubby plant with stiff stems, lantana does not combine well with other plants in containers. It is best grown on its own, with a single plant per hanging basket.

Hanging baskets of lantana and vinca ivy thrive in hot, sunny locations.

Lantana is one of the few annuals that is suited to growing in hanging baskets and does well in hot, dry conditions.

Larkspur

pink, purple, red, salmon

Consolida ambigua
(Delphinium ajacis)
Annual Delphinium,
Annual Larkspur

Height: 4 feet (120 cm)

Larkspur is a tall, stately plant with strong colours and delphinium-like blooms that are superb for cutting. These flowers have nostalgic appeal for people who remember it blooming in their parents' or grandparents' gardens. It is also a great addition to cottage gardens.

PLANTING

Seeding: Indoors 12–14 weeks before transplanting. Outdoors in the late fall.

Transplanting: 2 weeks after the average last spring frost. Space 10–12 inches (25–30 cm) apart.

Frost Tolerance: Moderate.

GROWING

Full sun.

At the back of borders, against a fence, in cottage gardens and cutting gardens.

Sometimes needs staking.

RECOMMENDED VARIETIES

Giant Imperial Series • the best variety for cooler climates; excellent quality flowers; blue, rose, scarlet, salmon and lilac.

TIPS

Larkspur can add striking height to fresh bouquets. Pick spikes when flowers on the lower half of the stem are open, and, for best results, re-cut the stems just before arranging them in a vase. The flowers last about 7–10 days after cutting.

When harvesting larkspur for drying, pick flowers at their peak of beauty, preferably in mid-morning after the dew has dried from the plants. Tie flower stems into small bunches and hang upside down to dry for about a week. The flowers retain their strong colours.

Larkspur used to be classified as *Delphinium*; some seed catalogues still list these plants under that heading.

Larkspur is one of the tallest annual plants (top). The blooms are wonderful in both fresh bouquets (above) and dried arrangements.

Lavatera

rose, pink, white

Lavatera trimestris
Annual Rose Mallow,
Tree Mallow

Height: 20–30 inches
(50–75 cm)

Lavatera makes a stunning border or background in flower beds because of its profusion of large, satiny flowers that can reach 4 inches (10 cm) in diameter. This plant is so showy in gardens that it draws attention from people passing by in cars. People often come into our greenhouse and say, 'I saw a big plant with beautiful pink flowers—do you know what it was?'

156

Lavatera is one of the showiest plants in the garden, and its blooms make outstanding cutflowers.

PLANTING

Seeding: Indoors 4–6 weeks before transplanting. Outdoors in the late fall.

Transplanting: 2 weeks after the average last spring frost. Space 15–24 inches (38–60 cm) apart.

Frost Tolerance: Moderate.

I once judged a gardening contest for residents of a trailer park in Edmonton. The first prize was 3 months free rent, and the winners were 2 young men who had grown the most beautiful, bushiest lavatera that I have ever seen.

GROWING

Sun.

Borders, backgrounds, hedges, screens, tall feature plant.

Water when dry but not parched.

Recommended Varieties

Beauty Series • showy mass of flowers; better mounding habit than other varieties; individually in rose, white or as a mixture of both plus light pink.

Tips

Lavatera's flowers are magnificent in mixed bouquets. I like to set off these large, showy blooms with tall spikes, such as bells of Ireland or dark-blue larkspur, and to add the delicate flowerheads of Queen Anne's lace as filler. Pick flowers for bouquets when they have begun to open but are not yet lying flat. The blooms last 7–10 days after cutting.

Lavatera has silken, cup-shaped flowers that resemble large single hollyhocks or hibiscus (above). The plants grow quickly from seed into well-shaped bushes that bloom like mad from early July through to the first fall frost (below).

Lavatera grows largest in sunny areas where it does not have vigorous rivals among neighbouring plants. We once saw a long row lining a pathway in a gardener's backyard that perfectly demonstrated this principle. The plants in full sun were huge, but the plants dwindled down to half the size at the opposite end of the row, where they were close to large trees which filtered out the sun and competed for moisture and nutrients.

Lavatera is gaining popularity at an amazing rate, because it is one of the largest annuals, has flamboyant flowers and is relatively undemanding in the garden.

Lobelia

light and dark blue, purple, lilac, wine-red, white

Lobelia erinus compacta
Border Lobelia, Bush Lobelia

Lobelia erinus pendula
Trailing Lobelia

Height: 4 inches (10 cm).
Trailing lobelia reaches a length of up to 12 inches (30 cm).

Lobelia is unmatched in hanging baskets and containers for the billowing clouds of colour provided by its tiny flowers.

A border of lobelia highlights a walkway (opposite, top). Even 'macho men' appreciate flowers. This tremendous display was discovered at our hometown rugby club (opposite, bottom).

Lobelia is famed as 'that little blue flower in hanging baskets,' although it also blooms in other colours and grows as a short, bushy plant that is great for uniform borders and in rock gardens. Lobelia produces a profusion of delicate flowers early in the season right through until fall.

PLANTING

Seeding: Indoors 8–10 weeks before transplanting.

Transplanting: 1 week after the average last spring frost. Space 6–8 inches (15–20 cm) apart in the garden.

Frost Tolerance: Poor.

GROWING

Full shade to partial sun. Avoid hot and dry locations.

Both types in windowboxes, planters, patio pots, as edging. Trailing type better for hanging baskets. Border lobelia for uniform borders and in rock gardens.

Recommended Varieties

Border types are listed first in each pair below, trailing types second.

True Blue

Blue Moon and Sapphire Pendula • the traditional deep indigo-blue; Blue Moon supersedes the traditional variety Crystal Palace with larger flowers, green foliage and earlier blooms; Sapphire Pendula has a striking white eye offsetting each flower.

Light Blue

Cambridge Blue and Blue Fountain • light-blue flowers on light-green foliage; Blue Fountain has a white eye in the centre of each bloom.

White

Paper Moon and White Fountain • pure white flowers.

Lilac

Lilac Fountain • trailing type; pastel mauve flowers. No bush variety yet developed in this colour.

Red

Rosamund and Red Fountain • wine-red flowers.

Mixture

Rainbow Mixture and Colour Cascade • striking blends of all the above colours.

Tips

Water frequently—lobelia is quick to show the effects of being allowed to dry out by turning brown and dying. Check hanging baskets daily, because they dry out most quickly. To keep lobelia from drying out as easily, arrange the plants toward the centres of planters or hanging baskets, rather than right at the edges.

Shear plants that become leggy. Use household scissors or garden shears to snip off the top one-third to one-half of growth. The plants will quickly regrow to become bushier with a greater number of blooms.

Lotus Vine

jade green, silvery-green, red, yellow

Lotus berthelotii
Parrot's Beak

Lotus maculatus
Gold Flash

Height: Trails up to 36 inches (90 cm)

Lotus vine is a bushy vine used in planters, hanging baskets and containers. It trails up to 3 feet (90 cm) long. Its needle-like foliage is soft to the touch. Gold Flash has jade-green foliage that is slightly coarser than Parrot's Beak, and it often produces bright-yellow blooms with orange markings. Parrot's Beak has silvery-green foliage and occasionally produces bright-red flowers that are shaped like the beaks of parrots. The vines cannot be relied on to produce flowers, however, and they are grown primarily for their attractive foliage.

PLANTING

Seeding: Not recommended, because it takes too long.

Transplanting: 1 week after the average last spring frost. Space 6–8 inches (15–20 cm) apart for a solid effect and up to 12 inches (30 cm) for individual plants.

Frost Tolerance: Moderate.

GROWING

Sunny locations.

Trailing in planters, windowboxes and hanging baskets.

The bushy foliage of lotus vine adds an exotic touch to containers and hanging baskets. This plant is excellent for hot, dry areas.

RECOMMENDED VARIETIES

Usually available only under one of the names listed above.

TIPS

Lotus vine can be used in combination with portulaca, ice plant and verbena in hanging baskets for hot, dry areas.

Parrot's Beak lotus vine billows from a windowbox (top). Gold Flash (above) often produces small, flame-like flowers.

Malva

purple

Malva sylvestris
  var. *mauritiana*
Hollyhock Mallow, Musk Mallow

Height: 4–6 feet (1.2–1.8 m)

Malva is similar in looks to lavatera, and the two are sometimes confused. Malva is generally taller and blooms in less profusion, but its flowers are a striking hue which is unavailable in lavatera. Malva's flowers are exquisite, with glossy petals of rich purple. People often choose to grow malva in combination with or as a substitute for lavatera, for variety in flower colour.

PLANTING

Seeding: Indoors 4–6 weeks before transplanting. Outdoors in the late fall.

Transplanting: 2 weeks after the average last spring frost. Space 12–20 inches (30–50 cm) apart.

Frost Tolerance: Poor.

GROWING

Sun to light shade.

Background or tall feature plant, for tall borders.

Plants in open areas may need to be staked.

RECOMMENDED VARIETIES

Bibor Felho • unique purple flowers with royal-pink veins and wavy petals; larger flowers than most varieties.

TIPS

Malva adds a dramatic flare to bouquets with its height and intense floral colour. For best results, cut the flowers when they are starting to open. Malva generally lasts 7–10 days after cutting.

One of our favourite gardeners owns a plot of land in the countryside, where there is an old, abandoned farmhouse surrounded by a wild meadow. Every year, at least one splendid malva plant appears in the midst of the wild-flowers, towering to 6 feet (1.8 m) tall, with a profusion of huge blooms. These marvellous plants are annuals that sprout from seed dropped the previous year, and they are the only reminder of the original farmer's garden, which was abandoned over 30 years ago.

Malva is outstanding for its exquisite, purple flowers that resemble large, single hollyhocks. It blooms from early June until frost.

Marigold

yellow, gold, orange, red

Tagetes erecta
African Marigold,
American Marigold,
Aztec Marigold

Tagetes patula
French Marigold,
Dwarf Marigold

Height: 6–36 inches
(15–90 cm)

Marigolds are one of the most popular annual flowers; in our greenhouses they are second only to petunias. African marigolds are tall plants that produce large, round flowers in solid, bright colours. The shorter French marigolds generally have smaller flowers with a greater variety of petal types, markings and colours. All marigolds are low-maintenance plants that stand up to heat, rain and windy conditions.

PLANTING

Seeding: Indoors, African marigolds 8 weeks before transplanting and French marigolds 10 weeks before transplanting.

Transplanting: 2 weeks after the average last spring frost. Space African marigolds 12–18 inches (30–45 cm) apart, and French marigolds 6–8 inches (15–20 cm) apart. The taller the plants, the further apart they should be spaced.

Frost Tolerance: Moderate.

Marigolds are exceptionally easy to grow, relatively free of insect pests and diseases, stand up well to all types of weather and bloom in radiant colours continuously until fall frosts.

GROWING

Sunny locations.

African for 12–36 inch (30–90 cm) high borders, mass plantings, backgrounds, annual hedges, feature plants.

French for 6–12 inch (15–30 cm) high borders, mass plantings, planters.

Marigolds grow well in poor soil.

RECOMMENDED VARIETIES

African

Climax Series •
36 inches (90 cm) tall; 5-inch (13 cm) flowers; gold, orange, pastel yellow, bright lemon-yellow and a mixture.

Jubilee Series •
24 inches (60 cm) tall; 3-inch (8 cm) blooms; yellow, gold, orange and a mixture.

African marigold flowers are twice as big as those of French marigolds.

Excel Series • 14 inches (35 cm) tall; 4-inch (10 cm) blooms; gold, pastel yellow, lemon-yellow and a mixture.

Discovery Series • 10–12 inches (25–30 cm) tall; 2½ to 3-inch (6–8 cm) blooms; orange and yellow.

French

Disco Series • 12 inches (30 cm) tall; the best single-flowered marigold yet; 2¾-inch (7 cm) blooms; 6 different colours, some with unique markings, and a mixture.

Safari Series • 12 inches (30 cm) tall; large 3-inch (8 cm), anemone-like flowers; 6 bright colours, some with outstanding markings, and a mixture.

Hero Series • 8–10 inches (20–25 cm) tall; 2¾-inch (7 cm), double flowers; 8 individual colours, some with striking markings, and a mixture.

Janie Series • 6–8 inches (15–20 cm) tall; 1¼-inch (3 cm) double flowers; 6 individual colours, including unique markings and colour combinations, and a mixture.

When marigolds are planted out in early spring, their foliage often turns a reddish-purple. This is because cool temperatures inhibit the uptake of phosphorous (one of the nutrients that is essential to plant growth). As temperatures warm and the plants mature, the burgundy tinge will disappear from the leaves, usually within only a week or two.

A mass planting of French marigolds creates an even sea of colour.

🌿*One year my husband Ted planted a hedge of African marigolds against a white-painted, wooden fence along the entrance to our driveway. The effect was so stunning that people driving by in cars would stop and come into the yard to remark on it. This was the year that we discovered the variety Jubilee as superior plants to the traditional variety Crackerjack.*

Tips

Marigolds do well in hot areas of the garden, such as near a heat-radiating brick wall, but the plants do not like to be parched. They will, however, tolerate short dry spells.

Pinching out the first central flower bud from African marigolds results in bushier plants. All new hybrid French varieties have been developed to grow into compact, well-branched plants without needing to be pinched back.

Marigolds make great cut flowers. I like the Africans on their own in a simple glass vase. Marigolds generally last about a week after cutting.

For apartment dwellers with windy but sunny balconies, French and shorter African marigolds are a good choice for containers.

Marigolds are reputed to repel insects. For this reason, some people like to plant a row of them as a bright border to the vegetable garden, or to add a few marigold plants around the bases of tomatoes and peppers growing in pots. Whether these plants actually do repel insects is sometimes disputed, but I have the attitude that they will certainly do no harm. If they do work, great; if not, you get the bonus of a more ornamental vegetable garden.

The foliage of some marigolds gives off a pungent fragrance when the leaves are brushed or crushed. I like the smell, but my son Bill dislikes it intensely; as with most scents, it is a matter of personal opinion. This scent has been bred away from some of the newer hybrids.

African marigolds are one of my all-time favourite flowers. Every year we plant a mass of them in a sunny bed at the front of our house.

Meadow Foam

white, yellow

Limnanthes douglasii
Fried Eggs, Poached Eggs

Height: 6 inches (15 cm)

Meadow foam is a marvellous plant for low-lying, wet areas of the garden. It produces small, daisy-like flowers on spreading plants with airy foliage. The flower petals are golden yellow with white tips, resembling the coloration of a fried or poached egg. Meadow foam blooms early in the season and continues throughout the summer.

PLANTING

Seeding: Indoors 4–6 weeks before transplanting.

Transplanting: Space 4–6 inches (10–15 cm) apart.

Frost Tolerance: Moderate.

GROWING

Full sun. Any shade at all detracts from this plant's performance.

Rockeries, low borders, edging along paths or in flowerbeds, at the edge of ponds or streams.

Water heavily; this is a marsh plant in its natural habitat and requires lots of moisture. Do not let plants dry out.

Meadow foam is one of the few annuals that will prosper in wet areas of the garden as well as in poor soil.

Recommended Varieties

Usually available only under one of the names listed above.

Tips

Meadow foam thrives only in sunny weather and must be grown in a spot fully exposed to the sunshine. It is a good choice to grow at the edge of a pond or stream.

Meadow Foam is also commonly known by the name 'Fried Eggs,' a somewhat humorous description of its flowers. In my mother's garden (above), these plants are often paired with anemones, which have a similar preference for moist conditions. The type of anemone shown here has tender tuberous roots that should be dug up in fall and stored for the winter.

Mimulus

orange, rose, yellow, scarlet, wine, ivory

Mimulus x hybridus
Monkey Face, Monkey Flower

Height: 10 inches (25 cm)

There are two attributes that place mimulus head and tails above many other annuals. The first is that it will thrive in almost any spot in the garden, even where little else will grow. The second is the appeal of its charming, tubular flowers, which bloom in some of the richest colours in the garden. Some varieties have flowers in solid colours, while others have attractive spots on their velvety petals.

The name 'mimulus' is derived from the word mimus, meaning 'buffoon,' which refers to the clown-like character of the flowers. This plant is known as 'monkey flower' or 'monkey face,' which reflects its, in my opinion, rather vague resemblance of the flowers to grinning monkeys. When mimulus is in full bloom, the flowers are irresistible!

PLANTING

Seeding: Indoors 6–8 weeks before transplanting.

Transplanting: 2 weeks after the average last spring frost. Space 6 inches (15 cm) apart.

Frost Tolerance: Poor.

GROWING

Full shade to full sun.

Mass plantings, as a border, in patio pots, windowboxes, planters, hanging baskets, at the edges of ponds or streams.

Recommended Varieties

Mystic Series • showy bright blooms without predominant spots; orange, rose, yellow and a mixture that also includes scarlet, ivory and wine.

Tips

Low-lying, wet areas are often the most frustrating parts of the garden. Mimulus is one of the very few annuals that will grow successfully in these conditions.

Keeping mimulus moist is critical. I have talked to many distressed gardeners whose plants have died for some unknown reason, which usually turns out to be simply that they did not water enough. Mimulus plants hate dry soil!

Mimulus is wonderful in a hanging basket, but unless you are very diligent about watering, hang the basket in a shaded area where it will be less likely to dry out.

If you are going away on holiday for a week or two, cut back mimulus plants by up to one-third before you leave. When you return home, the plants will greet you with a fresh flush of flowers.

Mimulus is highly effective in either a formal planting (above), shown here with dusty miller and English ivy, or an informal setting (opposite), as demonstrated in this garden in Whitehorse, Yukon.

Mimulus is native to Chilean bogs, which is why it does so well in wet areas. The hybrids that have been developed as bedding plants have larger flowers in a greater range of colours than do the wild plants.

Mimulus is one of the most versatile annuals. It grows almost anywhere—in full shade to full sun—and it will also thrive in wet areas of the garden.

Moon Vine

white

Ipomoea alba
   (Calonyction aculeatum)
Moonflower

Height: 8–10 feet (2.5–3 m)

The most spectacular feature of this fast-growing vine is the fragrant flowers that open each evening. The blooms unfurl in less than a minute, giving the observer an impression of watching a time-lapse film. Moon vine is great as a climber against a screen or trellis where you can savour the flower's fragrance on summer evenings. Moon vine's white flowers appear to glow in the moonlight.

PLANTING

Seeding: Indoors 3–4 weeks before transplanting.

Transplanting: 1 week after the average last spring frost. Space 12–18 inches (30–45 cm) apart to form a screen.

Frost Tolerance: Poor.

Moon vine is a fascinating annual vine, with fragrant flowers that open at sunset each evening, and close up by midday.

GROWING

Sunny locations; does well in hot areas of the garden.

Climbing against a screen or trellis, in large containers with a vine support.

Although moon vine is related to morning glory, its flowers are larger, from 4–6 inches (10–15 cm) across, and they open at a different time of the day.

RECOMMENDED VARIETIES

Usually available only under one of the names listed above.

TIPS

Moon vine climbs by twining tips, so it needs to be provided with a support. We grow moon vine in a whiskey-barrel planter with a tall wooden trellis set into the centre.

Morning Glory

blue, dark red, white

Ipomoea purpurea,
Ipomoea tricolour
Common Morning Glory

Height: 10 feet (3 m)

Morning glory is a fast-growing annual vine with decorative heart-shaped leaves. The progression of its large, tubular flowers opening and closing each day is fascinating. Each bloom lasts only a single day, but the flowers are produced in such profusion that there is almost always a good show of flowers. New blooms open afresh each morning and fade by late afternoon, to be replaced by others the next day.

PLANTING

Seeding: Indoors 3–4 weeks before transplanting.

Transplanting: 2 weeks after the average last spring frost. Space 12–18 inches (30–45 cm) apart. These plants do not mind being crowded, and they will knit together to form a dense vine cover.

Frost Tolerance: Poor.

GROWING

Sunny location.

Climbing against a screen or trellis, in large containers with a support on which to climb, trailing in a hanging basket.

RECOMMENDED VARIETIES

Heavenly Blue • very showy 4-inch (10 cm) flowers in a striking shade of sky-blue; one of the best annual vines and a prolific bloomer.

Morning Glory Mixture • 3-inch (8 cm) flowers in a mixture of sky blue, light blue with a star-shaped marking in darker blue, dark red and creamy white.

Scarlett O'Hara • 3-inch (8 cm) flowers in a rich, dark red.

Tips

Morning glory does not need deadheading. The finished flowers fold up into a tidy cone, and the floral show continues.

Morning glory is an extremely vigorous vine. We planted 6 small plants of the Morning Glory Mixture variety in an oak-barrel planter, 3 on each side of a 5-foot-high (150 cm) trellis. The plants quickly outgrew the trellis and the extension we wired onto it, and they became such an enormous tower of foliage that the trellis could no longer support their weight. We pounded steel stakes into the ground around the planter to solve this problem, but in future we will try fewer plants in a barrel, or else place 2 barrels on either side of an archway to provide a more sturdy support for the vines to climb.

Another experiment we tried was to plant the variety Heavenly Blue in a hanging basket. This had splendid results, with the vine climbing up the hanger of the basket and trailing over the sides. We hung the basket from the branch of a tree near our deck, where we could take full advantage of the beauty of these flowers both outdoors and indoors, from the view out of the windows.

Morning glory is a fast-growing annual vine with pretty, trumpet-shaped flowers that open afresh each morning, from July to frost.

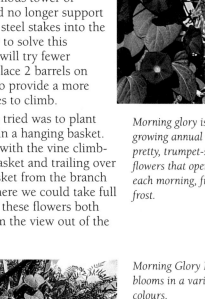

Morning Glory Mixture blooms in a variety of colours.

Nasturtium

burgundy, red, rose, orange, peach, yellow, cream

Tropaeolum majus
Common Nasturtium, Garden Nasturtium

Height: 8–12 inches (20–30 cm). Trailing types reach a length of up to 24 inches (60 cm).

Nasturtiums have a nostalgic appeal to many gardeners, who remember these flowers from childhood. Nasturtiums can be seeded directly into the garden and they grow quickly, do well in poor soil and need little maintenance other than watering. There are two types of nasturtiums: a rapidly spreading plant and a trailing type that looks attractive in a hanging basket.

PLANTING

Seeding: Indoors 2–3 weeks before transplanting. Outdoors 1 week after the average last spring frost.

Transplanting: 2 weeks after the average last spring frost. Space 6–8 inches (15–20 cm) apart.

Frost Tolerance: Moderate.

GROWING

Full sun to light shade.

In mixed beds, in rock gardens, edgings, borders, patio pots, windowboxes, planters, as an annual groundcover. Trailing types along stair railings, in hanging baskets and other containers, trailing over walls and ledges.

Water only when soil is dry.

Nasturtiums do well in poor soil.

Transplanting: Two to 3 weeks

Many people know that nasturtium flowers are edible, but few people actually eat them. All parts of the nasturtium are edible, including leaves, flower buds, unripened seed and flowers. The peppery leaves and flowers are good in salads, but only if no pest sprays have been used.

Recommended Varieties

Glorious Gleam Mixture • trailing type; large, slightly fragrant, semi-double and double flowers in a mixture of colours.

Whirlybird Series • an improvement on traditional types; semi-double flowers above mounding foliage create a spectacular display of colour; available as a mixture or in cherry, gold, mahogany, orange, peach and scarlet.

Tips

Nasturtiums are a good choice for children's gardens, because the pea-sized seeds are big enough to be easily handled by small fingers and the plants grow very quickly, with big, bright flowers.

Trailing types can be grown as climbers against a trellis if you tie the plants. This works well in a large barrel planter, and some plants can be allowed to trail over the edges. Try mixing in both types for a fuller display of flowers.

Nasturtium's flowers can be cut for short-stemmed bouquets. I know a gardener who has been cutting nasturtiums for years, and who insists that the addition of cedar greenery to the vase increases the vase-life of these flowers.

If you are going away on holidays for a week or two, cut back nasturtium plants by up to one-third before you leave. When you return home, the plants will welcome you with a fresh flush of flowers.

Recent breeding developments in nasturtiums have resulted in a wider range of flower colours, and in changes to the structure of the flowers. Classic nasturtium flowers have spurs that contain a nectar attractive to hummingbirds, but which force the flowers to face the ground. In the variety Whirlybird (above), these spurs are absent, the flowers face the sky and they are held well above the foliage, resulting in a more colourful display. The variety shown in the close-up (top) is Whirlybird Peach Melba.

Nemesia

red, orange, purple, pink,
yellow, white

Nemesia strumosa
Pouch Nemesia

Height: 8 inches (20 cm)

Nemesia is one of the few plants that grows as well in sun as it does in shade. A family friend used to plant a long border along the length of her driveway every year. The plants were as full of blooms and as evenly tall in the shaded area near her house as in the sunnier expanse near the bottom of the driveway.

Nemesia provides the answer for people who want a wide range of colours from a single plant. Its open-faced flowers resemble miniature orchids, and most varieties provide an outstanding mixture of hues. A more unusual look is provided by the variety Mello Red and White, which presents a rich contrast with its wonderful red and white flowers. Nemesia is easy to grow and blooms nonstop from June until fall frost.

PLANTING

Seeding: Indoors 6–8 weeks before transplanting.

Transplanting: 2 weeks after the average last
spring frost. Space 6 inches (15 cm) apart.

Frost Tolerance: Poor.

GROWING

Partial shade to full sun.

Borders, in rock gardens, containers, windowboxes.

Do not allow to dry out.

RECOMMENDED VARIETIES

Carnival Blend •
compact plants with
a mixture of flowers
in solid and 2-tone
contrasting colours;
white, yellow,
orange, pink, red
and purple.

Mello Red and White •
an unusual
contrasting colour combination; flowers are
half raspberry red and half white.

TIPS

Before you go away on holiday, cut back
nemesia plants by up to one-third. The plants
will welcome you back in a week or two with a
fresh flush of flowers.

Nemesia prefers cooler temperatures, making
it well-suited to northern gardens.

*Nemesia is a rather
uncommon flower, but
gardeners who discover its
charms tend to give it a
home in their garden, year
after year (top). Nemesia's
flowers look like tiny
orchids in rich, glowing
colours (above).*

Nemophila

sky blue, black and white

Nemophila menziesii
Baby Blue Eyes

Nemophila discoidalis
Pennie Black

Height: 4–6 inches (10–15 cm). Baby blue eyes spreads or trails to 18 inches (45 cm), and pennie black to about 12 inches (30 cm).

Nemophila appeals to many longtime gardeners who are attracted to plants that provide an uncommon touch in the garden. The two types of nemophila have distinctly different flowers that are equally appealing. The blooms of Baby Blue Eyes are larger, cup-shaped and pure sky blue. Pennie Black is less commonly found. Its blooms are penny-sized with scalloped petals, in hues of rich, deep purple to pure black ringed in silvery-white.

PLANTING

Seeding: Indoors 4–6 weeks before transplanting.

Transplanting: 2 weeks after the average last spring frost. Space 8 inches (20 cm) apart.

Frost Tolerance: Poor.

GROWING

Partial shade to partial sun. A site that is sheltered from wind is ideal.

Borders, rock gardens, as an annual groundcover, in windowboxes and patio pots.

Water regularly. Allowing the plants to dry out will greatly diminish the number of flowers.

RECOMMENDED VARIETIES

Usually available only under one of the names listed above.

TIPS

Pennie Black is splendidly set off by other brightly coloured flowers. Our on-staff photographer, Akemi Matsubuchi, (who also works in our greenhouses), planted it in her yard as part of a striking mixed border that included Livingstone daisies, Carnival Blend nemesia and tall stocks.

Pennie Black (above) provides a colour combination rarely found in flowers. The delicate flowers of nemophila add an uncommon touch to mixed flower beds and rock gardens.

Nicotiana

red, rose, lavender, purple, lime, white

Nicotiana affinis,
  N. alata,
  N. langsdorffii,
  N. sylvestris
Flowering Tobacco,
Tobacco Flower

Height: 12–36 inches
    (30–90 cm)

Nicotiana is a versatile plant that does well in most garden situations. I have seen attractive displays in mass plantings, borders, patio pots and window-boxes, in both sun and shade. One of the most charming effects we have seen was in two long, windowbox-type planters that had been attached to the top of a grey wooden fence, where a rose-flowered variety was planted with fragrant stocks and sweet alyssum.

PLANTING

Seeding: Indoors 8–10 weeks before trans-planting.

Transplanting: 2 weeks after the average last spring frost. Space 10–12 inches (25–30 cm) apart.

Frost Tolerance: Moderate.

GROWING

Partial shade to full sun.

Backgrounds, tall borders, mass plantings, containers, windowboxes.

Water frequently, especially during periods of hot weather.

Nicotiana has the dubious distinction of having the most mispronounced name of all the annual flowers. It is correctly pronounced 'nick-o-shana,' with a long 'o.'

Nicotiana is often called 'flowering tobacco' because it is related to the commercial tobacco plant. It is also related to petunias and has similarly fuzzy, somewhat sticky foliage.

Recommended Varieties

Nicotiana affinis

Usually available only under one of the names listed above. Highly fragrant; 36 inches (90 cm) tall; large, 3-inch (8 cm) icy-white flowers.

Nicotiana alata

Daylight Sensation Mix •
36 inches (90 cm) tall; shades of lavender, purple, rose and white.

Domino Series • 12–14 inches (30–35 cm) tall; 2-inch (5 cm) flowers; purple and picotee rose and white.

Starship Series • 12–14 inches (30–35 cm) tall; 2-inch (5 cm) flowers in lemon-lime, rose-pink, red, white or a mixture.

Tips

Just 2 or 3 stems of nicotiana make an attractive bouquet in a vase. Pick flowers for bouquets when 2 or 3 flowers in a cluster are open. They usually last 7–10 days in a vase.

Shorter varieties of nicotiana are splendid in container gardens. Nicotiana combines perfectly with rosy-hued impatiens and geraniums; the tiny flowers are lobelia (top). A mass planting of tall varieties (centre) makes a strong statement. Nicotiana affinis (left) bears a profusion of highly fragrant flowers. N. langsdorffii and N. sylvestris are the largest plants; see page 263 for more information.

🌿 *Nicotiana's flowers have a jasmine-like fragrance that is most intense in the evening. White-flowered varieties generally have the strongest perfume.*

Nierembergia

purple, white

*Nierembergia
  hippomanica*
Cupflower

Height: 4–6 inches (10–15 cm)

Nierembergia is an unusual plant to find in local gardens, most likely because not many people know about it, and because it looks rather dismal as a bedding plant on greenhouse shelves. Once it is planted into the garden, however, it undergoes an amazing transformation into a bushy mound that quickly becomes covered in masses of tiny, cup-shaped flowers, each marked with a golden eye.

PLANTING

Seeding: Indoors 8–10 weeks before transplanting.

Transplanting: About the date of the average last spring frost. Space 6 inches (15 cm) apart.

Frost Tolerance: Excellent.

Nierembergia spreads to almost twice its height, and forms a neat, dense mat that is covered in cup-shaped flowers.

GROWING

Partial shade to full sun.

Borders, edgings, rock gardens, mass plantings, annual groundcover, containers.

RECOMMENDED VARIETIES

Mont Blanc • 4–5 inches (10–13 cm) tall; awarding-winning variety; pure white, 1-inch (2.5 cm) blooms.

Purple Robe • 6 inches (15 cm) tall; regal, dark purple, 1-inch (2.5 cm) flowers.

Purple Robe nierembergia looks marvellous with white petunias.

TIPS

These plants do well in extreme weather conditions: heat and drought, wind and rain, cold temperatures.

Although it seems rather picky work to deadhead nierembergia's small flowers, the plants will repay you tenfold for each dead bloom that is pinched off.

Nigella

blue, rose, pink, purple, mauve, white

Nigella damascena
Fennel Flower, Love-in-a-Mist, Devil-in-a-Bush

Height: 18 inches (45 cm)

Nigella is a pretty flower with the most curious collection of apparently unrelated and somewhat uncomplimentary names. 'Love-in-a-mist' and 'devil-in-a-bush' are folk names which may be odd descriptions of the flowers and seed pods; 'fennel flower' and the French name cheveux de Vénus *('the hair of Venus') presumably relate to nigella's fine, feathery foliage.*

PLANTING

Seeding: Indoors 8–10 weeks before transplanting.

Transplanting: 2 weeks after the average last spring frost. Space 6–8 inches (15–20 cm) apart.

Frost Tolerance: Moderate.

GROWING

Sunny locations.

Cutting gardens, mixed flower beds, in cottage gardens, meadow gardens.

Recommended Varieties

Cambridge Blue • double flowers in shades of light and bright blue; interesting green seedpods with prominent purple veins.

Mulberry Rose • double flowers in shades of clear rose and light pink; interesting green seedpods with prominent purple veins.

Persian Jewels Mixture • semi-double flowers in a blend of pink, white, mauve, purple and some bicolours.

Tips

With its striking flowers and dainty foliage, nigella makes a good companion to roses in the garden.

For bouquets, cut when flowers are open but the petals are not yet separated from the centre. Change the water often to extend the vase-life. Flowers generally last up to 2 weeks after cutting.

Nigella's balloon-like seed pods add interest to dried arrangements. To dry them, simply tie the plants in small bunches and hang upside down for about a week. For best results, stagger the seed heads up the length of the bunch.

A cutting garden of nigella, cosmos, stocks and snapdragons (top) provides endless bouquets. Nigella also blooms in pink and white. Nigella seed pods transform a wreath of bay leaves (below).

Nolana

sky blue

Nolana napiformis
Chilean Bellflower, Cliffhanger
Height: 10 inches (25 cm)

In almost any hard-to-plant area of the garden, nolana will thrive. These tough plants grow in sun or shade, in dry or wet conditions, and in poor or sandy soil—even in gravel. Nolana's sky blue flowers resemble those of petunias, but they are produced in less profusion on dwarf, creeping plants.

Nolana has sky-blue, petunia-like flowers and does well in virtually any growing conditions.

PLANTING

Seeding: Indoors 6–8 weeks before transplanting.

Transplanting: 1 week after the average last spring frost. Space 12 inches (30 cm) apart.

Frost Tolerance: Moderate.

GROWING

Partial shade to full sun.

Edging along pathways, in rock gardens, trailing in hanging baskets and other types of containers.

You need to water nolana only when the soil becomes dry (but not parched), although these adaptable plants will also do well in low-lying, wet areas of the garden.

RECOMMENDED VARIETIES

Sky Blue • 2-inch (5 cm) sky blue flowers with distinct, large white centres.

TIPS

For apartment-dwellers with windy balconies, nolana is a good choice for containers and hanging baskets. Its sky-blue flowers are splendidly set off by blooms of bright yellow. Tagetes is a good partner in this situation.

Photo courtesy of Park Seed Co., Cokesbury Rd., Greenwood, SC 29647-0001.

A combination of nolana, annual daisies and red geraniums provides a bright, carefree garden (top). Nolana blooms in a shade of sky-blue rarely found in flowers (above).

Pansy

black, purple, lavender, deep and pale blue, light pink, rose, red, magenta, burgundy, bronze, orange, apricot, bright and lemon yellow, white

Viola x wittrockiana
Heartsease

Height: 6–7 inches (15–18 cm)

Pansies are among the most popular bedding plants, because they are extremely versatile and have a wide range of flower colours and patterns. Pansies are the first annual flowers we put into the garden in spring—often in early April, about a month before the average last spring frost in our area. With care, and under favourable conditions, pansies will bloom all summer and well into fall.

PLANTING

Seeding: Indoors 12 to 14 weeks before transplanting.

Transplanting: From 3 or 4 weeks before the average last spring frost. Space 6–8 inches (15–20 cm) apart.

Frost Tolerance: Excellent.

Pansies are hardy plants that bloom in almost every colour except green, from late April or early May and well into fall. They will survive several degrees of frost.

GROWING

Full sun to partial shade.

Uses: Borders, mixed flower beds, in rock gardens and cottage gardens, mixed or alone in windowboxes, planters, patio pots, in hanging baskets.

Water frequently. Do not let these plants dry out or they will quickly finish flowering and go to seed.

RECOMMENDED VARIETIES

Black Prince • the closest to pure black solid-coloured flowers available.

Crystal Bowl Series • the best pansies for hot areas; early blooming 2³/₄-inch (7 cm) flowers without blotches; 7 separate colours including orange.

Imperial Series • masses of 3¹/₂-inch (9 cm) flowers; 6 separate colours including unusual pastel shades.

Jolly Joker • a rare and startling colour combination of contrasting orange and purple; award-winning variety; 3-inch (8 cm) flowers.

Imperial Antiques Shades (above) blooms in soft pastels. Super Majestic pansies (below) are up to twice as large as other varieties.

Masterpiece Mixture • distinctive flowers with beautifully waved and ruffled petals showing unusual markings and colours; 2³/₄-inch (7 cm) blooms; shades of bright blue, purple and bronze.

Maxim Series • 2-inch (5 cm) flowers in 9 bright colour combinations.

Super Majestic • the largest flowers yet; huge 4-inch (10 cm) flowers all distinguished by dark blotches; colour mix includes blues, purples, reds and roses, scarlets and bronzes, whites and yellows.

Ultima Mixture • the most extensive colour mixture available; 2³/₄-inch (7 cm) flowers in a formula blend of 21 separate colours, including both blotched and clear faces.

Universal Series • masses of 3-inch (8 cm) flowers; 2 colours: solid dark purple, and bright violet with a darker blotch.

Pansies are usually the first plants to be set out in the spring, and one of the last to finish blooming in the fall. In general, pansies with flowers in solid blue and yellow hues are the toughest. Pansies have the greatest tolerance to frost of all the annuals.

TIPS

Pansies thrive in cool, moist soil. Sunnier locations result in more flowers, but hot sites are not recommended. The ideal site is one that is protected from the strong mid-afternoon sun.

Yellow and white pansies have a gentle fragrance. I often recommend using these flowers to brighten a potted herb garden.

Cut back pansy plants by up to one-third before you leave on vacation if you want to be greeted in a week or two with a fresh flush of flowers.

Pansies are a good choice for children's gardens. These plants are easy to grow, and young gardeners love the bright, friendly faces of the flowers.

We sometimes plant pansies with ornamental kale in late September to provide fall colour. Both plants still look beautiful over a month later after many frosts and a few overnight snowfalls. In the Pacific Northwest, both of these plants are planted in the fall, for winter gardens.

Pansies are usually treated as annuals or biennials because they produce their best flowers when relatively young. A friend who used to live in the Vancouver area had pansies that, with regular deadheading, lasted through 2 summers before the plants became too straggly. I recall as a child in Saskatchewan the excitement of discovering the odd pansy plant that had survived over a relatively warm winter.

🌿 *Pansies often re-seed themselves in the garden, resulting in new plants the following spring. Hybrids in the more unusual colours, such as pastel shades and orange, are less likely to reproduce in this manner than are plants with blue and yellow flowers.*

Jolly Joker (top) won the All-American Selections award in 1990 for its superb performance and outstanding flowers. Pansies make excellent short-stemmed cutflowers (above). Whoever said 'the more you cut, the more they bloom' must have had pansies in mind. Cut the flowers for bouquets often, or deadhead. Removing faded flowers and seed pods results in plants producing a greater number of blooms over a longer period.

🌿 *Pansies have a strange variety of less common names, which include ladies-delight, stepmother's flower, three-faces-under-a-hood, herb trinity, and love-in-idleness.*

Petunia

deep purple, lavender, purple-blue, sky blue, burgundy, red, rose, pink, deep coral, salmon, yellow, white

Petunia x hybrida

Height: 10–12 inches (20–30 cm). Grandiflora up to 16 inches (40 cm).

The petunia is the most popular annual flower in our greenhouses because it is fast-growing and blooms in a immense range of flower sizes, types and colours. It grows as either a spreading or cascading plant, and it does well in almost any garden. Petunias, like roses, are categorized by their flowering habits. Grandiflora petunias are the tallest and produce the largest flowers. Multiflora petunias are more compact and produce the greatest number of flowers, although the flowers are smaller than those of the grandifloras. Floribunda petunias combine the best attributes of multifloras and grandifloras by producing an abundance of larger flowers, and they generally have the best tolerance to poor weather. Double-flowering petunias have distinctive, carnation-like blooms; they spread less and produce fewer flowers than do the other types, but they are the best petunias for shadier locations.

Petunias are definitely one of my favourite flowers, because they can be grown almost anywhere, begin blooming in May and put on a nonstop floral show right through until frost.

PLANTING

Seeding: Single-petalled varieties indoors 10–12 weeks before transplanting. Double-flowering petunias are difficult to produce from seed and are best purchased as bedding plants.

Transplanting: 1 week after the average last spring frost. Space 8–12 inches (20–30 cm) apart.

GROWING

Sun to light shade. Double-flowering varieties up to partial shade.

Borders, mixed flower beds, mass plantings, containers of all types including hanging baskets.

Double-flowering petunias require frequent applications of fertilizer to develop and maintain fully double flowers.

RECOMMENDED VARIETIES

Single-Flowered Petunias

Dreams Mixture • grandiflora; beautiful mix of solid bright colours; 12 inches (30 cm) tall; deep blue, pink, red, salmon and white.

Hulahoop Series • grandiflora; distinct flowers with a white outer edge; 12 inches (30 cm) tall; ruffled 3½-inch (8 cm) blooms in 4 separate colours.

Magic and Supermagic Series • grandiflora; unusual colours; 12 inches (30 cm) tall; 4-inch (10 cm) flowers; black, cherry-red and yellow.

Orchid Daddy • grandiflora; striking colour; 12–14 inches (30–35 cm) tall; recommended over the traditional variety Sugar Daddy; large 4-inch (10 cm) ruffled, pale burgundy blooms with darker veins.

Ultra Series • grandiflora; 12 inches (10 cm) tall; loads of blooms; excellent weather tolerance; uniform blooming time between all colours (traditionally, white and paler shades bloom before other colours); large 4-inch (10 cm) flowers in 9 different colours, including 2 that are marked with a white star.

Madness Series • floribunda; the best petunia available; 10–12 inches (20–30 cm) tall; masses of 3-inch (8 cm) flowers so prolific that they produce a solid carpet of colour above the foliage; superb performance in poor weather; particularly noted for their ability to bounce back after heavy rains; 17 colour choices including 2 with stars; plus 2 separate mixtures, Just Madness (only veined flowers) and Total Madness (a mix of all colours).

Pearls Series • multiflora; 10–12 inches (25–30 cm) tall; great performance in adverse weather conditions, especially hot spells; 2-inch (15 cm) flowers with distinctive creamy throats; 7 individual colours and a mixture.

Dreams petunias (above) are a 'formula blend,' with a guaranteed percentage of each colour. Lilac Madness petunias (opposite) perform outstandingly in all kinds of weather.

Double-Flowering Petunias

Double Madness Series • the first double floribunda; 10–12 inches (25–30 cm) tall; more flowers and better performance in poor weather than other double types; 5 individual colours and a mix.

Nocturne • 12 inches (30 cm) tall; fragrant, 3- to 4-inch (8–10 cm) dark violet-blue flowers.

Purple Pirouette • 12 inches (30 cm) tall; award-winning flower; lightly fragrant, bicoloured, 4-inch (10 cm) flowers in violet-purple and white.

Sonata • 12 inches (30 cm) tall; fringed, 3- to 4-inch (8-10 cm) white flowers.

Valentine • 12 inches (30 cm) tall; the best red yet developed in double petunias; 3-inch (8 cm) light salmon-red flowers.

If someone offered you the choice of an ounce of petunia seed or an ounce of gold, which would you choose? If your choice was based solely on price, the correct answer would be the ounce of petunia seeds—at market rates current at the time of writing, petunia seeds were approximately CDN$3,500 per ounce compared to about $480 per ounce for gold.

A bed of petunias (top) with French marigolds and Salvia farinacea *provides vivid colour. Many of the double-flowered petunias (above) available today originated from the painstaking efforts of an Edmonton grower whom Ted and I knew, the late Robert Simonet. He could only carry out cross-pollination when the sun was shining, using tweezers to remove stamens from single-flowering petunias and then brushing their pistils with pollen from the double-flowering plants that he had developed. Mr. Simonet was a largely self-taught plant breeder and won several awards for his work.*

TIPS

Choose stocky plants with dark-green leaves when purchasing petunias as bedding plants. Petunias often bloom in cell-packs, a trait that makes it easy to choose colours. With double-flowering petunias, do not be concerned about the flower size of the bedding plants. Double-flowering plants often produce single-petalled or smaller flowers in cell-packs, but they attain full size once they are planted in the garden.

Before you leave on a holiday, cut back all of your petunias to about half their height, water them very heavily and fertilize. By the time you return home, they will be bushier than ever and loaded with new buds and flowers.

Double-flowering petunias grow well in most types of containers, but because they are more upright than other types, we do not usually recommended them in hanging baskets.

Blue and purple varieties have a heavenly fragrance. Plant these in a flower bed near an open window or outdoor sitting area, or set a pot full of them near a patio door, where you will be able to enjoy their fragrance both indoors and out. Some pink- and white-flowered petunias have a more subtle scent.

Petunias are remarkably resilient. These plants (above) seemed destroyed by a hail storm just two weeks before this photo was taken. Petunias do well in sunny locations. Red and white petunias (below) thrive alongside salvia and alyssum in matching hues.

🌿 *Petunias and geraniums are the most popular choices in annual flowers with professional land-scapers, because they produce splendid floral shows and are relatively easy to grow. Bryan Fischer, horticulturist for the Silver Springs Golf Course in Calgary, filled the course's huge beds with Midnight Madness and Simply Madness petunias. He rated their performance as outstanding.*

Phlox

crimson, rose, salmon, light
blue, white

Phlox drummondii
Annual Phlox, Drummond
Phlox, Texan Pride

Height: 6–8 inches (15–20 cm)

Phlox is a traditional garden flower that has become less popular over the past few years, but I think that it deserves to be re-examined. Phlox is easy to grow and produces appealing flowers in large clusters. It does well in hot, sunny locations, and also has a high tolerance to frost and cool temperatures. Phlox makes a wonderful, colourful border.

PLANTING

Seeding: Indoors 10–12 weeks before transplanting.

Transplanting: On or near the date of the average last spring frost. Space 6–8 inches (15–20 cm) apart.

Frost Tolerance: Moderate.

GROWING

Sun to light shade.

Edging, borders, rock gardens, mass plantings, containers.

Add a handful of sand to the planting hole to improve drainage and prevent plants from rotting.

Phlox is picky when it comes to moisture. It enjoys frequent watering, but not being waterlogged. If it dries out, it will finish blooming and produce seed.

Phlox blooms throughout the summer and continues well into the fall, with its display undiminished even after several mild frosts.

RECOMMENDED VARIETIES

Palona Series • compact plants produce loads of flowers about 10–14 days earlier than do traditional varieties; all flowers are marked with darker centres; available in 4 individual colours and as a mixture.

TIPS

One of the nicest displays of phlox that I have seen was on the cool, windy balcony of a seventh-floor apartment. Rose-coloured phlox filled the planter, and thrived in conditions that would deter many other plants.

Phlox has a good resistance to frost and can be planted in the garden in early spring.

Phlox is a pretty annual flower that is well-suited to northern climates, with its long blooming season and tolerance of both heat and frost.

Poppy

red, pink, salmon, orange, yellow, cream, white

Eschscholzia californica
California Poppy

Papaver commutatum
Flanders Poppy

Papaver rhoeas
Shirley Poppy, Corn Poppy

Height: 16–24 inches
(40–60 cm)

The flowers of annual poppies have splendid, striking colours and shapes. California poppies have the longest blooming period of all these poppies, with silky blooms in bright colours set off by feathery, grey-green foliage. Flanders poppies are blazing red, with distinctive markings in black or white. Shirley poppies are delicate flowers in strong pastel hues.

PLANTING

Seeding: Indoors 4–6 weeks before transplanting. Outdoors as soon as the ground is workable in spring.

Transplanting: 1 week after the average last spring frost. Space 10–12 inches (25–30 cm) apart.

Frost Tolerance: Moderate.

Poppies are beautiful flowers that are easy to grow from seed and likely to self-seed in great numbers.

GROWING

Sunny locations.

Grouped in flower beds for splashes of colour, in borders, mass plantings, rock gardens, as edging along pathways, as backgrounds, in meadow gardens, in large containers.

Water only when dry. California poppies are the most drought-tolerant.

The blooming season of poppies can be greatly prolonged by deadheading.

Recommended Varieties

Mission Bells Mixture • California poppy; 18 inches (45 cm) tall; semi-double flowers in rose, gold, cherry, scarlet and pink.

Danish Flag (Danebrög) • Flanders poppy; 24 inches (60 cm) tall; blood-red flowers each vividly marked with a distinct white iron cross in the centre; laced or fringed petals; an incredible display when flowers are in full bloom.

Ladybird • Flanders poppy; 18 inches (45 cm) tall; bright, shining, crimson flowers with a distinct black blotch on each petal; very striking.

Shirley Double • Shirley poppy; 16–20 inches (40–50 cm) tall; double flowers in shades of salmon, pink, rose and scarlet.

Shirley Single • Shirley poppy; 16–20 inches (40–50 cm) tall; delicate, single flowers in pink, red or salmon with a white patch in centre.

The Clown • Shirley poppy; 18 inches (45 cm) tall; unusual, tulip-flowered, multicoloured flowers; very unique.

Tips

Poppies self-seed readily, which means that you will have new plants appearing in the garden each year after the first planting. To encourage self-seeding, stop deadheading the plants toward the end of the season. To discourage self-seeding, simply remove seedpods as they appear.

Poppies make good cutflowers as long as the stems' milky sap is prevented from sealing the cut end. To alleviate this problem, re-cut the stem and immediately afterward, singe the stem ends in a candle until they blacken, or immerse the stem ends in boiling water for 20–30 seconds.

After blooming slows, cut back California poppies to a couple of inches above the ground and they will bloom again with a burst of colour.

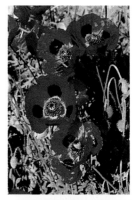

201

'Ladybird' is the British term for ladybug, and an apt description of these poppies (top). This entire bed of California poppies in my mother's garden (above) is filled with volunteer plants: plants that re-seeded themselves from plants grown the previous year. Although new breeding innovations have resulted in red, yellow and cream flowers, most often the flowers of self-seeded plants revert to orange, the traditional poppy colour.

Portulaca

purple, fuchsia, orange, hot and light pink, scarlet, yellow, white

Portulaca grandiflora
Moss Rose, Sun Moss

Purslane oleracea
Hybrid Portulaca, Purslane, Rose Moss

Height: 5 inches (13 cm). The trailing type reaches a length of up to 18 inches (45 cm).

The two species of portulaca are not closely related, although their flowers look remarkably similar. In the greenhouse, we usually differentiate between the two by referring to Portulaca grandiflora simply as 'portulaca,' and to Purslane oleracea as 'portulaca from cuttings.' Portulaca grandiflora is low-growing, with bright flowers that resemble tiny roses, and it is best suited to open gardens. Portulaca from cuttings is a trailing plant with smaller, single-petalled, open flowers on stiff, succulent stems, and it is best in hanging baskets and containers. Both have excellent heat, drought and wind tolerance. Their flowers close up at night, in shade and on cloudy days.

PLANTING

Seeding: Sow *Portulaca grandiflora* indoors 8–10 weeks before transplanting. Portulaca from cuttings should be purchased as a bedding plant later in the season.

Transplanting: 2–3 weeks after the average last spring frost. Space 6 inches (15 cm) apart.

Frost Tolerance: Poor.

Portulaca is one of the least demanding annuals. It thrives in hot, dry areas and is relatively free of plant diseases and insect pests. Its flowers fall cleanly as they fade so that no deadheading is required.

GROWING

Hot and sunny locations.

Borders, as edgings in flower beds, in rock gardens, in windowboxes, patio pots and planters. Trailing types at the edges of containers, in rock gardens and in hanging baskets.

Water only when dry (but not parched).

RECOMMENDED VARIETIES

Portulaca (Portulaca grandiflora)

Sundial Series • blooms 2 weeks earlier than most; bushy plants that branch and spread more quickly than most varieties; available individually in fuchsia, orange, pink, scarlet, white, yellow and as a mixture.

Portulaca from cuttings (Purslane oleracea)

Usually available only under one of the names listed above. Produced only from cuttings so more expensive than *Portulaca grandiflora*; available in 5 intense colours; purple, hot pink, orange, red and yellow.

The variety Sundial is an example of recent breeding developments. These new plants (top) are far more vigorous and produce a greater number of large flowers than do traditional varieties.

TIPS

We often grow portulaca from cuttings in hanging baskets, where the plants grow into a thick carpet that hugs tight to the sides of the containers. These plants look splendid on their own, but can also be mixed with other plants with similar growing requirements, such as ice plant, verbena and lotus vine.

Queen Anne's Lace

white

Ammi majus
White Lace Flower

Height: up to 24 inches
(60 cm)

Queen Anne's lace is unmatched for the splendour of its lacy flowers in fresh bouquets and dried arrangements, so it is one of the most popular annual flowers for cutting. Its name is familiar to many gardeners who have never grown it, but, more often than not, after people grow Queen Anne's lace once they want to grow it every year.

PLANTING

Seeding: Sow indoors 8 weeks before transplanting.

Transplanting: 1 week after the average last spring frost. Space 12 inches (30 cm) apart.

Frost Tolerance: Moderate.

GROWING

Sun.

In cutting gardens, in cottage gardens, meadow gardens, as background plants.

RECOMMENDED VARIETIES

Snowflake • white, dainty flowers in huge clusters.

The dainty flowers of Queen Anne's lace are wonderful in both fresh and dried floral arrangements.

TIPS

Queen Anne's lace grows quickly as a bedding plant, and the seedlings in cell-packs are often tall and thin. At this stage, the seedlings are still fine for transplanting.

Queen Anne's lace can be sown directly into the garden, but it takes about 12 weeks from seeding to flowering. If you can get into the garden in the early spring, scatter the seed in a 1-foot-wide (30 cm) band to create a miniature meadow.

Avoid planting Queen Anne's lace in windy or exposed areas, because this often results in the plants flopping over. An alternative is to stake the plants or use peony rings for support.

The flowers of Queen Anne's lace act as an airy filler in bouquets that enhances larger, more showy flowers. I like to mix Queen Anne's lace with blooms of vibrant colours, or sometimes, for a simple but elegant effect, with only white-petalled flowers.

To dry Queen Anne's lace, simply tie about 5 stems in a bunch and hang them upside down. For best results, stagger the flowerheads up the length of the bunch.

Queen Anne's lace and fragrant freesias make an elegant bouquet that lasts ten or more days.

Salpiglossis

purple, rose, red, orange, yellow

Salpiglossis sinuata
Painted Tongue, Velvet Flower

Height: 24 inches (60 cm)

The velvety flowers of salpiglossis offer some of the richest colours in the garden, dazzlingly overlaid with golden veins and intricate markings. Salpiglossis is an uncommon plant, a factor that I think is most likely due to its unappealing name. In the garden, however, salpiglossis provides masses of colour in a variety of situations. Its preferred growing conditions of fairly cool nights and not-too-hot days are perfectly matched to those found in most northern gardens.

PLANTING

Seeding: Indoors 8–10 weeks before transplanting.

Transplanting: 2 weeks after the average last spring frost. Space 8–12 inches (20–30 cm) apart.

Frost Tolerance: Moderate.

Most flowers that are best for bouquets need a sunny location. Salpiglossis is one of the few annuals that makes a wonderful cutflower and grows well in shaded areas.

GROWING

Partial shade to partial sun.

Backgrounds, feature plant, mixed flower beds, tall borders, in containers.

Recommended Varieties

Splash Mix • huge 3½-inch (9 cm) flowers; compact plants; masses of gorgeous colours in red, yellow, orange, rose and purple.

Tips

Salpiglossis is splendid in containers. We grew it in an oak-barrel planter at the edge of the parking lot outside the green-house, where its exotic flowers drew a lot of attention.

Salpiglossis is stunning in bouquets. Its flowers are borne in loose clusters on the tops of long stems. Arrange a vase with just salpiglossis, or mix it with other flowers. Blooms of solid yellow, such as calendula or snapdragons, are particularly good partners, because their colour enhances the golden veins of salpiglossis. Pick salpiglossis for bouquets when the blooms are just starting to open. These flowers generally last 7–10 days after cutting.

Salpiglossis blooms all summer long.

Salpiglossis, yellow calendula and purple statice go well together.

Salvia

red, dark and light salmon, pink, lilac, purple, deep blue, cream, white

Salvia splendens
Salvia, Scarlet Sage

Salvia farinacea
Mealy Cup Sage

Salvia horminum
Clary Sage

Height: 10–24 inches
(20–60 cm)

Salvia is distinctive for its spiky flowerheads in vivid colours. Salvia splendens is the most common type, and is the perfect plant for those people who prefer an orderly garden, because it is so tidy, compact and uniform. Its flowers are most often an intense scarlet, but you can also find newer varieties in shades of salmon, purple and white. Salvia farinacea bears narrow flower spikes that are profusely covered in tiny flowers. Salvia horminum has long flower spikes with widely-spaced, flat petals that protrude from the stalks.

PLANTING

Seeding: Indoors, *S. splendens* 7–8 weeks before transplanting, and the other 2 types 8–9 weeks prior.

Transplanting: *Salvia farinacea* and *S. horminum* 1 week after the average last spring frost, and *S. splendens* 2 weeks later. Space *S. splendens* 6–8 inches (15–20 cm) apart. Because the variety Flare is twice the usual height, it should be spaced 10 inches (25 cm) apart. *S. farinacea* and *S. horminum* can be planted 12 inches (30 cm) apart.

Frost Tolerance: Moderate (*S. farinacea* and *S. horminum*) to poor (*S. splendens*).

GROWING

S. splendens in partial shade to full sun; *S. farinacea* and *S. horminum* need a sunny location.

Backgrounds, mixed flower beds, mass plantings, in containers. *S. splendens* for borders. *S. farinacea* and *S. horminum* in cottage gardens, cutting gardens and meadow gardens.

Remove the first central flower spikes from *S. splendens* as soon as it forms. This encourages the plants to bush out immediately and produce many more flowers, resulting in a much better show of flowers.

RECOMMENDED VARIETIES

S. splendens

Flare • 18 inches (45 cm) tall; twice the usual height; bright-scarlet flower spikes.

Empire Series • 10 inches (20 cm) tall; dark and light salmon, lilac, purple, red and white.

S. farinacea

Victoria Series • 18–20 inches (45–50 cm) tall; grey-blue leaves; blooms continuously; deep violet-blue and silvery white.

S. horminum

Oxford Blue • 24 inches (60 cm) tall; deep-blue flower spikes.

Pink Sundae • 18 inches (45 cm) tall; rose-pink flower spikes.

Horminum Tricolour Mixture • 18 inches (45 cm) tall; blue, pink and cream.

Salvia farinacea (above) has lavender-like flower-spikes and sage-scented leaves. S. splendens (opposite) is the most common type of salvia, and for years red was by far the most common colour. Plant breeders have recently developed varieties of S. splendens in an array of other colours (top).

Salvia splendens is one of the most uniformly even annuals available.

TIPS

S. splendens is what we call a heavy feeder. It needs lots of nutrients, more than most annuals, and responds to a regular fertilizing program by producing more flowers in brighter hues. Fertilize these flowers once a week throughout the summer for the best results.

Plant red *S. splendens* with bright yellow marigolds or silvery dusty miller for a very showy display.

S. farinacea looks superb combined with yellow African marigolds. The blue variety is also striking in flowerbeds with Tango or Katie geraniums.

We once spotted a stunning display outside a restaurant in Skagway, Alaska, with double planters of the Tricolour Mix bordered by bright-pink and blue petunias.

The flowers of both *S. farinacea* and *S. horminum* are splendid in bouquets. Cut when the flowers are starting to open. They generally last 7–10 days after cutting.

The flowers of *S. farinacea* and *S. horminum* are easily dried for use in permanent arrangements. Pick for drying when the bottom half of flower spikes are open. To dry them, tie about 5 stems in a bunch and hang them upside down for about a week. For best results, stagger the flowerheads up the length of the bunch.

Salvia farinacea *and* S. horminum *do well in dry areas of the garden and produce flowers that provide beautiful accents to both fresh and dried bouquets (above, left).* S. horminum *(above) looks best* en masse *or in groups among other flowers.*

Scabiosa

burgundy-black, rose, coral, salmon, crimson, purple, lavender, deep blue, white

Scabiosa atropurpurea
Mourning Bride, Pincushion Flower, Sweet Scabious

Scabiosa stellata
Paper Moon, Star Flower

Height: 18–36 inches (45–90 cm)

The flowers of the two types of scabiosa are similar in shape, but there the resemblance stops. Scabiosa atropurpurea *has beautiful, large, colourful flowers that are showy in the garden and splendid in bouquets.* S. stellata *has small, white flowers that quickly mature to decorative seedpods, shaped like geodesic domes. It is for these seedpods that* S. stellata *is most often grown.*

PLANTING

Seeding: Indoors 8–10 weeks before transplanting.

Transplanting: 2 weeks after the average last spring frost. Space 10–12 inches (25–30 cm) apart.

Frost Tolerance: Poor.

GROWING

Sunny locations.

Backgrounds, mixed flower beds, cutting gardens. *S. stellata* is less showy and would be better planted in an inconspicuous area of the garden.

The round blooms of the pincushion flower have entrancingly detailed petals and are stunning in bouquets.

RECOMMENDED VARIETIES

Imperial Giants • *S. atropurpurea*; 24–36 inches (60–90 cm) tall; a mixture of burgundy-black, rose, coral, crimson, purple, lavender, deep blue, salmon and white.

Ping Pong • *S. stellata*; 18–20 inches (45–50 cm) tall; bronze, globe-shaped seed pods with an intricate design, each segment with a maroon star.

TIPS

Pincushion flower's blooms are beautiful in bouquets. Cut when they are just starting to open for best results. The flowers generally last about a week. Re-cutting the stems helps to extend the vase-life.

We usually allow the seedpods of *S. stellata* to dry on the plants before harvesting them.

Scabiosa stellata is most often grown for its bronze, globe-shaped seed pods, which are used in dried arrangements.

Annual scabiosa looks splendid in a bouquet with perennial statice and baby's breath from the garden.

Scaevola

sky blue

Scaevola aemula
**Australian Blue Fan Flower,
Fairy Fan Flower**

**Height: 8–10 inches
(20–25 cm)**

Scaevola is the type of plant that endears itself to gardeners for its ability to thrive in hot, dry situations. It produces tiny, blue, fan-shaped flowers on curving branches throughout the season. Scaevola is a fast-growing and undemanding plant native to Tasmania and parts of Australia. People who discover this plant generally grow it year after year.

PLANTING

Seeding: Not recommended; usually propagated from cuttings.

Transplanting: 2 weeks after the average last spring frost. Space 12 inches (30 cm) apart in the garden, or use 3 plants per 10-inch (20 cm) hanging basket.

Frost Tolerance: Poor.

GROWING

Partial to full sun.

Hanging baskets, windowboxes, patio pots, planters.

RECOMMENDED VARIETIES

Blue Wonder • sky blue, fan-shaped flowers.

Scaevola is one of the best annuals for hanging baskets and containers in hot, dry areas.

TIPS

For apartment dwellers with windy balconies that get a lot of sun, scaevola is a wonderful plant. It will do well in planters and tubs as well as in hanging baskets in these sorts of locations, where many other plants would wither and die from lack of water.

Scaevola is a tough plant that can withstand some abuse. I have seen plants that have been allowed to dry out until they are wilting that bounce back amazingly well after a good watering.

A hanging basket of scaevola thrives in a sunny location near white, heat-reflecting walls.

Scaevola does well in a mixed planter with geraniums and dracaena.

Schizanthus

red, magenta, pink, blue,
yellow, white

*Schizanthus x
wisetonensis*
Butterfly Flower, Poor Man's
Orchid

Height: 10–12 inches
(25–30 cm)

*Schizanthus at its peak of splendour is irresistible.
A woman once told me that after seeing a pot filled
with these plants in full bloom, she wanted to buy
every single schizanthus plant in the greenhouse.
The showy flowers bloom in dense clusters and
resemble brightly coloured orchids with contrasting
markings. Fringed, fern-like foliage perfectly sets
off the blooms.*

PLANTING

Seeding: Indoors 6–8 weeks before transplanting.

Transplanting: 2 weeks after the average
last spring frost. Space 8 inches
(20 cm) apart.

Frost Tolerance: Poor.

GROWING

Sun to light shade.

Borders, mass plantings, rock gardens,
windowboxes, planters, patio pots,
hanging baskets.

Keep well-watered. These
plants suffer in dry conditions.

*Schizanthus is
smothered in
blooms throughout the
summer. These plants
love a bright location
with moist conditions
and cool nights,
making them ideal for
northern climates.*

RECOMMENDED VARIETIES

Hit Parade Mixture • mound-shaped plants covered with blooms in white, blue, pink, yellow, red and magenta.

TIPS

A planter overflowing with schizanthus is spectacular. Fill a garden pot with only these flowers, or set off their exotic markings by combining them with bright, solid-coloured flowers, such as geraniums or marigolds.

The blooms of schizanthus are stunning in bouquets. For best results, cut them when clusters are at least half open, as far down the stem as possible. The blooms generally last 7–10 days after cutting.

Schizanthus in full bloom, petunias and dusty miller (top) create a traffic-stopping display. Schizanthus is also striking in a hanging basket (above).

Snapdragon

bronze, light orange, scarlet, rose, crimson, light and medium pink, lavender, purple, yellow, white

Antirrhinum majus

Height: 6–36 inches
(15–90 cm)

To me, the sight and subtle scent of these velvety flowers evokes childhood memories of summer days happily spent in my mother's garden. Snapdragons bloom in an immense range of colours on plants of various heights. The traditional snap-jawed blooms are familiar to most people, but there are also varieties with open-faced, ruffled-edged blooms and others with double flowers that resemble miniature roses. All make wonderful, long-lasting cutflowers.

PLANTING

Seeding: Indoors 10–12 weeks before transplanting.

Transplanting: As soon as the ground is workable in the spring, up to 2 weeks before the average last spring frost. Space most snapdragons 10–12 inches (25–30 cm) apart. Dwarf types can be planted 8 inches (20 cm) apart.

Frost Tolerance: Excellent.

GROWING

Sunny locations.

Borders, backgrounds, feature plants, in windowboxes, planters, patio pots, for mass plantings, edgings.

RECOMMENDED VARIETIES

Varieties are listed from tallest to shortest.

Rocket Series • 36 inches (90 cm) tall; traditional flower-type; extra-long flower spikes; 4 individual colours and a mixture.

Bright Butterflies Mixture • 30 inches (75 cm) tall; open-faced flowers; bushy, stocky plants with lots of long-stemmed flowers; mixture of 8 colours.

Madame Butterfly Mixture • 30 inches (75 cm) tall; extra-large, double, azalea-type flowers; flowerstalks are 8–10 inches (20–25 cm) long; mixture of 7 colours.

219

Liberty Series • 18–20 inches (45–50 cm) tall; traditional flower-type; early-blooming; extra-long, shapely flower spikes easily 12–14 inches (30–35 cm) long; 9 individual colours and a mixture.

The flowers of Sweetheart snapdragons resemble azaleas or miniature roses.

Princess White with a Purple Eye • 18 inches (45 cm) tall; traditional flower-type; especially bred for cutting; stunning in bouquets; an unusual variety with pure-white blooms highlighted by distinct purple eyes.

Sweetheart Mixture • 12 inches (30 cm) tall; azalea-type flowers on medium flower spikes; superb tolerance to wind; mixture of 6 colours.

Snapdragons are one of the first annuals that can be planted out in the spring, and they bloom from early summer to mid-fall.

Floral Showers Series • 6–8 inches (15–20 cm) tall; traditional flower-type; short, stocky plants that begin to flower in late May; plants perform well even in poor weather; 9 individual colours and a mixture.

Snapdragons such as the varieties Liberty or Floral Showers are good candidates for mass plantings on commercial sites because they provide a solid carpet of showy colour, even where deadheading on a regular basis is impractical. The trick to obtaining a mass of blooms is to pinch the central flower shoot at the time of planting.

TIPS

With snapdragons, it is fairly easy to determine whether the bedding plants you are purchasing have been hardened off. Gently run your hand across the tops of the plants. If they feel sturdy, they most likely have been hardened off; if they feel somewhat floppy and soft, they most likely have not. Bedding plants that have been hardened off are also often a darker green with thicker stems than those that have not been through this process.

Pinch out the central flowerstalk after planting snapdragons. This encourages the plants to bush out more quickly and produce multiple flower spikes instead of only a single stalk per plant.

Snapdragons make excellent, long-lasting cutflowers. Cut flower spikes for bouquets when flowers on the lower half are open. Snapdragons last 2 weeks or longer after cutting. Frequent re-cutting of stems extends the flowers' vase-life.

221

The results of extra attention are especially evident with snapdragons. By pinching after planting, cutting or deadheading regularly and watering and fertilizing often, you will be rewarded by many more flowers and sturdy plants that do not flop over in the garden.

Cut flowers for bouquets often, or deadhead plants regularly. Removing the finished blooms results in increased production of flowers. Snapdragons really respond to this treatment— the more you cut, the more they bloom.

With snapdragons, even an apartment dweller or someone without an open garden can have a source of flowers for bouquets. One of our staff members who grew Madame Butterfly snapdragons in a large oak barrel planter cut the flowers for fresh bouquets one after the other all summer long. The plants bloomed so profusely that there were always enough flowers left on the plants to provide a showy display, despite (or as a result of) the frequent cutting.

The subtle scent of a snapdragon still brings me back to my mother's garden. Snapdragons were one of my favourite flowers as a child, because each bloom could be made to talk by squeezing it at the back so that its mouth would open and shut.

Spider Plant

green, white

Chlorophytum comosum

Height: 6 inches (15 cm)

We first started using spider plants in outdoor planters after experimenting with various candidates as accent plants for shady areas. Spider plant won out over the others because it performs so well outdoors, is easy to grow and often has attractive, variegated foliage. It provides height with the graceful upward arch of its lance-shaped leaves, and it sometimes produces trailing runners with baby spider-plantlets.

Spider plants make wonderful additions to patio planters and hanging baskets, and they serve double-duty as houseplants at the end of the season.

PLANTING

Seeding: Not recommended, because it takes too long.

Transplanting: 3 weeks after the average last spring frost. Space 6–8 inches (15–20 cm) apart in planters or pots.

Frost Tolerance: Poor.

GROWING

Full to partial shade.

As accent plants in windowboxes, patio pots, planters and hanging baskets.

Recommended Varieties

Usually available only under one of the names listed above. Various spider plants do, however, have different appearances to their leaves. Some are solid green, some are variegated (creamy white with a green stripe) and others are reverse-variegated (green with a white stripe).

Tips

We recommend spider plant as a houseplant, not only because it is attractive and easy to grow, but also because it has the ability to purify indoor air. It is surprising to discover the number of air-pollutants that are commonly found in most homes. New or newly-renovated houses especially, with their freshly painted walls and brand-new carpeting, can have a high level of potentially harmful pollutants.

You can compensate for contaminants, in part, by filling your home with attractive houseplants. Studies by the U.S. National Aeronautics and Space Administration (NASA) have found that certain houseplants actually clean harmful chemicals, such as benzene, trichloroethylene and formaldehyde, from the air. Spider plant is on NASA's 'Foliage for Clean Air' list.

The ideal site for spider plant is one that receives morning sun. Tuberous begonias, asparagus fern and English ivy (above) make ideal partners.

Geraniums will do well with spider plants in lightly shaded areas. The variety shown is Blues.

Statice

dark and light blue, purple, pink, apricot, yellow, white

Limonium sinuata
Annual Statice, Mexican Statice, Sea Lavender

Limonium suworoii
Pink Poker Statice, Pink Pokers, Rat-tail Statice, Russian Statice

Height: 18–24 inches
(45–60 cm)

Statice is one of the most popular everlasting flowers. Annual statice is the type commonly found in florists' arrangements. These plants have sturdy, triangular stems rising from rosettes of thick, flat leaves. Russian statice is more unusual, with long, branched, gracefully curved spikes of bright rose-pink flowers. Both types look equally pleasing in fresh or dried arrangements, or growing in your garden.

PLANTING

Seeding: Indoors 8–10 weeks before transplanting.

Statice is one of the best flowers for drying, because its papery petals retain their vivid colours indefinitely. The plants are among the easiest of the everlastings to grow.

Transplanting: 2 weeks after the average last spring frost. Space annual statice 12 inches (30 cm) apart, and Russian statice from 8–12 inches (20–30 cm) apart.

Frost Tolerance: Moderate.

GROWING

Sunny and hot locations.

Backgrounds, cutting gardens, mass plantings, mixed flower beds. Annual statice for tall borders and hedges.

Recommended Varieties

Annual Statice

Fortress Series • 24 inches (60 cm) tall; large flower clusters on long, strong stems; 7 individual vibrant flower colours and a mixture.

Russian Statice

Usually available only under one of the names listed above.

Statice flowers have dry, papery petals even while growing.

Russian statice brings vibrant colour to the garden. Both it and the bachelor's buttons in the background provide flowers for cutting.

TIPS

Statice does well in hot locations, but the plants must be kept well-watered. Statice reacts to drought in a manner similar to a cactus: it does not die, but it stops growing to conserve energy until moisture returns. Regular watering results in better flowers.

Annual statice can be relied on to produce strong, straight flower stems that never need staking. This trait makes it one of the most desirable flowers for cutting, and it is the reason that many people who grow vegetables for sale at farmers' markets include a few rows of statice. We once grew half an acre of statice in one of our fields to sell in bouquets throughout the summer.

Statice is one of the easiest flowers to dry, and it is just as easy to use in arrangements. This plant's stems were simply tucked into a grapevine wreath, where they will stay in place and retain their colours indefinitely.

Annual statice displays its flowers in a bush-like fashion on the tips of branched stems. These sturdy plants can set in a long row to form a striking temporary hedge.

Statice is often added to fresh bouquets. Cut the stems when most of the flowers have just opened and are showing colour. Statice lasts 2 weeks or longer after cutting, and it can be easily dried once other flowers in the bouquet are finished.

The best way to dry statice is to tie the stems in small bunches and hang them upside-down for about a week. For best results, stagger the flowerheads up the length of the bunch. Use stems with flowers that are fully open, and harvest in mid-morning, after the dew has dried from the plants.

Unlike most of the everlasting flowers, statice withstands mild frost and light snowfalls without noticeable effects.

Statice can also be successfully dried by simply placing the cut stems in a vase with about an inch (2.5 cm) of water in it. As the water evaporates, the stems slowly dry and the flowers keep their vibrant hues. This method does, however, sometimes result in less-upright flowers than does hang-drying.

Stock

blue-purple, deep purple, soft mauve, deep wine, rose, pink, apricot, white

Matthiola incana
Common Stock, Gillyflower

Height: 18–24 inches
(45–60 cm)

Stocks are among the most beautiful flowers in the garden, with their long, dense flowerstalks set off by grey-blue foliage. They are especially noted for their strong, clove-like fragrance. When we first started in the greenhouse business, stocks were almost as popular as petunias. Since then, their popularity has taken a dip, but stocks are now making a resurgence as people rediscover the value of these flowers for cutting.

228

PLANTING

Seeding: Indoors 6–8 weeks before transplanting.

The beauty of stocks is in their long, dense spikes of double flowers; occasionally, however, these plants produce less-attractive single blooms. The key to attaining only double flowers is to keep only the yellow-green, palest seedlings and discard the others. Single-flowered seedlings are easier to detect by lowering temperatures to 45–50° F (7–10° C) as the seedlings appear.

Transplanting: 2 weeks after the average last spring frost. Space 10–12 inches (25–30 cm) apart.

Frost Tolerance: Moderate.

GROWING

Sunny location.

Borders, mixed flower beds, near decks, patios or outdoor sitting areas, as background plants, in windowboxes, patio pots, planters.

Do not allow plants to dry out.

The scent of stocks reminds my son Bill of our visits to the city farmers' market when he was a boy. Many farm women used to grow stocks to sell in bouquets, and their spicy-sweet perfume filled the air for quite a distance from the booths.

An attractive swag can be easily created by tying twigs in a bunch and gluing flower stems of dried stocks in place. Finish with a bright bow.

RECOMMENDED VARIETIES

Our best recommendation is to choose a tall, double mix.

TIPS

Plant stocks near a pathway or an outdoor sitting area where you will be able to enjoy their perfume. Our photographer, Akemi Matsubuchi, grew stocks in a mixed border outside her back door, and she told us that everyone who visited remarked on their fragrance as they came into the house.

Stocks are the most fragrant annual cutflower, with a heavenly, spicy, clove-like fragrance that fills the entire house.

Stocks are wonderful in bouquets and showy enough to be displayed on their own. Cut them when nearly half of the buds on each stalk are open. Stocks last 7–10 days after cutting. To extend their vase-life, re-cut the stem ends and remove leaves before placing the stems in the vase. Frequently re-cutting the stems and adding flower food also helps.

Stocks provide flowers for cutting, vibrant colour and a wonderful fragrance.

A bouquet of stocks can easily be dried. Arrange the fresh flowers in the vase, then pull the entire bunch out and fasten an elastic band around the stem ends. Turn the intact bouquet upside down to dry for about a week. Once the flowers have dried, return them to the dry vase.

Strawflower

purple, pink, silvery rose, red, orange, salmon, frosted sulphur, bright yellow, lemon, white

Helichrysum bracteatum
Everlasting Flowers

Height: 24–40 inches
(60–80 cm)

Strawflowers are one of the best everlasting flowers. Their large flowerheads are round and full, similar in shape to chrysanthemums, and they bloom in an extensive range of intense colours, which are retained indefinitely after drying. The crisp, pointed petals have a satiny sheen, and they are papery to the touch.

PLANTING

Seeding: Indoors 6 weeks before transplanting.

Transplanting: 2 weeks after the average last spring frost. Space 8–12 inches (20–30 cm) apart.

Frost Tolerance: Moderate.

GROWING

Sunny and hot locations.

Mixed flower beds, cutting gardens, backgrounds.

RECOMMENDED VARIETIES

Finest • a superior mix with extra-large flowers on very stiff stems; many unusual hues; 8 individual colours and a mixture.

Strawflowers are one of the best flowers for drying! Their flowers are larger and more durable than many of the other everlastings, and they bloom in a more extensive range of vivid colours.

TIPS

I like to plant flowers specifically for cutting (whether for fresh or dried bouquets) in a long row in the back garden. That way, I can cut happily away for bouquets by the armload, without disturbing the show in the main flower garden. This method works particularly well with flowers that are grown for drying, since the entire lot must sometimes be harvested in one fell swoop when they reach their peak of bloom.

Strawflowers can be added to fresh bouquets. Cut the flowers before they are fully open. They generally last 10 days to 2 weeks after cutting.

To dry strawflowers, cut the blooms when only the outer petals are open and the centres remain tightly closed. Strip off the foliage from the stems, tie them into bunches of about 5 stems, and hang them upside down for about a week. For best results, stagger the flowerheads up the length of the bunch.

Another method of drying is to snip the stems off at the base of the flowerheads. Some people then use a fine florists' wire to attach in place of the stems, but my daughter-in-law Valerie simply chops off flowerheads and tosses them into wicker baskets. The baskets have adequate air circulation to permit the flower-heads to dry in place, and the result is a splendid display that is effortless to create.

Strawflowers traditionally bloom in bright, sunny colours (left). Newer varieties include more unusual hues (opposite), such as purple-black and silvery rose.

The ideal time to harvest strawflowers is at the stage shown above, when the outer petals are open but before the central petals are fully opened. This is important because these flowers will continue to open as they dry, and flowers at a more mature stage produce a rather unattractive, protruding centre that can open to release fluffy seeds like those of a dandelion.

Sunflower

bright yellow, red

Helianthus annuus,
  H. debilis

Height: 1–6 feet (30–180 cm)

Sunflowers are traditional favourites for flower gardens because they have such showy flowerheads and are so easy to grow. As well as the traditional type of sunflowers, there are some wonderful and very different-looking varieties that make marvellous additions to any sunny garden. Most people think of sunflowers as towering plants with large, sunny, yellow flowers, but some varieties bloom in shades of red, with smaller or double-petalled flowers on shorter plants.

PLANTING

Seeding: Outdoors as soon as the ground is workable.

Transplanting: 2 weeks after the average last spring frost. Space tall varieties 24 inches (60 cm) apart, and short varieties 18–20 inches (45–50 cm) apart.

Frost Tolerance: Moderate.

Sunflowers have huge, showy flowerheads that are stunning in bouquets. These plants are easy to grow from seed sown directly into the garden in the early spring.

GROWING

Full sun.

Backgrounds, borders, annual hedges, children's gardens. Dwarf varieties also in large containers. Tallest varieties also as windbreaks, screens.

Taller varieties may require staking.

RECOMMENDED VARIETIES

Big Smile • 12–15 inches (30–38 cm) tall; makes an excellent and unusual border; great for children's gardens; large, 6-inch (15 cm) wide, golden yellow flowers with distinct black centres.

Big Smile sunflowers have full-sized flowerheads on plants just 3 feet (1 m) tall. They are superb growing in large containers.

Teddy Bear • 3 feet (90 cm) tall; similar flower type to that illustrated in Van Gogh's famous painting; makes an exceptional, fun, fast-growing border; bushy, very sturdy plants; huge, 6-inch (15 cm) wide, fully double, bright-yellow flowers like fluffy chrysanthemums.

Florastan • 3 feet (90 cm) tall; masses of extremely pretty blooms; dark central discs bordered by reddish-brown petals with golden tips.

Russian Mammoth • 6 feet (180 cm) tall; huge, 10-inch (25 cm) flowers; traditional flower type.

Florastan is a branching variety with unusual flowers that make wonderful bouquets.

TIPS

If you are short on garden space, plant sunflowers on the north side of cucumbers, where they will provide an attractive shelterbelt and aid the growth of these vegetables. Do not plant sunflowers near corn, because they attract birds.

Even the homeowner without a garden can grow sunflowers by planting dwarf varieties in containers. We found that the variety Big Smile provided a splendid display in an oak-barrel planter. Six plants were arranged in a circle, with bright-yellow French marigolds planted around the rim.

Sunflowers are a wonderful choice for children's gardens. Their seeds are big enough to be easily handled by little hands, the plants have a fantastic growth rate, and the splendid, huge flowers provide edible seeds. The dwarf variety Big Smile provides the advantage of full-sized flowerheads at a height easily accessible to children.

*Teddy Bear
sunflowers look
marvellous in
bouquets. The
flowers last up to
two weeks after
cutting.*

Sunflowers are easily grown from seed, but if you are late putting in your garden and want to be assured of the plants obtaining their full size, choose bedding plants for plantings in June.

Sunflowers make excellent cutflowers. The smaller-flowered varieties are often most manageable in vases. Cut when the blooms are open but the centres are still tight. They last 10 to 14 days after cutting.

To dry sunflowers, hang individual stems upside down for about a week, arranged so that they do not touch each other. Harvest flowers for drying at the same stage you would for fresh bouquets. For best results, cut them about mid-morning, after the dew has dried from the plants.

Sunflowers frequently re-seed themselves each year, so you may discover new plants appearing in your garden each spring, some-times from seeds dropped by birds feeding at nearby birdfeeders.

In the fall, leave the flowerheads on the plants until the back of the seedhead is brown and dry. Allow the seeds to dry all the way to the centre of the disc; cover them with cheese-cloth if you do not want to share your harvest with the birds. Remove the seeds by brushing them out with your hand or a stiff brush.

Sweet Pea

sky-blue, purple, lavender,
maroon, red, rose, pink,
salmon, white

Lathyrus odoratus

Height: 15 inches to 6 feet
(38–180 cm)

A woman who was the stage manager for the opera once called because she had her heart set on carrying sweet peas in her wedding bouquet. Unfortunately, it was too late in the season to find these flowers in the garden, but we were able to find a grower in Holland.

Sweet peas have sweetly-scented flowers that can be cut throughout the summer for fragrant bouquets.

Sweet peas are a traditional garden favourite because they are easy to grow, sprout quickly from seed and have sweetly-scented blooms that can be cut often for fragrant bouquets. Most varieties are tall-growing and need a support for their tendrils to cling to, but there are also dwarf varieties available that produce a solid bush of airy blooms and are ideal for small gardens.

PLANTING

Seeding: Indoors 3–4 weeks before transplanting. Outdoors as soon as the ground is workable.

Transplanting: 1 week after the average last spring frost. Space the taller, vining varieties 6–8 inches (15–20 cm) apart. Dwarf varieties should be planted 12–15 inches (30–38 cm) apart.

Frost Tolerance: Moderate.

GROWING

Sunny locations.

Backgrounds, screens, against a wall, fence or trellis. Dwarf varieties for a colourful, scented border, in mixed flower beds. Both types in large containers.

Water heavily and frequently. Sweet peas like to have cool, moist roots.

RECOMMENDED VARIETIES

Continental Mixture • 15–18 inches (38–45 cm) tall; extra-long stems for a bush variety of sweet pea; large flowers in a full colour range including pink, white, rose, red, blue, purple and salmon.

Cuthbertson Floribunda Series • up to 6 feet (180 cm) tall; extra-long flower stems make this variety excellent for cut flowers; 6 or 7 blooms per flower stem; excellent heat tolerance; 4 individual colours and a mixture.

Pick sweet peas when the buds at the tips of flower clusters are not yet open. Sweet peas last a little more than a week after cutting.

Bush varieties of sweet peas are shorter plants with the same flowers, and need no support.

TIPS

Some people soak seeds before planting to speed germination. I think soaking seed is unnecessary and can create problems. Tender sprouts will die if allowed to dry out, and uncooperative weather can create problems: too dry, and you will need to water daily to keep sprouts alive; too wet, and you will be unable to get into the garden to plant the already sprouted seed. Instead of soaking seed, I simply plant into warm, moist soil and use a garden inoculant.

Inoculants are naturally-occurring materials that contain soil bacteria. They help sweet pea plants use nitrogen (a nutrient that is essential to plant growth), resulting in bigger plants with more flowers that grow more quickly. Simply mix this dry, sooty powder with your seed before planting. Use a thick coating, buy fresh inoculant each year and avoid exposing it to heat and sunlight. Excess inoculant can be worked into the soil or used for your bean and pea crops. If you plant in the same spot each year, using an inoculant is unnecessary.

Fertilizing regularly results in the best flowers. Sweet peas are what we call heavy feeders, which means that they need extra nutrients to support the production of a large amount of blooms. If you discontinue fertilizing, the size and number of flowers will decrease.

Sweet peas climb by curling tendrils that need a support to cling to. Almost anything will do: a trellis, an arbour, chicken wire, netting, string or a chain-link fence. We recently saw a garden where seeds had just been tossed in a shrub bed; the sweet peas climbed up the cedars.

Sweet peas are marvellous climbing over the garden gate.

You can easily create a stunning column of flowers by placing a tomato cage in the centre of a large pot, such as an oak half-barrel. Sweet peas will entwine themselves into a colourful and fragrant display. A similar effect can be achieved in the garden, using a tube of chicken wire as the support. The plants will completely cover the wire.

Sweet peas are useful as screens to hide unattractive areas. My husband Ted has used these flowers for this purpose in various locations over the years: beside the culvert, along a chain-link fence, and against a shed. He also planted them in a flowerbed next to a raised back porch to hide the space underneath, and, in that location, we had the bonus of enjoying the perfume of the sweet peas both indoors and out.

The more often you cut sweet peas for bouquets, the more flowers the plants produce. Pick bouquets often, and remove any faded blooms or seedpods. Sweet peas and annual baby's breath are one of my favourite combinations in bouquets.

Edmonton, Alberta, gardener John Jordan grows prizewinning sweet peas from seed that he imports from England each year. His backyard contains an amazing display of these scented blooms, all carefully labelled, staked and pruned to produce extra-large, perfect flowers.

Tagetes

lemon yellow, golden orange, red

Tagetes tenuifolia
  (*T. signata*)
Dwarf Marigold, Rock Garden Marigold, Signet Marigold

Height: 12 inches (60 cm)

Deliciously fragrant, lacy, fern-like foliage and masses of tiny, bright flowers make tagetes a wonderful plant for sunny gardens. I like to plant tagetes as a border along pathways, or in a pot near the doorway, to enjoy the fresh, clean scent that is released whenever the foliage is brushed. This plant is a member of the marigold family.

PLANTING

Seeding: Indoors 4–6 weeks before transplanting.

Transplanting: 2 weeks after the average last spring frost. Space 6–8 inches (15–20 cm) apart.

Frost Tolerance: Poor.

GROWING

Sunny locations.

Accent plants, uniform borders, in rock gardens, in containers.

Tagetes is covered in dainty, dime-sized flowers throughout the summer until fall frost.

Tagetes grows well in poor soil.

Water when fairly dry. Tagetes does well in hot areas of the garden, but does not like to be parched.

These plants do not need deadheading.

RECOMMENDED VARIETIES

Gem Series • available individually in lemon (yellow), paprika (orange-red), tangerine (golden orange) and as a mixture.

TIPS

Tagetes grows into a small, rounded bush if provided with sufficient space. A row of these flowering balls creates a lovely border. To attain this effect, allow up to 12 inches (30 cm) between plants.

For apartment dwellers with windy but sunny balconies, tagetes are a good choice for growing in containers.

Closely spaced plants result in a continuous mass of flowers (top). Tagetes is a member of the marigold family. The pungent, lemony scent of its foliage is reputed to repel insects.

Torenia

dark and light blue, violet, burgundy, rose, white

Torenia fournieri
Wishbone Flower

Height: 6–8 inches (15–20 cm)

Gardeners looking for something different to plant in a shady area should be tempted to try torenia. These uncommon plants produce a profusion of open-faced flowers that resemble small gloxinias, in unusual 2-toned colour combinations atop neat, bushy foliage. A pot filled with torenia and set on a shaded doorstep will intrigue your visitors.

PLANTING

Seeding: Indoors 10 weeks before transplanting.

Transplanting: 3 weeks after the average last spring frost. Space 4–6 inches (10–15 cm) apart.

Frost Tolerance: Poor.

GROWING

Shady locations.

Shade gardens, low borders, rock gardens, windowboxes, planters, patio pots.

Water only when dry.

RECOMMENDED VARIETIES

Clown Series • bushy, compact plants; 5 unique and colourful combinations of flower colours.

TIPS

In an unseasonably cool spring, delay planting until shady areas have had a chance to warm.

Torenia will withstand partial sun only if the location does not get too hot. A location that receives early morning sun is fine. If the area is too hot, sunny or windy, the leaves become sunburnt and turn brown.

Torenia can be brought indoors in the fall as a houseplant in a sunny location.

Torenia is an unusual plant, with charming, velvety flowers.

Torenia is a real gem for shaded locations, where few other flowers will grow.

Verbena

purple, purple-blue, scarlet, rose, carmine, pink, coral, peach, cream, white

Verbena hortensis
   (syn. *V. hybrida*)
Common Garden Verbena

Verbena peruviana
Peruvian Verbena,
Trailing Verbena

Height: 8–15 inches
   (20–38 cm).
   Trailing types reach
   a length of up to
   20 inches (50 cm).

Verbena is a good plant for hot, dry areas of the garden. Its tiny flowers bloom in eye-catching clusters and provide a splendid carpet of colour in mass plantings. Trailing verbena can be used in place of an ivy for a beautiful display in patio containers and hanging baskets. Verbena flowers early in the season and continues throughout the summer until frost.

PLANTING

Seeding: Garden verbena from seed indoors 8–10 weeks before transplanting. Trailing verbena is propagated from cuttings.

Transplanting: 2 weeks after the average last spring frost. Space garden verbena 8–10 inches (20–25 cm) apart. Use 3 plants of trailing verbena per 10-inch (25 cm) hanging basket, or space 12 inches (30 cm) apart in the garden.

Frost Tolerance: Moderate.

GROWING

Sunny and hot locations.

Edging, borders, flower beds, annual groundcover, rock gardens, mass plantings, containers, hanging baskets. Trailing types best in containers, hanging baskets, as an annual groundcover.

Water only when dry.

Verbena has pretty clusters of flowers, and it is one of the best plants for hot, dry areas of the garden.

RECOMMENDED VARIETIES

Garden Verbena

Novalis Series • 10 inches (25 cm) tall; good tolerance for summer heat; plants maintain their compact, mounding growth habit even in the hottest conditions; available in deep purple-blue, rose-pink and salmon, with a distinct white eye in centre of each bloom.

Romance Series • 8–10 inches (20–25 cm) tall; excellent garden performance; flowers in solid white or red, with white eyes in carmine or violet, plus a mixture.

Peaches and Cream • 8 inches (20 cm) tall; excellent heat tolerance but poor weather tolerance; award-winning plant; unusual colour combination in sensational blend of pastel salmon and apricot.

Trailing Verbena

Usually available only under one of the names listed above. 8–15 inches (20–38 cm) tall; 2-inch (5 cm) clusters of flowers in pink, purple, red or white.

TIPS

Mix both types of verbena in hanging baskets for a beautiful display from basket edge to the tips of the vines.

Garden verbena can be cut for bouquets. The flowers generally last about a week after cutting.

Romance Carmine with a white eye (top). Peaches and Cream (middle) provides pastel shades. Romance Mix (bottom) is a formula blend of colours.

Viola

purple, lavender-blue, yellow, cream

Viola tricolour
Johnny Jump Up

Height: 4–7 inches (10–18 cm)

Viola's charming little flowers look like miniature pansies. These plants produce an abundance of flowers bloom early in the season and continue throughout the summer and well into fall. A pot spilling over with violas will brighten a doorstep or balcony well before many other flowers can be planted out, and long after the others finish blooming. One gardener we know grew violas in a terra-cotta pot in a sheltered spot outside her front door, where these plants continued blooming into early November.

PLANTING

Seeding: Indoors 10–12 weeks before transplanting.

Transplanting: 3–4 weeks before the average last spring frost. Space 4–6 inches (10–15 cm) apart.

Frost Tolerance: Excellent.

Violas have very pretty flowers, and an extremely high tolerance to frost. These plants withstand temperatures of 15–20° F (-8 to -10°C) without any problem at all.

GROWING

Sun to partial shade.

Low borders, rock gardens, in mixed flower beds, in windowboxes, patio pots, planters and in hanging baskets.

Water frequently. If violas dry out, they quickly go to seed. Don't plant violas in hot locations.

Cut tall plants back to keep them neat and promote bushiness.

Recommended Varieties

Helen Mount • the classic Johnny Jump Up; 7 inches (18 cm) tall; flowers are tricoloured: violet, lavender and yellow.

Yellow Charm • 7 inches (18 cm) tall; masses of 1-inch (3 cm) pure golden-yellow flowers.

Princess Series • 4–6 inches (10–15 cm) tall; better heat tolerance than most other violas; 3 individual colours, each marked with distinct black whiskers: blue; cream and yellow; and dark blue with a white face and yellow eye.

Tips

Violas make excellent miniature cut flowers. Cut for bouquets when the flowers are starting to open. Violas generally last 5–7 days after cutting.

Violas are almost guaranteed to self-seed, with the result that you often discover new plants appearing in the garden the following spring. When blue or yellow-flowered violas are grown as well as the tricoloured Helen Mount, many varied natural crosses result from self-sown seed.

Violas are a good choice for children's gardens. The tiny faces of the flowers appeal to young gardeners, and the plants are easy to grow. Flowers left on the plant quickly develop into seedpods, which open to expose the tiny seeds they contain. This transformation is fascinating to children, who are equally excited to discover new plants growing from self-sown seed the following spring.

Helen Mount's flowers (top) have the classic viola face. These flowers make charming mini-bouquets (centre). Remove finished flowers (above) to extend blooming.

Viscaria

pink, rose, lavender

Viscaria oculata
  (syn. Silene coeli-rosa,
  Lychnis coeli-rosa)
Silene, Catchfly, Campion

Height: 6–16 inches
        (15–40 cm)

Viscaria is another plant with a confusing assort-ment of names that sometimes make it difficult to find in seed catalogues. It is, however, easy to grow and bears delicate, airy sprays of flowers on long, slender stems. Viscaria is too thin as a single plant, but it produces a splendid display when planted in groups.

PLANTING

Seeding: Indoors 3–4 weeks before trans-planting. Outdoors about the date of the last average spring frost.

Transplanting: 2 weeks after the average last spring frost. Space 8–10 inches (20–25 cm) apart.

Frost Tolerance: Moderate.

GROWING

Sun to partial shade.

Rock gardens, against walls, borders, cottage gardens, meadow gardens, in planters and pots.

Water only when dry.

Viscaria is easy to grow, and produces a mass of pretty flowers throughout the summer.

A fountain provides a whimsical setting for viscaria's delicate flowers.

RECOMMENDED VARIETIES

Usually available as a 'Hybrida Mix' or under one of the names listed above.

TIPS

Do not over-fertilize viscaria. It is an exception to most plants in that an abundance of nutrients will diminish rather than increase the floral display. A general rule for this plant is to fertilize it every other time that you fertilize other annuals.

Viscaria produces its best show when planted in groups.

Wee Willie

scarlet, crimson, salmon, pink, white

Dianthus barbatus
Annual Sweet William

Height: 3–4 inches (8–10 cm)

Wee Willie is one of the plants that we have grown since our early days in the greenhouse business. We often mix it with other flowers in containers for bright splashes of colour. Many gardeners tell me that they like wee Willie because it is like a miniature version of the perennial sweet William, but as an annual, wee Willie has the added benefit of blooming nonstop throughout the summer.

PLANTING

Seeding: Indoors 8–10 weeks before transplanting.

Transplanting: As soon as the ground is workable in the spring. Space 4–6 inches (10–15 cm) apart.

Frost Tolerance: Excellent.

GROWING

Sunny locations.

Dwarf borders, in rock gardens, as accent plants for planters and hanging baskets.

Keep well-watered; these plants do not like to dry out.

Wee Willie is relatively untroubled by plant diseases and insect pests.

Wee Willie is an old-fashioned favourite that blooms in clusters the size of a fist, from late May throughout the summer until fall frost.

RECOMMENDED VARIETIES

Usually available only under one of the names listed above.

TIPS

Plant wee Willie in a pot or windowbox in the early spring to brighten the doorstep or apartment balcony. It looks pretty on its own or mixed with bright pansies, which are even more tolerant of frost.

Wee Willie's charming flowers (above) have an interesting mix of colours and markings. These plants are good companions for pansies (above, left) since both annuals are highly tolerant of frost.

Xeranthemum

rose, pink, lilac, white

Xeranthemum annuum
Immortelle, Paper Daisy,
Paperflower

Height: 36 inches (90 cm)

The star-shaped flowers of xeranthemum are everlasting, which means they remain in a near-perfect stage indefinitely after drying. The plants are as easy to grow as their name is difficult to recall. ('Xeranthemum' rhymes with 'chrysanthemum,' with the 'x' pronounced as a 'z.') Xeranthemum waits until midsummer before blooming, but then it produces loads of flowers, enough for both fresh bouquets and drying.

Xeranthemum has wiry-stemmed, crisp-petalled flowers that resemble tiny stars, and it is the oldest known everlasting flower.

PLANTING

Seeding: Indoors 8–10 weeks before transplanting.

Transplanting: 2 weeks after the average last spring frost. Space 8–12 inches (20–30 cm) apart.

Frost Tolerance: Poor.

GROWING

Sunny locations.

In mass plantings, cutting gardens, meadow gardens, backgrounds.

Recommended Varieties

Usually available only under one of the names listed above.

Tips

Xeranthemum makes a splendid addition to fresh bouquets. Mix these flowers with white or pink blooms, such as cosmos, lavatera, asters or snapdragons and use baby's breath or Queen Anne's lace as a filler.

An entirely different effect can be created when xeranthemum is contrasted with bright-yellow calendula, with asparagus fern tucked in to soften the effect.

To dry xeranthemum's flowers, simply tie about 5 stems in a bunch and hang them upside down. For best results, stagger the flowerheads up the length of the bunch. Cut the plants when the flowers are fully open. The best time for harvest is mid-morning, after the dew has dried from the plants.

Pick xeranthemum for bouquets when the flowers are mostly open (above). The flowers last 7–10 days after cutting.

'Xeranthemum' is one of those words that does not easily come to mind. We tell new staff in the greenhouse that when customers ask for 'the little star-shaped flower that is everlasting,' this is usually the plant that they mean (below).

Zinnia

scarlet, red, rose, pink, coral, orange, gold, yellow, ivory

Zinnia elegans
Common Zinnia

Height: 8–36 inches
(20–90 cm)

The array of colours in zinnia's tidy flowers provide a splendid burst of colour that continues nonstop throughout the season. I love to see a huge mass of these plants in the garden. Zinnia plants grow sturdy and bushy, in a great range of heights. The flowers can be dahlia-like, with round, full blooms, or cactus-like, with spiky-petalled, solid flowerheads, and they vary from small to huge. Zinnias begin to flower early in June and continue until frost.

254

PLANTING

Seeding: Indoors 4–6 weeks before transplanting. Outdoors from a few days after the average last spring frost until the first week in June.

Transplanting: 2 to 3 weeks after the average last spring frost. Space 10–12 inches (25–30 cm) apart.

Frost Tolerance: Poor.

Zinnia's brilliant blooms are as wonderful in bouquets as they are in the garden.

GROWING

Full sun.

Borders, backgrounds, cutting gardens, in windowboxes, planters and patio pots.

Water zinnias in the morning, from the base of the plants. Avoid wetting the foliage to help prevent disease.

RECOMMENDED VARIETIES

State Fair Mixture • 30–36 inches (75–90 cm) tall; the best giant-flowered zinnia; huge 6-inch (15 cm), dahlia-type blooms; colours include scarlet, cerise, pink, cream, orange, gold and yellow.

Dreamland Series • 12 inches (30 cm) tall; 4-inch (10 cm) dahlia-type flowers; very showy; available individually in coral, ivory, pink, rose, scarlet and yellow.

Short Stuff Mixture • 8 inches (20 cm) tall; extra-large, dahlia-type blooms; outstanding garden performance; a bright mix of colours including pink, red, yellow, cream and orange.

For spectacular colour, plant a mass of Dreamland zinnias.

TIPS

Pinch out the first flower shoot that forms to encourage plants to bush out more quickly and produce a larger flush of flowers.

I often ask Ted, my husband, to include a long row or two of zinnias when he sows our vegetable garden, so that I can cut the flowers by the armload for fresh bouquets throughout the summer, without disturbing the show in the flower garden.

Never crowd zinnias. These plants are susceptible to powdery mildew, which is warded off by good air circulation.

In my opinion, zinnias are—in a vase on their own—one of the prettiest cut flowers. Cut the flowers when they have fully opened but their centres are still tight. Remove foliage. Zinnias last 7–10 days after cutting.

State Fair zinnias thrive in a sunny garden with asters and marigolds.

I have often sown zinnia seed directly into a container with splendid results.

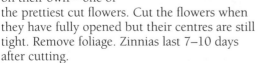

APPENDIX 'A'
PLANT LISTING BY COLOUR OF BLOOM.

 WHITE

Ageratum
Alyssum
Aster
Baby's Breath
Bachelor's Button
Balsam
Begonia
Black-Eyed Susan
   Vine
Carnation
Clarkia
Cleome
Coleus
Cosmos
Dahlia
Daisy
Datura
Dianthus

Flowering Cabbage
   and Kale
Four O'Clock
Fuchsia
Gazania
Geranium
Godetia
Helipterum
Hollyhock
Impatiens
Lavatera
Lobelia
Meadow Foam
Moon Vine
Morning Glory
Nicotiana
Nierembergia
Nigella

Pansy
Petunia
Phlox
Poppy
Portulaca
Queen Anne's Lace
Salvia
Scabiosa
Schizanthus
Snapdragon
Statice
Stock
Strawflower
Sweet Pea
Verbena
Viola
Wee Willie
Xeranthemum
Zinnia

White snapdragons make a beautiful sight in any room of the house.

🌿 PINK

Alyssum
Aster
Bachelor's Button
Balsam
Begonia
Brachycome
Candytuft
Carnation
Celosia
Clarkia
Cleome
Cosmos
Dahlia
Dianthus
Flowering Cabbage
and Kale
Four O'Clock
Fuchsia
Gazania
Geranium
Godetia

Gomphrena
Helipterum
Hollyhock
Ice Plant
Impatiens
Larkspur
Lavatera
Nasturtium
Nemesia
Nicotiana
Nigella
Pansy
Petunia
Phlox
Poppy
Portulaca
Salpiglossis
Salvia
Scabiosa
Schizanthus
Snapdragon

A handmade cart overflows with lobelia, fibrous begonias and impatiens.

Statice
Stock
Strawflower
Sweet Pea
Torenia
Verbena
Viscaria
Wee Willie
Xeranthemum
Zinnia

🌿 PURPLE

Ageratum
Alyssum
Aster
Bachelor's Button
Brachycome
Browallia
Candytuft
Clarkia
Cleome
Cobaea
Datura
Dianthus
Evening Scented Stock
Four O'Clock
Fuchsia

Geranium
Gomphrena
Heliotrope
Ice Plant
Impatiens
Larkspur
Lobelia
Malva
Morning Glory
Nemesia
Nicotiana
Nierembergia
Nigella
Pansy
Petunia

Portulaca
Salpiglossis
Salvia
Scabiosa
Schizanthus
Snapdragon
Statice
Stock
Strawflower
Sweet Pea
Torenia
Verbena
Viola
Viscaria
Xeranthemum

🌿 RED

Amaranthus
Aster
Bachelor's Button
Begonia
Carnation
Celosia
Clarkia
Cleome
Coleus
Cosmos
Dahlia
Dianthus
Flowering Cabbage and Kale
Four O'Clock
Fuchsia
Geranium

Godetia
Gomphrena
Helipterum
Hollyhock
Ice Plant
Impatiens
Lantana
Larkspur
Lobelia
Marigold
Morning Glory
Nasturtium
Nemesia
Nicotiana
Pansy
Petunia

Phlox
Poppy
Portulaca
Salpiglossis
Salvia
Scabiosa
Schizanthus
Snapdragon
Stock
Strawflower
Sunflower
Sweet Pea
Tagetes
Verbena
Wee Willie
Zinnia

🌿 ORANGE

African Daisy
Balsam
Begonia
Black-Eyed Susan Vine
Calendula
Carnation
Celosia
Coleus
Cosmos
Dahlia
Four O' Clock
Fuchsia
Gazania
Geranium

Impatiens
Lantana
Marigold
Nasturtium
Nemesia
Pansy
Poppy
Portulaca
Salpiglossis
Snapdragon
Statice
Strawflower
Tagetes
Zinnia

Nasturtium supplies a brilliance of colour in shades of reds and oranges.

YELLOW

African Daisy
Bachelor's Button
Begonia
Black-Eyed Susan
Vine
Calendula
Canary Bird Vine
Carnation
Celosia
Coleus
Cosmos
Dahlberg Daisy
Dahlia

Daisy
Datura
Four O' Clock
Gazania
Hollyhock
Ice Plant
Lantana
Marigold
Meadow Foam
Nasturtium
Nemesia
Pansy
Petunia

Poppy
Portulaca
Salpiglossis
Schizanthus
Snapdragon
Statice
Stock
Strawflower
Sunflower
Tagetes
Viola
Zinnia

GREEN

Asparagus Fern
Bells of Ireland
Castor Bean
Citrosa
Coleus

Dracaena
Flowering Cabbage
and Kale
Ivy
Kochia

Lotus Vine
Nicotiana (lime-green
flowers)
Spider Plant
Zinnia (lime-green
flowers)

BLUE

Ageratum
Aster
Bachelor's Button
Brachycome
Larkspur
Lobelia
Morning Glory

Nemophila
Nigella
Nolana
Pansy
Petunia
Phlox
Salvia

Scabiosa
Scaevola
Statice
Sweet Pea
Torenia
Viola

SILVER

Dusty Miller
Ivy (nepeta and
lamiastrum have
silvery markings)
Lotus Vine (silvery-
green)

BLACK

Nemophila (black and
white)
Pansy (as close to pure
black as you can
get in a solid flower
colour)

Scabiosa (burgundy-
black)
Strawflower (purplish-
black)

The most impressive hanging baskets, in my opinion, contain a mixture of plants that perform all season long. The flowers provide lots of colour without fading, and the plants cascade over the sides of the basket without becoming 'leggy.' Almost any plant can be successfully grown in a hanging basket, and experimenting with different combinations is fun and can result in a creation that you absolutely love.

THE BEST ANNUALS FOR HANGING BASKETS

Alyssum	Lobelia
Begonia	Lotus Vine
Brachycome	Mimulus
Browallia	Nasturtium
Coleus	Petunia
Dahlberg Daisy	Portulaca
Fuchsia	Scaevola
Geranium (ivy types are best)	Verbena
	Viola
Impatiens	Wee Willie
Ivy	

I first became enamoured of fragrant flowers the summer that we planted evening scented stocks outside the back porch. On warm evenings, their heavenly scent would drift into the house through open windows and fill every room with sweet perfume.

THE BEST ANNUALS FOR FRAGRANCE

The following flowers have the strongest fragrance.

Alyssum (especially white flowers)	Stock
	Sweet Pea
Carnation (certain varieties only)	
Evening Scented Stock	
Heliotrope	
Nicotiana (especially white flowers)	
Pansy (only the yellow and white blooms are scented)	
Petunia (dark purple flowers only)	

Both fragrance and beauty are provided by this window box display of heliotrope, petunias and pansies.

THE BEST ANNUALS FOR DRIED FLOWERS

Drying flowers is not something that I often do. Instead I rely on a staff member who has been with us since she was a young girl. Janelle Grice is an artist with flowers; she now runs our floral department. These are her recommendations on the best flowers for air-drying.

All of them retain their colours beautifully; individually, they provide the variety of shapes, sizes and textures needed to make wonderful mixed arrangements. To dry these flowers, simply hang small bunches upside down for about a week. Janelle says she gets the best results by staggering the flowerheads up the length of each bunch. The best time to pick flowers for drying is mid-morning, after the dew has dried from their petals.

Strawflowers are excellent in dry bouquets year 'round (above). Celosia makes an unusual addition to your decore all year (below).

Bells of Ireland (for striking accents)

Carnation

Celosia

Gomphrena

Helipterum

Larkspur

Nigella (both the flowers and the pretty seed pods)

Queen Anne's Lace (a favourite as a filler)

Salvia (*S. farinacea* and *S. horminum*)

Scabiosa (the seed pods of *S. stellata*—Paper Moon)

Statice

Stock

Strawflower

Sunflower

Xeranthemum

For years Ted has used flowering annual vines in various locations around our property to transform somewhat unsightly areas into glorious displays of colour. We've had sweet peas beside the culvert, outside the back door, along a chain link fence and against a shed. This year we tried something new: hanging baskets of morning glories and black-eyed susan vines from branches of trees near the back deck. The effect of the flowers against the green leaves of the trees was splendid. We recommend these flowering annual vines:

FLOWERING ANNUAL VINES

Black-Eyed Susan
  Vine

Canary Bird Vine

Cobaea

Moon Vine

Morning Glory

Sweet Pea

Gardeners often ask for the largest annuals, to act as centrepieces in flowerbeds, to provide a screen for privacy or to hide unattractive areas. The final height of plants varies according to the season, the location, amount of water and fertilizer, and if growing in a container, the size of the pot.

GIANTS OF THE ANNUAL GARDEN

These plants grow the tallest, to a height of 4 feet (120 cm) or more in a single season. Vines which require support have not been included.

Amaranthus

Castor Bean

Cleome

Datura

Hollyhock

Larkspur

Malva

Nicotiana (*N. langsdorffii* and
  N. sylvestris)

Sunflower

Nicotiana langsdorfii (*shown here with my son Bill, who is 6' 5"*) *bloom from mid-June to frost.*

The Earliest Annuals to Plant Out

Some annuals are highly tolerant of frosts. Every year at the beginning of April we move the pansies from the greenhouses to outdoors. Sometimes, the temperatures drop drastically, and the entire family has to get outside in the dark to cover the flats of plants with burlap to protect against the frost. Most often with these plants, unless it's an especially hard frost, this is not necessary.

These are the plants that I recommend for someone who wants the yard to look nice for a May wedding or anniversary party in early June, or just an earlier start to the garden.

Seed	*Transplant*
Baby's Breath	Carnation
Bachelor's Button	Dianthus
Cosmos	Dracaena
Poppy	Dusty Miller
Sunflower	Flowering Cabbage
Sweet Pea	and Kale
	Pansy
	Snapdragon
	Viola
	Wee Willie

Sweet peas are easy to grow from seed and provide endless bouquets throughout the summer. The more often you cut the flowers, the more blooms are produced.

bract: a modified leaf at the base of the flower-head, which appears to be part of the flower (e.g. strawflower)

calyx: a whorl of leaves forming the outer case of a bud or enveloping the flower (e.g. bells of Ireland)

corolla: a ring whorl of petals, separated or combined, forming the inner envelope of the flower (e.g. fuchsia)

corona: appendage on top of seed or inner side of corolla (e.g. fuchsia)

cultivar: a cultivated variety that has been named (e.g. Madness petunias)

everlasting: a flower with papery petals that keep their shape and colour when air-dried for winter decoration (e.g. statice)

eye: a circle of colour in the centre of the flower petals, of a different hue than the rest of the petals (e.g. verbena)

face: a distinct marking of contrasting colour on the petals of a flower (e.g. pansy)

floret: a small, individual flower that makes up a compound flower or dense flowerhead (e.g. geranium)

harden off: to gradually acclimatize plants from indoor to outdoor temperatures, in order to increase their resistance to low temperatures and drought

hybrid: the offspring of two plants of different genetic make-up

picotee: a flower of a light colour with a darker edging to its petals (e.g. Pin-up begonia)

variegated: patterned with two distinct colours or shades of colour; mostly used to describe foliage (e.g. vinca ivy)

Select
Glossary

265

Select Index

moonflower
see moon vine

morning glory 174–175

mosquito repellent plant
see citrosa

moss rose
see portulaca

mourning bride
see scabiosa

musk mallow
see malva

❦ N–O ❦

nasturtium 176–177

nemesia 178–179

nemophila 180–181

nepeta
see ivy

New Guinea impatiens
see impatiens

nicotiana 182–183

nierembergia 184–185

nigella 39, 186–187

night scented stock
see evening scented
stock

nolana 18, 188–189

ornamental cabbage
see flowering cabbage
and kale

ornamental kale
see flowering cabbage
and kale

❦ P ❦

painted tongue
see salpiglossis

pansy 34, 39, 43,
190–193

Papaver commutatum
see poppy

Papaver rhoeas
see poppy

paper daisy
see xeranthemum

paper moon
see scabiosa

paperflower
see xeranthemum

parrot's beak
see lotus vine

patience plant
see impatiens

Pelargonium citrosum
see citrosa

Pelargonium peltatum
see geranium

*Pelargonium x
domesticum*
see geranium

Pelargonium x hortorum
see geranium

pennie black
see nemophila

petunia 13, 43, 194–197

phlox 198–199

pincushion flower
see scabiosa

pink pokers
see statice

pink tassels
see celosia

poached eggs
see meadow foam

poor man's orchid
see schizanthus

poppy 39, 200–201

portulaca 37, 202–203

pot marigold
see calendula

Prince of Wales feather
see celosia

purple climber
see cobaea

Purslane oleracea
see portulaca

❦ Q–R ❦

Queen Anne's
lace 204–205

ragged sailor
see bachelor's button

red summer cypress
see kochia

rhodanthe
see helipterum

Ricinus communis
see castor bean

rock garden marigold
see tagetes

rocky mountain garland
see clarkia

rose impatiens
see balsam

rosebud impatiens
see impatiens

rose mallow
see lavatera

rose moss
see portulaca

❦ S ❦

sage
see salvia

salpiglossis 206–207

salvia 208–211

Salvia spp.
see salvia

satin flower
see godetia

scabiosa 212–213

scaevola 214–215

scarlet sage
see salvia

schizanthus 216–217

sea fig
see ice plant

269

Lois Hole and her husband Ted started selling vegetables out of their red barn over 30 years ago; today Hole's Greenhouse & Gardens Ltd. is one of the largest greenhouse and garden centres in Alberta. It remains a family business, owned and operated by Lois, Ted, their sons Bill and Jim, and Bill's wife Valerie.

Lois was born and raised in rural Saskatchewan, and she later moved to Edmonton, Alberta. She attained a degree in Music from the Toronto Conservatory of Music. Neither she nor Ted had lived on a farm before starting Hole's, but soon they were growing grain and raising livestock. They planted their first vegetable garden out of necessity.

Lois is often asked to talk with groups and share her knowledge. She is known for her enthusiastic involvement in all that she does, and is a familiar face in the greenhouses to many customers who seek out her friendly advice and gardening tips.

Lois and Ted continue to live and work on the same site they started out on, by the river in St. Albert, Alberta.

Dig in with more books from Lone Pine Publishing

Lois Hole's
Northern Vegetable Gardening
By Lois Hole
With growing tips, variety recommendations, recipes and nutritional hints, Lois Hole describes how to grow, harvest and use more than 30 vegetables and 117 varieties in a temperate climate. Suggestions about composting, fertilizing, pest control and small-space gardening make this colourful and inspirational guide a horn of plenty.
5.5" x 8.5" 160 pages 44 colour photographs
51 B & W illustrations 33 colour illustrations
Softcover $14.95 CDN $11.95 US
ISBN 1-55105-029-3 **A Bestseller**

Annuals for the Prairies
By Edgar W. Toop
An invaluable photographic reference to hardy annuals. More than 150 annuals suitable for the prairies or Great Plains are featured with colour, size, culture, use and maintenance tips. Beautifully illustrated with more than 300 colour photographs.
8.5" x 11" 224 pages
more than 300 colour photographs
Softcover $29.95 CDN $24.95 US
ISBN 1-55105-034-X
Published in association with the University of Alberta Faculty of Extension and the University of Saskatchewan Extension Division

Perennials for the Prairies
By Edgar W. Toop and Sara Williams
This is the ultimate book on growing, maintaining and enjoying over 200 perennials suitable for a prairie climate. With advice on planting and transplanting perennials and rejuvenating old beds, and with extensive descriptions of cultivars and their uses.
8.5" x 11" 190 pages
more than 300 colour photographs
100 illustrations
Softcover $29.95 CDN $24.95 US
ISBN 1-55091-005-1
A University of Alberta Faculty of Extension and University of Saskatchewan Extension Division Publication

Rose Gardening on the Prairies
By George W. Shewchuk
Develop a productive, gorgeous rose garden with the help of this book, brimming with detailed information on starting, maintaining and improving rose gardens in a prairie climate. Topics include planning, selection, planting, mulching, over-wintering, display and more.
8.5" x 11" 80 pages 50 colour photographs
numerous illustrations
Softcover $18.95 CDN $15.95 US
ISBN 0-88864-140-0
A University of Alberta Faculty of Extension Publication

Gardening in Toronto
By Pat Tucker
If you want to improve your flowerbeds or increase your vegetable harvest, this guide is for you. It will guide you through the planting season with special sections on gardening in small spaces, lawns, trees and shrubs.
5.5" x 8.5" 160 pages 60 colour photographs
Softcover $12.95 CDN ISBN 0-919433-68-5

Gardening in Vancouver
By Judy Newton
Create lush and healthy gardens with the aid of this guide full of "perennial" advice. Climate, small spaces, fruit growing, woody ornamentals, pests, lawns, soil improvements and vegetables—its all here.
5.5" x 8.5" 176 pages 61 colour photographs
45 illustrations
Softcover $14.95 ISBN 0-919433-74-X

Look for these and other Lone Pine books in your local bookstore or contact Lone Pine Publishing for a complete catalogue of nature, recreation and outdoor titles.

Edmonton
206 10426 81 Avenue
Edmonton AB T6E 1X5
Ph (403) 433-9333
Fax (403) 433-9646

Vancouver
202A 1110 Seymour Street
Vancouver BC V6B 3N3 Ph
(604) 687-5555
Fax (604) 687-5575

Washington State
16149 Redmond Way, #180
Redmond WA 98052
Ph (206) 343-8397

or call toll-free today! 1-800-661-9017

VINEGAR

Over 400 Various, Versatile & Very Good Uses You've Probably Never Thought of

by

Vicki Lansky

illustrations by Martha Campbell

€€€€€€€

distributed by Publishers Group West, Berkeley, CA

BOOK PEDDLERS

Editorial thanks to Kathryn Ring, Dana Lansky and Abby Rabinovitz
Cover designer: Laurie Ingram-Duren
Illustrated by Martha Campbell

ISBN 0-916773-53-1

(UPC 607966 53104)

Copyright © 2004 by Vicki Lansky
First printing January 2004

Publisher's Cataloging-in-Publication
(Provided by Quality Books, Inc.)

Lansky, Vicki
    Vinegar : over 400 various, versatile & very good
uses you've probably never thought of / by Vicki Lansky:
illustrations by Martha Campbell.
    p. cm.
    Includes bibliographical references and index.
    ISBN 0-916776-53-1

    1 . Home economics. 2. Vinegar.   I. Title

TX158.L357 2004   640'.41
                         QBI03-200148

BOOK PEDDLERS
15245 Minnetonka Blvd, Minnetonka, MN 55345
952/912-0036 • fax: 952/912-0105
www.bookpeddlers.com
vlansky@bookpeddlers.com

PRINTED IN THE USA

05 06 07 08 09 9 8 7 6 5

Dear Reader,

I became interested in great ways to use vinegar because of what I learned when writing about and talking about—for the last 5 years—my book, *BAKING SODA Over 500 Fabulous, Fun and Frugal Uses You Probably Never Thought of.* And I learned a lot.

It would be fair to say that I now use a LOT of baking soda and a LOT of vinegar around my house. I love their economy and I love their multipurpose qualities.

This is far from a complete discussion of *everything* there is to know about vinegar. If you want to know more there are additional books that can give you: a more detailed history, more recipes, more about various vinegars and more in-depth technical details.

I love vinegar for what it can do for me on a daily basis and that is what I have shared with you here.

Vicki Lansky

€€€€€€€

...a word to the wise

I can't tell you how every idea here works. Nor have they all been used by me. But each has worked for someone, which is how I learned of it, and it just might be useful to you. Conditions and situations are unique to each of us. Keep in mind that home remedies can not take the place of competent medical advice. I can not guarantee each and every tip. Use common sense and use this book to increase your repertoire of great uses for vinegar and—I believe—you'll enhance your home, health and happiness.

Table of Contents

VINEGAR

A BIT OF BACKGROUND

€€€€€€€

Vinegar has been used in many different ways by many different peoples for thousands of years. In ancient Rome, bowls of vinegars made from wine, dates, figs and other fruits were used for the dunking of breads. Rice vinegar has a long history in China, going back 3000 years. Japanese samurai believed a rice vinegar drink would boost their strength. Vinegar is mentioned in early Middle Eastern writings for medicinal uses ranging from a clotting agent to a digestive aid to an expectorant. It was used in dressing wounds and was valued as both a medicine as well as a condiment.

Cleopatra demonstrated its solvent property by dissolving precious pearls in vinegar to win a wager that she could consume a fortune in a single meal. Vinegar is mentioned as often in the Bible as is wine. In the New Testament, it is said

that a sponge soaked in vinegar was held to the lips of Jesus to ease his thirst while on the Cross.

Doctors tending those who were contagious during the Black Plague rubbed vinegar, infused with essential oils and herbs, over their own bodies. They also used it inside their hooded cloaks as an inhalant for their own protection. A variation of this practice was common in the eighteenth century when vinegar-dipped sponges were held to the nose to offset odors of raw sewage and the lack of indoor plumbing.

George Washington in his final illness was given a gargle concoction of vinegar and sage. During the American Civil War vinegar was used on wounds as a healing agent. Soldiers also drank it in an attempt to ward off scurvy—a vitamin C deficiency. *(I'm assuming it was cider vinegar.)*

Vinegar has been a mainstay of many folk recipes that have been handed down for generations. Today modern industry uses vinegar in dozens of ways—from reducing microorganisms in slaughter houses and poultry plants to cleaning equipment in the construction industry.

Vinegar *(which literally means 'sour wine')* results when wine or another alcoholic liquid is allowed to ferment a second time, turning it acetic. If you let wine be exposed to the bacteria in the air, it will ferment and eventually turn into vinegar.

The word vinegar comes from the French word "vinaigre" ("vin" *for wine and* "aigre" *for sour)*. It is actually

bacteria spores that convert a fermented liquid into vinegar. It then becomes a weak form of acetic acid. It is formed through this second fermentation of sugars or starches. Vinegar can come from the juice of sweet fruits and grains such as barley (malt beer), apple (cider) and grape (wine), yet it can also be made from roots or wood (often the base of white distilled vinegar). Filipinos use coconuts as their vinegar base; Mexicans use the cactus fruit that is the base for tequila.

One hundred grams of basic distilled white vinegar has 16 calories. It contains small amounts of protein and starch. It has no vitamins but does contain trace amounts of various minerals. Vinegars made from other bases will contain some of the nutrients of the plant or fruit from which it was derived.

VINEGAR IN THE KITCHEN

Vinegar has been a kitchen staple for many generations. It is a trusted health remedy, a neutralizer, a cleaner, a condiment and a preservative. Its acetic quality enables it to kill bacteria, mold and germs while being safe enough not to harm the body or the environment. According to the Heinz Company *(maker of one of the most popular consumer brand name vinegars)*, numerous studies show that their straight 5 percent acetic solution of distilled white vinegar, found in supermarkets, kills 99 percent of bacteria, 82 percent of mold and 80 percent of germs. Sometimes you may see the acid measured in grains. 50 grains is the same as a 5 percent acid level, and is the most common percentage. Since distilled white vinegar is not registered as a pesticide the label cannot

claim it as a disinfectant. Vinegar is available in higher acetic concentrations, but this is not easy to find in consumer outlets as it can be more hazardous and needs to be handled with appropriate precautions.

A FOOD FAVORITE

Vinegar is safe and edible, and it cannot harm your stomach when ingested in small amounts. When it comes to food enhancements and vinaigrettes, multiple types and flavors of vinegars are available. The world of culinary vinegars is a large one. Many types of vinegar are flavored by the addition of herbs or fruits; raspberry vinegar is one of the most popular. For the diet conscious, vinegar is fat free and low in sodium.

Use simple white distilled vinegar when a sharp acidity is needed without any other characteristics. The distilling process destroys its nutrients, making it a purer and more tart acetic acid as well as clear in color. Many vinegars in stores today also have preservatives added.

Vinegars made from other bases have different flavors. Common types of culinary vinegar include balsamic *(often used for oil and vinegar salad dressings)*, red wine, white wine, rice wine, sherry, champagne, Chinese red and, of course, cider vinegar. Malt vinegars and brown rice vinegars are most often used with "fish and chips." Distilled vinegar used in making pickles works best with at least a 5 percent or higher acidity level. Read your labels when making your choices.

Do not confuse rice wine with rice wine vinegar. Read the label carefully. If it says wine vinegar, then it is vinegar, not wine. Asian grocery stores usually carry three basic types of rice vinegar—white, red and black. Rice vinegars tend to be milder as rice *(the base)* has a lighter taste. Rice vinegar is a byproduct of sake or Japanese rice wine. The popular seasoned rice vinegars have a blend of sweeteners and salt added giving it a light taste. It has become a healthy alternative for many, as a salad dressing and a flavor enhancer.

Balsamic vinegar—*true* balsamic vinegar—will have the word "traditional" or "natural" on the label. It will be aged about 50 years and come from Modena Italy's Trebbiano grapes, and it will most likely be *very* expensive. The affordable supermarket types of balsamic vinegars are factory-made, even the ones you see that have Modena on the label. These are usually imported from Italy but are commercially made. They are not bad vinegars; they are just not the premiere vinegar of that town. Taste and quality vary from brand to brand, and bottle to bottle. The key is to find one that suits you and your budget.

HEALTHFUL BENEFITS

Before the advances in modern medicine, vinegar, being available to the general population, was used as a curative in many ways. It was—and still is—the basis for many home remedies. One could dispute many of the curative remedies attributed to vinegar however vinegar certainly has properties that have helped in many different situations. There are claims that vinegar can lengthen life, reduce osteoporosis,

treat dementia and arthritis, and improve hearing, vision and mental powers. While all this might be well beyond its realistic properties, there are still many ways that vinegar can be healthful both internally and externally.

Most of the health benefits linked to vinegar are associated with cider vinegar made from apple cider or a base of processed apple parts. Apple cider vinegar has the same advantages of other vinegars and differs only in that it is made from the actual juice pressed from apples. Cider vinegar is most common in America due, no doubt, to the abundance and availability of apples. Hard cider *(historically a homemade, American alcoholic drink)* gave rise to the common use of cider vinegar.

You can't make cider vinegar from most store-bought apple juices. The preservatives and pasteurization process prevent it from happening. Organic apple cider that you find in the health food store is not processed the same way, which is why you will usually find sediment at the bottom of those bottles. Check also for "use by" or "sell by" dates on labels.

Probably the most unusal use of vinegar—though I don't know if this qualifies as a health benefit—is one in which you can help choose the sex of your unborn baby, or more specifically to help you choose to conceive a baby girl. In this low tech method—which is not a guarantee but may make the odds more favorable—some doctors, including Dr. Landrum Shettles in his book, *How to Choose the Sex of Your Baby*—recommends a diluted vinegar douche 15-30 minutes before intercourse. This creates a preferred acidic environment for the X female sperm. For the Y male sperm prefer-

ring a more alkaline environment, using a douche with a solution of baking soda will favor conception of a boy. Obviously it is also important to time this extra step to the 4 to 5 day period before—and 1 day after—ovulation. *(Ovulation is generally 12 to 16 days before a woman's next period.)* Before exploring this method, it would be advisable to check Shettles's book for all the details.

AS A LIQUID CLEANER

Each vinegar, as we have noted, has some use to which it is especially suited. For cleaning purposes, it's best to use distilled 5 percent acid white vinegar. Cider or brown vinegar should be avoided for cleaning because it could cause certain surfaces (especially porous ones) to stain. No vinegar should be used on marble surfaces, in metal goblets or on unglazed pottery that might be decorated with leaded paint. It can leach into the liquid.

If you find that straight vinegar or a vinegar and water solution doesn't clean as you had hoped, it might be due to a slight residue previous commercial cleaners have left. In that case you may need to add 1/2 teaspoon of detergent to your water and vinegar solution. A cleaning solution can range from 2 parts water to 1 part vinegar or 3 or 4 parts water to 1 part vinegar, depending on the strength you wish to use.

Vinegar is a safe and inexpensive cleaner that can be used in place of many other commercial cleaning supplies. Actually a bottle of vinegar, a box of baking soda and a jug of bleach can fill most of your household cleaning needs—despite what commercials tell you.

Spray Bottles

Vinegar can work full strength or diluted with water. A splash straight from the bottle works just fine in many situations. Spray bottles are a great way to dispense vinegar full strength. Whether you reuse small bottles you've cleaned out, or purchase new ones—*check out travel bottles or spray bottles in the drug store cosmetic area*—you may wish to keep spray dispensers of full strength vinegar by each sink. In the kitchen you may prefer a larger, colored one on your counter. This is good for spraying the counters or spraying peeled potatoes that will be used in potato salad to keep them from discoloring. Use a permanent marker to clearly label "vinegar" on any bottle in which it is stored.

Consumer History

Vinegar is a large business. Supermarket sales of all types of bottled vinegar is over $220 million a year. Almost 40 percent of these sales are of white distilled vinegar, 20 percent cider vinegar and the balance goes to red wine vinegar, balsamic vinegar, rice vinegar and all the others.

Today few people make their own vinegar. We generally look to store shelves to find vinegar. There are many active vinegar makers, many of which are small companies. Most of the vinegar is made by a few large companies, H.J. Heinz being the one that comes to mind for most Americans.

The H.J. Heinz company was founded in 1869 by Henry John Heinz (1844-1919). He cultivated horseradish on a less than one-acre plot in Sharpsburg, PA. Heinz and his then-partner L.C. Noble started a company they named the Anchor Pickle and Vinegar Works. The company quickly

expanded in acreage, employees and new products. The Panic of 1873 caused the Heinz, Noble & Company to go bankrupt by 1875. Two months later Heinz and some family members began the business anew. Within the year they introduced tomato ketchup to the Heinz product line using basically the same recipe that is used today. It became the standard by which other ketchups are rated. *(Ketchup, by the way, now uses 10 percent of the vinegar market.)* By 1888 H.J. bought the controlling interest in the company and continued his expansion of factories and employees in the Pittsburgh area. When H.J. died of pneumonia at the age of 75, his company had over 6500 employees, 25 branch factories, 85 salting stations, 53 tomato receiving stations and 11 pickle receiving stations. The business had also expanded to sales in England and Europe. His son, and later his grandson, continued to run the family business from 1941 to 1966. It became a public corporation in 1946. Today it has 100 major locations world-wide and is the corporate parent to over two dozen entities.

H.J. Heinz's keen marketing sense in those early years was very important for his fledgling company. He adopted the Heinz 57 Varieties slogan. His was the first mass-produced vinegar to be made with all-natural ingredients. Pure food was at the center of Heinz's product development and promotion. He put his products in clear glass jars to show their purity when others masked their products in tinted bottles. H.J. Heinz was considered somewhat of a traitor by other food purveyors at the time for using purity as a sales differential. He was one of the leaders who pushed for the Pure Food Act, which ultimately led to the creation of the Food and Drug Administration (FDA).

Fleischmann's entered the vinegar business in the 1920's as a way to utilize the excess alcohol produced by their bakers' yeast growth. Consequently, vinegar production units were installed at a number of yeast plant locations. By the mid 1930's Fleischmann's had become a major vinegar supplier mainly in the industrial or wholesale area. By the 1950's technological advances in the production of bakers' yeast reduced the production of alcohol as a bi-product. Alcohol was then purchased instead of being produced on site and the vinegar link to yeast weakened. Today Fleischmann's is the largest vinegar producer in the world. Fleischmann's Vinegar Company, Inc. entered the specialty vinegar business in 1990 when the parent corporation purchased Waylon Foods, a cider vinegar operation. Since then they have created a complete line of specialty vinegars including wine, rice, malt, balsamic and others. They are the leading manufacturer and marketer of industrial vinegar in North America.

Nakano Foods was established in California in 1981 as the American division of Japan's Mitsukan Group which first produced rice vinegar in Japan over 200 years ago. Nakano operates in all segments of the vinegar business across the US and Canada. They are the largest supplier of private label vinegar to the supermarket industry and the Asian food service industry, and the second largest supplier of industrial vinegar. Today they are located in Mt. Prospect, IL. They offer seven different flavored, seasoned rice vinegars and two additional seasoned red wine vinegars. Nakano is the only company in the US to produce rice vinegar with real whole rice instead of rice syrup.

To Thine Own Taste be True

So how can you tell the difference, other than depending on the label or a recommendation, as to which vinegar you prefer? It's expensive to buy a dozen bottles of assorted vinegars only to find out you like some more than others. Often we are *"sold"* by the look of the bottle and its label. All balsamics are not equal, nor are all raspberry-flavored vinegars. Wine tasting parties are definitely more popular than vinegar tasting parties so it's seldom you have a chance to try different ones. If you have a chance to go to vinegar tastings or have one yourself, this is how it is done.

Vinegar can't be tasted "straight." *(I found that out the hard way.)* With your first taste the acid closes your taste buds for 10 to 15 minutes. The correct technique is to pour a small amount of room temperature vinegar in a shallow dish just prior to tasting. You then place a sugar cube in the vinegar and in a second the sugar cube drinks up the vinegar. You now suck on the sugar cube and the flavor is released without the acidic side effect. You may wish to drink or rinse your mouth with water between tastings. Another useful method is to mix some of the vinegar with a tablespoon of mayonnaise and taste it on a bland cracker or a celery stick.

Build It and They Will Come

There are, to date, three actual vinegar museums. The only one in the US is the International Vinegar Museum in South Dakota. It opened in June of 1999 and is attracting thousands of visitors. Its owner hopes to attract vinegar fans from around the world. Displays feature the different ways

vinegar is made all over the world, explanations of how to make your own and taste offerings from an exotic vinegar collection. The museum also houses a large research kitchen. The Vinegar Man and creator of the museum, Lawrence J. Diggs, has a mission to make people more aware of "the sour power" of vinegar. It is open from June until October. Information can be found at the website: www.vinegar man.com, or you can contact the museum at PO Box 41, 30 Carlton St, Roslyn, SD 57261. You can also call toll free 1-877-486-0075 for a copy of their free catalog. How Diggs ended up in a small town in South Dakota which then helps him open a vinegar museum is a unique tale in itself. Ask him about it should you get to South Dakota.

In Japan you can visit the Mitsukan Vinegar Museum in Handa-shi Aichi-en, near the JR Handa Station. It includes the history of vinegar dating from the Edo period. There is a display and information about the Japanese vinegar making process.

In 2001 China opened its own vinegar museum in Qingxu County in the northern Shanxi Province, the country's largest vinegar production area. Shanxi has over 100 vinegar factories and supplies over one fifth of the national vinegar output in China. One can find over 50 kinds of vinegar products. Chencu, or mature vinegar, has been used for more than 1000 years in China. It has a delicate fragrance and a dark caramel color. It is used by many for it's health value, similar to how apple cider vinegar is used in America.

The uses for vinegar are endless. You may find many in this book that you've probably never thought of or dreamt were possible.

CHAPTER ONE

COOKING WITH VINEGAR

€€€€€€€

    Vinegar is a common culinary ingredient for several reasons.

    First, since vinegar tenderizes meat, it is a common ingredient in meat marinades. It is always a good addition when slow cooking any tough, inexpensive cuts of meat.

    A sugar and vinegar combination (2:1) is the basis for an easy sweet-and-sour taste, which is another reason it is found in many recipes. Lemons are available year round today, which was not always the case. Vinegar was often used as a lemon taste substitute. Though vinegar does not have the Vitamin C value of lemon, its acid base performs the same taste function.

    Vinegar was and is used as a preservative, especially important before refrigeration. Our fondness for pickling recipes derives from this tradition.

Egg-citing Ideas

- Replace an egg when baking, if you are short one egg for a recipe, with—*really*—a tablespoon of white wine vinegar. This will work only if there's another rising agent present, such as baking powder, baking soda or self-rising flour.

- Add a tablespoon or two of white vinegar to water when boiling eggs to help keep them from cracking and to limit the whites from leaking, if the shells crack.

- Add a little vinegar to the water when poaching eggs. The whites stay better formed. You can use an empty tuna can *(top and bottom removed)* for a quick poached egg form.

- Make creamy scrambled eggs. As eggs thicken when scrambling, add a tablespoon of vinegar for every two eggs used and stir until eggs are done.

Meat Magic

- Consider a vinegar wash for any meat, including poultry, to kill bacteria.

- Rub vinegar on the cut end of uncooked ham to prevent mold.

- Add a couple of tablespoons of either white or cider vinegar to boiling ham to reduce the salty taste and make the meat more flavorful.

- Marinate meat in vinegar both to kill bacteria and to tenderize the meat. A quarter-cup of vinegar, added to any

other liquid ingredients called for, is enough for a two- to three-pound roast. Include favorite herbs to add flavor to the dish. Wine vinegars are good for marinating.

- Add a tablespoon of vinegar when boiling ribs or stew meat for extra tenderness.

MARINATING AND BASTING MEATS

Let less tender meats rest a few hours in a glass dish or a sturdy plastic bag in a marinade before cooking. Flank steak, for one, benefits from this process. You can also marinate meat in a zip closing bag and store it (meat and marinade) in the freezer until ready to use. Or a marinade can be used just to baste meats as they cook in the oven or on a grill.

Basic Beef Marinades
Mix 1/2 cup white or rice vinegar, 1/4 cup oil, 1/4 cup ketchup, 1 cup brown sugar and 5 tablespoons soy sauce.

Or make a quick marinade sauce using equal parts of a prepared barbecue sauce and vinegar. You may need to add more sugar to taste. (*This has more of a smoky flavor.*)

Meat Basting Sauce
Mix 1/2 cup sugar (white or brown), 1/4 cup rice vinegar, 1/4 cup ketchup, 2 tablespoons soy sauce, 2 crushed garlic cloves, 1 teaspoon fresh ginger (or 1/4 teaspoon ginger powder) and 2 tablespoons cornstarch. Cook on medium heat until it boils. Stir until it thickens a bit.

Fish

- Try adding a tablespoon of white vinegar (and an equal amount of sherry, if you wish) to any fish or seafood you're frying or poaching to make it more tasty.

- Season fish with a tablespoon of an herbal flavored vinegar such as tarragon for a different taste.

- Marinate canned fish or seafood beforehand about 20 minutes in vinegar and water to make it taste fresher.

- Rub fish with vinegar a few minutes before scaling, to make the process easier.

- Create a nice sauce for serving over hot, cooked fish by combining 2 teaspoons white wine vinegar with 1/2 cup heavy cream.

AH SO!

Japanese cuisine has always depended on vinegar—rice vinegar. Its antiseptic qualities prevent germs from growing on raw fish. It tenderizes meats and vegetables used in stir fry dishes. It also helps eliminate fishy odors from fish dishes.

Fruits...

- Improve the flavor of any fruit you're cooking by adding a little vinegar.

- Create a quick fruit dressing by adding a few tablespoons of a fruit-flavored vinegar *(strawberry, raspberry, etc.)* with either a cup of sour cream or vanilla yogurt.

- Splash a little rice or balsamic vinegar on fresh fruits such as pears, cantaloupe, honeydew or others to add a zesty new taste. Serve immediately to avoid the fruit from becoming mushy.

- Flavor a bowl of fresh strawberries *(whole or cut up)* that have been washed by sprinkling them with 2 or 3 spoonfuls of balsamic or rice vinegar. Allow to stand for 5 to 10 minutes before adding sugar or artificial sweetener to taste. Mix and serve.

...and Veggies

- Get rid of bugs in any fresh vegetables with a short soak in water with a good dash of vinegar and salt. *(Vinegar is a great replacement for expensive fruit and vegetable washes.)*

- Freshen wilted vegetables by soaking them in cold water to which you've added a spoonful or two of vinegar.

- Add a tablespoon or two of vinegar to the water when boiling or steaming cauliflower, beets or other vegetables. It will help keep their color, improve the taste and reduce gassy elements. This is also true when cooking beans and bean dishes.

- Top cooked, chilled asparagus with a vinaigrette of your choice. See page 12 for ideas.

- Store fresh bell peppers in sterilized jars, and top off with boiling vinegar. Seal tightly. Store 2 weeks before serving.

- Olives and pimentos covered with vinegar can be kept almost indefinitely if refrigerated.

- Make an excellent, non-creamy coleslaw dressing by combining:
  > 1 tablespoon vegetable oil
  > 2 tablespoons sugar
  > 1/4 cup seasoned rice vinegar
  > 1/2 teaspoon dry mustard
  > salt and pepper to taste

- Or try a Colonel's kind of coleslaw dressing by combining:
  > 1/3 cup sugar
  > 1/4 cup milk
  > 1/4 cup buttermilk
  > 1-1/2 tablespoons white vinegar
  > 2-1/2 tablespoons lemon juice
  > 1/2 cup mayonnaise
  > salt and pepper to taste

- Make a sweet marinade for cooked vegetables or for a three-bean salad *(using one or more cans of at least 3 of these: green beans, string beans, yellow beans, pinto beans or cut corn)* by combining:
  > 1 cup white or brown sugar
  > 1 cup vinegar
  > 1 cup vegetable oil
  > salt and pepper to taste

Heat in a microwave just until sugar has dissolved. Add this to a mixture of drained, canned vegetables—plus one thinly sliced onion—and refrigerate for a few hours or overnight before serving.

THE BEST GAZPACHO SOUP

This cold Spanish soup can be made many ways but this version is easy, versatile and a great way to use up—*or just take advantage of*—summer vegetables.
In a blender or food processor place:

> 1/3 cup oil
> 1/4 cup vinegar *(plain or flavored)*
> 1 garlic clove
> slice of onion
> 2 ice cubes

Liquefy. Now add:

> 1/2 *(more or less)* of a cut up cucumber
> 1/2 cut-up green pepper *(minus the seeds)*

Blend again. Now slice up as many as you have from:

> 1 to 4 tomatoes *(If you only have one tomato,*
> *add a small can or two of tomato juice or V-8.)*

Blend tomatoes only long enough to process them. *(It's best when the tomatoes are not completely blended.)*

Top soup bowls with seasoned croutons, chopped cucumbers, chives or anything you like for texture.

Carb Ideas

• Turn out great rice by adding a teaspoon of vinegar to the boiling water.

• Add just a dash of vinegar to pasta as it cooks, to make it less sticky and to cut some of its starch.

• Season cold pasta with any vinaigrette (see page 12). Make it a full meal by adding cubes of meat, ham or chicken as well as cheese and colorful cooked vegetables such as peas and shredded carrots.

• Keep peeled potatoes from discoloring for short term use (or even for days, if you wish, by storing them in the refrigerator), by covering them with cold water to which some vinegar has been added.

• Give homemade bread a shiny crust by brushing the top of a loaf with vinegar a few minutes before baking is finished. Return to the hot oven to complete.

• Make any dried bean dish less gassy by adding 1/8 to 1/4 cup vinegar to the soaking water. Rinse thoroughly after an overnight soak, then add a dash of vinegar to the cooking water.

• Make a perfect picnic potato salad with cooked, peeled and cubed potatoes with the following for a dressing:
> 1 cup mayonnaise
> 3 tablespoons vinegar
> 1 tablespoon sugar
> 1/2 teaspoon salt

Optional items to add to the potatoes: 2 chopped, hard-cook eggs, match-stick carrots, diced celery, cut-up green onion tops, and crumbled, cooked bacon.

Dairy Do's

- Keep cheese fresh longer by wrapping it in a cloth moist-ened with vinegar. For extra protection, store the cheese in a sealed container.

- Give some extra zest to your white sauce by adding 1/2 teaspoon of your favorite vinegar.

- Make a buttermilk substitute by adding a tablespoon of vinegar to a cup of fresh milk and let stand long enough to thicken—5 to 15 minutes. Speed the process up by microwaving the mixture for 30-40 seconds.

- Make a substitute, low-fat sour cream, by blending in a food processor a 12 oz. container of small curd cottage cheese with 1/4 to 1/3 cup skim milk, 2 teaspoons vin-egar, and 2 teaspoons sugar.

Condiments

- Try cider or malt vinegar instead of ketchup with french fries—that's how the British like to eat them. Either one is great on fish or any fried or broiled meat.

- Make ketchup and other condiments last longer when the bottle is almost empty by adding a little vinegar and shaking or mixing it well.

- Use up little packages or last bits of ketchup, mustard, soy sauce and other bottled sauces by mixing them with some vinegar, and adding onion, garlic and herbs of your choice to make a marinade.

- Create your own unique mustard by using 2 to 4 table-spoons mustard *(dry or from a jar)*, 2 tablespoons honey and up to 1 tablespoon of vinegar *(flavored or not)* to create a taste and texture of your choice. Experiment by adding powdered ginger, garlic and salt. Heat to blend. Add a spoonful of flour if you need to thicken the mixture.

- Experiment with different kinds of vinegars in the stores to find your favorite. Cider vinegar and distilled white vinegar are strong tasting. Rice wine vinegar, rice vinegar and many other flavored vinegars are "softer" and may be used in most any recipe where you prefer their taste. Refrigerate. *(Write down details if you wish to make it again.)*

Pickling

Pickling with vinegar is a centuries old method of pre-serving food. It is used less today for preserving food than for making pickles. Vinegar creates an environment in which bac-teria can't live because of the acid content. This is the reason you want to use glass or ceramic containers for pickling as the acid won't react with it while it can react to metal and even some plastic containers.

There are three kinds of vinegar used in putting up pick-les. Most recipes call for *white distilled* vinegar, which has a tart flavor and a distinctive aroma. It will not change the color of pale veggies or fruits. *Apple cider vinegar*, often used in pick-ling, has its own special fruity flavor and it may cause many foods to darken. (*Apple cider _flavored_ vinegar* combines the lat-

ter two and may be used as regular apple cider vinegar is.)

All three of these vinegars are 5 percent acetic acid; 4 percent acetic vinegar is weaker and should only be used for salad dressing. It will not make good pickles.

Follow pickling recipes carefully. Do not use any flavored vinegars, and don't dilute the vinegar with water unless that's specifically called for. There are entire books available about how to make pickles. Maybe there are some favorites in your family that you should be sure to write down. *(By the way, kosher pickles do not use vinegar.)* Picking the right size and type of cucumber is part of the art. Smaller pickle cukes, for instance, make crisper pickles. (If working in quantity when making pickles, you can wash a whole load of cukes in your top loading clothes washer. Just remember to line the bottom with a towel, use a cold water wash, gentle cycle, and no soap, please, though a splash of vinegar won't hurt.)

- Make a large jar of refrigerator pickles. First place in a large, wide-mouth glass jar, 1 cup of sugar and 1 cup of very hot water. Stir until the sugar dissolves. Add 1/2 cup of white vinegar and stir again. Now add to the jar thin, circle-sliced pieces of 2 cucumbers and one bunch of green onion tops cut in 1-inch pieces. Cover the container and store in the refrigerator at least a half day before serving. This makes an excellent sweet and sour pickle that lasts up to one week in the refrigerator.

- Try pickling eggs. These will keep for two months in the refrigerator. Put a dozen small, hard-cooked, peeled eggs in a wide-mouth jar with a small sliced onion. In a pan, bring to a boil and simmer over low heat for about 5 minutes: 3 cups vinegar, a 3-inch cinnamon stick, 1 tablespoon honey, 1 teaspoon each whole spice and whole

clove, 1/2 teaspoon whole coriander seeds *(optional)*, a slice of fresh ginger the size of a quarter and a bay leaf. Once cooled, pour this mixture over the eggs and refrigerate for a week before using.

Kitchen Odor Eaters

- Remove kitchen odors that come from burnt pots or when cooking certain vegetables by bringing to a boil a small amount of water with 1/4 cup vinegar so that the steam circulates in the room. Add a few shakes of cinnamon or potpourri to the water for extra fragrance.

- Put a little vinegar in a small bowl *(don't use styrofoam, because the vinegar will eat through it)* anywhere in the house to eliminate odors as it evaporates.

- Use up flavored vinegars you purchased but decided you don't really like as odor eaters. Let them evaporate in small dishes in areas that need some "help."

- Or dampen a cloth with vinegar and wave it through a room to rid it of the smell of smoke.

- Rub vinegar on your hands to make onion odor disappear, as well as stains from fruits such as berries.

Vinaigrettes as Salad Dressings

Experiment with different kinds of vinegars in the stores to find your favorite. Cider vinegar and distilled white vinegar are strong tasting. Rice wine vinegar, rice vinegar and many other flavored vinegars are "softer" and may be used in most any recipe where you prefer their taste.

The basic vinaigrette salad dressing proportion is:
1 part vinegar to 4 parts oil
(This means 1 tablespoon of vinegar to 4 tablespoons oil, or 1/2 cup
vinegar to 2 cups of oil, etc.)

- Adding 1/3 to 1/4 teaspoon salt to a vinegar cruet will keep the vinegar clear and give it a bit of seasoning.

- Any plain vinaigrette can *(and should)* be seasoned to taste with any of the following used in modest amounts *('modest' translates to 1 to 2 teaspoons):*
  - salt   • pepper   • dry or Dijon mustard
  - dried tarragon   • garlic (powder or fresh pressed)
  - basil (dried or minced fresh—fresh being stronger, so use less)

- Put some balsamic vinegar, which has a more intense flavor and can be more expensive, in a clean glass spray bottle. Now it is easier to dispense small amounts.

- Create your own flavorful citrus vinaigrette by first combining 1 part balsamic vinegar with 2 parts olive oil. To that add 1 teaspoon sugar, 1 teaspoon mustard, 1 crushed garlic clove and orange juice equal to the amount of the vinegar used. Lemon juice can be used instead of orange juice.

- Make a creamy vinaigrette by adding some plain or whipped cream to a mixture of 1 part vinegar to 3 parts oil.

- Create a tasty and attractive vinaigrette with zing by combing in a blender or food processor: 1/4 cup raspberry vinegar, 1/2 cup olive oil, 1/4 cup water, a garlic clove and 1-8 oz. jar of pickled beets, drained.

- Use seasoned rice vinegar (and oil) when you use the prepared *Good Season's Italian Dressing* salad dressing mix. It creates a new taste flavor.

Making Flavored Vinegar

You can flavor any basic vinegar of your choosing. When doing this, it is best to use as your base unseasoned rice vinegar, white wine vinegar or distilled white vinegar, as these will not compete with the seasonings you are adding. You can use such things as sprigs or leaves of herbs, raw garlic, hot peppers or lemon peel to make your own flavors. If using fruits such as raspberries, you should first cook down the fruit adding a tablespoon of sugar or honey to the mixture before putting it in a wide mouth jar *(the wide mouth makes it easier to remove your additives later or strain out the fruit)* and covering it with vinegar. Cool, cap and label, and give it a week or two before tasting. When stored in a cool dry place flavored vinegars should last at least 2 years. Berry fruits can change color but they don't spoil as the vinegar is a safe preservative.

- Choose the vinegar you want to flavor by what you wish to add to it. Apple cider vinegar compliments fruits; white vinegar goes well with many herbs; and wine vinegars work well with stronger herbs such as garlic and tarragon. Other items you can use to flavor food vinegars are: cloves, cinnamon, or even horseradish.

- Or flavor vinegar without heating and just adding herbs of your choice. Use 3 tablespoons dried herbs to each pint of vinegar. Use 3 to 4 sprigs fresh herbs. When the vinegar has reached the desired flavor, strain the vinegar and return it to a clean and labeled container.

- Create your own spicy vinegars by gently heating 1 qt of vinegar *(or smaller amounts if you're experimenting)* to which you've added dry spices such as peppercorns, whole cloves, cinnamon sticks or others alone or in any combination. Cool, strain, bottle and label. No aging time necessary.

- Place the peeled cloves of garlic from a whole garlic bulb in a quart glass jar. Fill it with white vinegar or white wine vinegar and let this sit covered tightly for a least 2 weeks. *(If you only have a metal jar lid, place a small plastic sandwich bag under the lid so the vinegar doesn't come in contact with it.)* Pour the vinegar into another glass bottle or decanter and strain out any residue. It will have a strong garlic taste. One teaspoon garlic powder will substitute for 1 garlic clove.

- Create quick fruit-flavored vinegars by just adding 2 tablespoons preserves or jam to 1 cup red or white wine vinegar. Let this stand for a week before using. No need to strain it.

- Make your own serving of wine vinegar *(especially if you have none on hand)* by adding a tablespoon of white or red wine to two tablespoons of white vinegar. To make a larger amount use 1/4 to 1/2 cup of red or white wine to 1 cup of white vinegar or cider vinegar. Experiment to find the combination you like.

- Or if you don't have wine on hand to create your own wine vinegar, you can use a blend of white grape juice and vinegar (1:2), or a little apple cider with vinegar (1:2) for creating cider vinegar when you need to make do.
- Sterilize new containers that you are using for flavored vinegars to prevent the vinegars from clouding.

- Lavender vinegar is made with unseasoned rice vinegar with sprigs of lavender, left to stand, capped, for a few weeks. This vinegar is not for adding to food but to use as a mild scented splash, cleaner or deodorizer.

- Or use rose petals or any sweet smelling flower to give a lovely aroma to a white vinegar.

- Recycle glass bottles previously used for wine coolers, sauces, or olive oil to hold your homemade vinegars. Close bottles with a cork, not a metal lid. Craft stores sell corks in a large array of sizes and shapes.

- If you find that your own seasoned vinegars are particularly nice, bottle them and give them as gifts. A pretty glass container, a handmade label and a tie of raffia are good finishing touches!

- Order your own, personalized labels for vinegar bottles from www.myownlabels.com, or make some on your computer.

- Don't display flavored vinegars in direct sunlight. It can change the flavor, acidity and color of your vinegar. They do make attractive displays on kitchen counters if not in direct sunlight.

Flavored vinegars for purchase are referred to as specialty vinegars. They are favorites of the gourmet market. You don't have to make your own to enjoy the variety of tastes available. And they are wonderful to give as gifts as we tend not to treat ourselves to them.

Using Flavored Vinegars

- Make marinated mushrooms that have been rinsed and stems trimmed by first bringing them to a boil and simmering in a sauce pan for 10 minutes: 3/4 cup vegetable or olive oil, 1/2 cup of an herb flavored *(be it chive, garlic, basil, or thyme)* vinegar, 1 teaspoon salt, 1 teaspoon sugar, 1 bay leaf and a few peppercorns. Add a pound or so of mushrooms and simmer for 3 minutes uncovered. Pour mushrooms and liquid into a bowl. Cover and chill for several hours or overnight. Remove bay leaf and peppercorns and drain mushrooms. Serve as an appetizer or on a relish tray.

- Add a dash of any herb flavored vinegar when making tuna salad.

- Try a citrus flavored vinegar in place of lemon juice called for in a recipe.

- Save the juice from fish cooked in vinegar and add some to a basic vinaigrette. Use it on the salad you serve with the fish for a complementary taste.

- Marinate sliced tomatoes in an herb flavored vinegar and some olive oil for a few hours before serving, or overnight.

- Make a quick vegetable or cracker dip by combining 2 oz. (4 tablespoons) mayonnaise with 1 teaspoon of your flavored vinegar of choice.

- Give a new flavor to your favorite potato salad recipe calling for white vinegar by using an herb flavored or seasoned rice one in its place.

RECIPES FOR MAKING FLAVORED VINEGARS

Here's a selection of do-it-yourself recipes to let you begin creating your own favorites *(with thanks to the H.J. Heinz Company):*

Basil Garlic Vinegar
Use in dressings for rice, pasta, antipasto salads or in flavored mayonnaise.
Place 1/2 cup coarsely chopped fresh basil leaves and 2 garlic cloves, peeled and split, in a sterilized pint jar. Heat wine vinegar or white vinegar to just below the boiling point. Fill the jar with vinegar and cap tightly. Allow this to stand for 3 to 4 weeks. Uncap, strain vinegar and discard basil and garlic. Pour the vinegar into a clean sterilized jar, adding some fresh basil garnish, if desired. Seal tightly.

Orange Mint Vinegar
Use in dressing for tossed green salads with orange and grapefruit sections or in marinades for chicken or lamb chops.
Remove peel (colored portion only) from 1 small orange in a thin spiral and place in a sterilized pint jar. Lightly bruise 1/2 cup fresh mint leaves and add to jar. Heat apple cider or white vinegar to just below the boiling point. Fill jar with vinegar and cap tightly. Allow to stand 3 to 4 weeks. Strain vinegar, discarding peel and mint. Pour vinegar into a clean sterilized jar, adding fresh mint and peel for garnish, if desired. Seal tightly.

Raspberry Vinegar
Perfect for mixed greens, fruit salads or in marinades for chicken.

Bruise 1 cup fresh raspberries lightly and place them in a sterilized pint jar. Heat white or wine vinegar to just below the boiling point. Fill the jar with vinegar and cap tightly. Allow this to stand for 2 to 3 weeks. Uncap and strain the vinegar, discarding the fruit. Pour the vinegar into a clean jar and seal tightly.

Lemon Thyme Vinegar
Use in dressings for tossed green salads or marinades for vegetables.

Remove peel (colored portion only) from 1 lemon in a thin spiral and place in a sterilized pint jar with 4 to 5 springs of thyme or lemon thyme. Heat white vinegar to just below the boiling point. Fill jar with vinegar and cap tightly. Allow to stand 3 to 4 weeks. Strain vinegar, discarding peel and thyme. Pour vinegar into a clean sterilized jar, adding fresh thyme sprigs and peel for garnish. Seal tightly.

Jalapeno Garlic Vinegar
Use in dressings for taco, tomato and onion or avocado salads, or when making salsa.

Cut a few small slits in 2 small jalapeno peppers and place in a decorative bottle with 2 cloves peeled garlic. Heat wine or apple cider vinegar to just below the boiling point. Fill bottles with vinegar and cap tightly. Allow to stand 3 to 4 weeks.

MAKING YOUR OWN VINEGAR

Depending on which source you read, making your own vinegar is either very easy or sounds more complicated than you care to know. If you enjoy any form of home brewing and go to home-brew supply sources, you will be able to find materials there to help you make your own vinegar.

Basically you start with a sweet based liquid of your choice as it can be made from anything containing sugar or starch. Cider (unpasteurized from a health food store) or old wine or another fruit juice is usually the easiest to use.

The top of your container (*glass or stainless steel is best*) should be covered with cheesecloth to keep out fruit flies, but not air tight as you need the bacteria in the air to allow it to ferment. You do not cap this fermenting solution.

Unprocessed fermenting vinegar contains a cobweb-like gel called "mother vinegar" which is a mat that forms the basis for the fermentation. It may look bad but it is good.

You keep this vinegar-to-be solution in a dark, warm area. This is not a fast process. It takes many weeks to many months—or longer—to produce a satisfactory vinegar, they say. This process is not to be confused with just leaving wine or ale exposed to the air. It may taste vinegary but it is just sour wine or ale.

If you have noted a less than enthusiastic tone on my part, you can tell that making vinegar is not my thing. I actually tried one simple method but it was less than appealing so I stopped there. Do read up on it. Many can tell you a variety of ways to make vinegar. There are many sources available from books and also on the Internet (*start with: www. vinegarman.com/VinegarMaking.html*). Lawrence Diggs' book, *VINEGAR*, has lots of information too.

THE 'CLASSIC' PUDDLE CAKE

Here's a recipe that is easy to make *(it only requires one dish to clean—other than the measuring utensils)* and it is also milk-free.

Combine and mix the following dry ingredients in an 8"x 8" ungreased baking pan:

> 1 cup sugar
> 1 -1/2 cups flour
> 1 teaspoon baking soda
> 4 tablespoons cocoa powder

Next create 3 holes in the dry mix. Put one of the following in each "hole":

> 1 teaspoon vanilla flavoring
> 1 tablespoon vinegar
> 4 tablespoons cooking oil

Now pour 1 cup water over everything and stir with a fork until evenly blended with the dry ingredients. Bake at 350° for 40 minutes.

Desserts

- Keep molded gelatin desserts and salads from sagging or melting in the summer heat by adding a teaspoon of vinegar for each box of gelatin used.

- Add a spoonful of vinegar to any chocolate cake—home-made or from a box—for extra moistness and taste.

- And add a drop of vinegar to icing to keep it from sugar-ing. It will also help keep white frostings white and shiny.

- Try a tablespoon of vinegar in pie crusts for great flavor and texture.

- Make perfect, fluffy meringue by adding a teaspoon of vinegar for every 3 to 4 egg whites used.

VINEGAR PIE

This simple, sweet *(and delicious)* pie is not very vinegary. It is more of a custard pie. It's a classic that is necessary to include. *(It is even good cold for breakfast!)*

4 eggs
1-1/2 cups sugar
1 teaspoon vanilla
2 tablespoons vinegar (white, cider, balsamic or rice)
1/4 cup butter or margarine, melted
9-inch frozen pie shell, defrosted

Preheat oven to 350°. In a large mixing bowl combine eggs, sugar, vanilla, vinegar and butter. Mix well and pour into the defrosted (or home made) pie shell. Bake 50-60 minutes until firm. Cool. Top, if desired, with whipped cream.

A Miscellany of Kitchen Vinegar Ideas

- You've burned yourself in the kitchen? Pour a dash of white vinegar on a small cloth and lay it over the burn. This works for sunburn as well.

- Rub your hands with vinegar to remove berry stains.

- Relieve thirst with a drink of a spoonful or two of apple cider vinegar in very cold water.

- Remove smells of mayonnaise or peanut butter in jars you've washed and want to save by rinsing with vinegar.

- Add a tablespoon to 1/4 cup white vinegar to soup stock you're preparing (depending on the size of your pot), in order to pull every bit of calcium from the bones as they cook down.

- Perk up any can of soup or sauce with a teaspoon of red or white wine vinegar.

- Substitute your favorite flavored vinegar for most of the wine called for in a Coq au Vin *(chicken-in-wine)* recipe.

- Save money *(and perhaps "the day")* by substituting 1 teaspoon vinegar for each teaspoon of lemon called for in any recipe. Of course if you really need the flavor of the lemon, this won't work well.

- Avoid the greasy taste in food cooked in a deep fryer by adding a dash of vinegar.

- Wipe off the outsides of canned jars of fruits or vegetables with white vinegar so mold doesn't grow if stored in a damp area.

- Whoops! You added too much salt to a recipe. Add a spoonful of vinegar and sugar to try correcting the taste.

CHAPTER TWO

A CLEAN KITCHEN

€€€€€€€

Sink and Countertops

- Shine up chrome sink fixtures that are marred with stains or lime buildup by cleaning them with a paste made of 2 tablespoons salt and 1 teaspoon distilled vinegar.

- Let a vinegar-soaked cloth lie on a stubborn water stain or mineral deposits for an hour or so, then scrub with the salt/vinegar mixture again.

- Or try heating the vinegar just to the boiling point, then pour it on fixtures to soften such deposits.

- Make your own scouring cleanser by combining 1/4 cup baking soda with 1 tablespoon liquid detergent. Add just enough white vinegar to give it a thick but creamy texture.

- Spray vinegar full strength on a cutting board after its last use at night and don't rinse it off. The smell will evaporate and the acidic energy will have done its job.

- Or rub it down first with baking soda and spray the surface with full strength vinegar. It will bubble for a bit and then subside. Let this set for 5 to 10 minutes before rinsing it clean with water.

- Clean counter tops and make them smell sweet again with a cloth soaked in undiluted white vinegar.

- Or keep an attractive spray container of full strength vinegar on your counter. Spray and wipe down counters at the end of each day. This will also help keep crawling critters at bay.

- Make your own stronger-than-5-percent acetic vinegar solution *(should you wish to use some)* by simmering a pan of white vinegar down by 1/3 to 1/2 of the amount of liquid. The water will evaporate and the remaining solution will now be between 5 and 10 percent acetic acid.

Down The Drain

- Clean and deodorize a drain by pouring in 1 cup baking soda, then 1 cup hot vinegar. (Your microwave is perfect for heating the vinegar.) Let this sit for 5 minutes or so, then run hot water down the drain. This same process *(cutting the amount to 1/2 cup baking soda and 1/2 cup hot vinegar)* will also clean and deodorize the garbage disposal.

- Or try vinegar ice cubes to deodorize and clean the garbage disposal. Make them by freezing vinegar in a molded ice cube tray. Run several cubes down the disposal while flushing with cold water. As the vinegar freezes it will deodorize the freezer as well!

Appliance Applications

- Wash appliance exteriors with a mixture of 1/2 cup baking soda, 1/2 cup vinegar, 1 cup ammonia and a gallon of hot water.

- Clean the microwave oven by mixing 1/2 cup vinegar and 1/2 cup of water in a microwave-safe bowl or glass mixing cup and bringing it to a rolling boil so the inside streams up. Baked-on food will be loosened. Wipe clean. Odors will disappear too.

- Or try this slightly different method. Mix a tablespoon of vinegar and a drop or two of liquid dish soap with a cup of water and bring it to a boil in the microwave. Let it stand for about 15 minutes before wiping clean.

- Clean the shelves and walls of the refrigerator with a half-and-half solution of water and vinegar.

- Wipe clean the top of the refrigerator with a paper towel or cloth using full strength vinegar. It will cut the grime.

- Avoid that bad smell when you heat up a newly cleaned oven. Make your final rinse a wipe out with a sponge wet with undiluted vinegar.

- Soak oven racks in a large, heavy garbage bag, with a solution of 1/4 cup dishwasher detergent, a cup of vinegar and very hot water. Set the bag in the garage or outside and let the racks soak for a few hours or overnight before finishing the cleaning job in the sink.

- Saturate a grease-splattered window of an oven door with full strength white vinegar *(let the door lie open)* for 10 to 15 minutes before cleaning it with a scrub sponge.

- Pour a cup of vinegar into the dishwasher and run the empty machine through a whole cycle each month to get rid of soap buildup and odors.

- Clean your glass cook top with a cloth or sponge dipped in warm sudsy water to which a splash of white vinegar has been added.

Glass Aware

- Add 1/2 cup vinegar to the dishwasher rinse cycle to get dishes and glassware sparkling.

- Remove the chalky deposit sometimes left on dishes in the dishwasher. Place the dishes on the lower rack and run the machine for about five minutes with a cup of vinegar added. Then run a complete cycle with your regular detergent.

- Prevent good glassware from getting etched by minerals when running them through your dishwasher by *not* running them through your dishwasher. Wash them by

hand in a sink full of hot water to which you've added a small amount of dishwashing soap and 1 cup vinegar. Rinse and towel dry.

- Spray washed glassware with full strength vinegar using that spray bottle you now keep by the kitchen sink. Give glasses one quick hot water rinse before you let them drip dry or drying them with a clean towel.

HOW TO BE A *FILM* STAR

Vinegar, due to its mild acid content, is excellent for removing stains, grease and mineral deposits from glass surfaces. The white film that builds up on glassware is an all too common experience. A periodic vinegar bath for glassware is helpful for keeping film at bay or for removing it. For seriously cloudy glassware, soak paper towels or a cloth in full strength vinegar and wrap around the inside and outside of the glass. Let sit for awhile before rinsing the glassware clean.

If the white film doesn't disappear, you are probably too late. The minerals in your water have etched the glassware and you will have to live with this or move on to a new set of drinking glasses.

Kitchen Perks

- Get rid of lime deposits in a teakettle by adding 1/2 cup vinegar to the water and letting it sit overnight. If more drastic action is needed, boil full strength vinegar in the kettle a few minutes, let cool and rinse with plain water. That should do the trick!

- Check owners' manuals before trying to remove mineral deposits from coffee makers with vinegar. If its use is approved, fill the water reservoir with 1 cup or more of vinegar and run it through a whole cycle. Run it once or twice more with plain water to rinse clean.

- Clean a percolator coffee maker by filling it with vinegar and simply letting it sit overnight. Oils and coffee residue should disappear.

Assorted Containers

- Remove stains from coffee and tea cups by scrubbing them gently with equal parts of salt (or baking soda) and vinegar, using a sponge or brush. Rinse clean.

- Clean a bread box and get rid of that stale odor by wiping it out with a cloth dampened with vinegar. Do the same for stained and smelly plastic food containers.

- Remove odors from a lunch box by enclosing within it a vinegar-soaked slice of fresh bread and leaving it overnight.

- Clean a thermos by filling it with 1/4 cup white vinegar and then hot tap water. Use a bottle brush or cloth to whisk the insides before rinsing it clean.

- Remove ugly film in narrow necked glass jars, flower vases and bottles by letting undiluted vinegar sit in them for a few hours. Add a little rice or sand and shake vigorously to loosen stubborn stains. Repeat if necessary.

- Wipe down the outsides of glass jars of home-canned preserves and other foods with vinegar to avoid mold-producing bacteria.

Pots and Pans and Such

- Use a paste with equal amounts of vinegar and table salt for cleaning not only cooking pots, but also tarnished brass, copper, and pewter. *(There is also a popular folk remedy for cleaning pewter using cabbage leaves dampened with vinegar and dipped in salt to rub on the pewter.)*

- Or do the job on copper pots by spraying with a mixture of hot vinegar and a tablespoon or two of salt on the object, then rinsing and drying it.

- Make a metal cleaner by adding enough vinegar to 2 tablespoons cream of tartar to make a paste. Rub it on and let it dry on the surface. Wash it off and dry with a soft cloth.

- For brass, spread on a paste of equal parts of salt and flour with enough vinegar to get the desired consistency. Apply the paste and let sit for 15 minutes (or rub briskly on the brass) before rinsing it off and wiping the surface dry.

- Polish brass and copper with a mixture of 2 tablespoons of ketchup and 1 tablespoon of vinegar. Rub it on with a clean cloth until dry and the surface will shine.

- Remove dark stains on an aluminum pot by boiling in it a mixture of 1 cup white vinegar and 1 cup of water.

- Or boil an entire small utensil in a larger pot filled with the aforementioned solution.

- For pots of other metals, try using a solution of 3 table-spoons vinegar to a pint of water.

- Or simply fill the pots with vinegar and let them stand for a half hour. Wash with soap and water.

- Clean the inside of cast-iron pans (the outside is best done with oven cleaner) with a solution of water and 2 table-spoons white vinegar, boiled together in the pan. Re-season the pan with cooking oil. Store it with a piece of waxed paper in it, especially if you are placing something on it when it is not in use.

Miscellaneous Kitchen Aids

- Discourage ants by spraying undiluted vinegar outside doorways and window sills, around appliances and wherever you find the pests coming in.

- Get rid of fruit flies by setting out a small dish of undi-luted vinegar. It will attract and drown them.

- Clean the wheel of a can opener using vinegar and an old toothbrush.

- Remove the smell of spoiled food (that could occur after a power failure) from a freezer by first rinsing the emptied area with soap and water. Then spray surfaces with full strength vinegar and wipe them down with a damp cloth

or sponge. Fill some open containers with cat litter and/or baking soda. Close freezer door and leave for a few days.

- Soak a sponge in distilled vinegar and wipe grease off exhaust fan grids, air conditioner blades, the inside of your oven or anywhere grease gathers.

- Keep a spray bottle of a vinegar solution (half water and half white vinegar) next to your outdoor grill—whether it is gas or charcoal. Spray the cooking surface before heating and/or after cooking for easier cleanup.

- Spread a cloth soaked in vinegar over a label, decal or price tag you want to remove. Leave the cloth on overnight and the label should slide off.

- Renew sponges and dish rags by letting them soak overnight in enough water to which 1/4 cup vinegar has been added to cover them.

CHAPTER THREE

IN THE BATHROOM

€€€€€€€

Bathroom Sinks

- Get rid of calcium deposits on faucets by soaking a cloth, paper towel or even strips of toilet tissue in vinegar and wrapping the area tightly. Let this sit for a couple of hours or overnight.

- Remove soap buildup from faucets by scrubbing them with a solution of 1 part salt to 4 parts vinegar.

- Rid a faucet of lime deposits by tying a plastic bag containing 1/3 to 1/2 cup of vinegar around it and leaving it there for two or three hours. If mineral deposits don't wipe off, scrubbing with an old toothbrush should complete the job.

- Shine up colored porcelain sinks by scouring them with undiluted white vinegar.

- Rinse away soapy film on countertops with a solution of vinegar and water.

- Clean grout by letting full-strength vinegar sit on it for a few minutes and scrubbing it with an old toothbrush. Bleach is also effective but there are times you may not wish to use it.

- Kill germs all around the bathroom with a spray of full strength vinegar. Wipe clean with a damp cloth.

Tub and Shower Savers

- Wipe tub, tile and shower curtain or door with undiluted vinegar to remove grime, mildew and scum. Rinse with water.

- Give a little preventive maintenance to shower doors by spraying them with full strength white vinegar after you've squeegeed the glass (which is helpful to do after each shower), or even before you are about to step in and turn on the water. It will help release the hard water deposits so they don't remain on the glass.

- Mix up a cheap and super tile cleaner by adding 1/2 cup baking soda, 1 cup white vinegar and 1 cup ammonia to a gallon of warm water.

- Get rid of stubborn bathtub film by first wiping the ring

with vinegar, then scouring with baking soda.

- Spray full strength white vinegar along the bathtub ring after each bath and it will make clean-up a breeze.

- Clean a fiberglass tub almost effortlessly by sprinkling it liberally with baking soda, then wiping it down with a vinegar-soaked cloth. Rinse and wipe dry for a spotless shine.

- Soak a sponge or loofah in a strong vinegar-water solution overnight to remove dirt and slime. Rinse several times with cold water and let air dry—and in the sun if possible.

- Clean shower door tracks by filling them with white vinegar and letting this sit for a few hours. Pour hot water into the tracks and with a brush, wash and scrub away the scum.

Shower Head Hints

- Pour 1/2 cup baking soda and 1 cup vinegar into a strong, sandwich-sized plastic bag *(quart-sized if needed)* and tie it onto and over a scummy shower head. Let this set for an hour after the bubbling has stopped. Remove the bag and then turn on the water. Hard water buildup will be gone and your showerhead will sparkle again.

- Give a clogged, detachable showerhead a thorough clean-out by first removing it , then "simmering" it in a pot filled with equal parts of vinegar and water for 5 to 20 minutes. Be sure to remove the rubber washer first.

Toilet Tips

- Deodorize the toilet bowl by allowing 3 cups white vinegar to sit in it for about a half hour, then flushing.

- Make the toilet bowl sparkle by pouring in a cup or more of undiluted vinegar and letting it sit for several hours or overnight. Scrub well with the brush and flush.

- Pour 1 cup vinegar and 1 cup borax into the toilet bowl. Let this sit for awhile before using a toilet brush to scrub the bowl and up under the rim.

- Spray full strength vinegar on the toilet rim occasionally. Lift up the seat, spray the inside bowl rim and don't bother to rinse it off. The smell will also help deodorize odors as it evaporates.

- Get rid of a lime deposit ring in the bowl by first removing as much water as possible from the bowl. This can be done by pouring a bucket of water into the bowl *(yes, strange as it sounds, it does work)* or literally 'pushing' the water down the neck of the bowl with a johnny mop. Soak rolled-up paper towels in vinegar and lay them on the ring. Leave on for an hour or more or until the ring is easy to scrub off. Using a pumice stone at this point makes the job easy.

- Or bring a gallon of white vinegar to a boil and pour it into the almost-empty bowl. In a few hours, the ring should disappear with a quick scrub of the brush.

- Freshen air in the bathroom by spraying into the air a

solution of 1 teaspoon baking soda and 1 tablespoon vinegar and 1 cup water. (Any empty, clean spray dispenser will do.) Shake the spray bottle well after the mixture stops foaming.

- Or just lightly spray the air with full strength vinegar. You can add a drop of your own perfume fragrance, or herbs, or spices or vanilla extract to the vinegar—*or not*—depending how you feel about the aroma of vinegar.

CHAPTER FOUR

ALL THROUGH THE HOUSE

€€€€€€€

Starting at the Bottom

- Clean any floor that can be cleaned with a wet solution with a mixture of 2 gallons water, 1/2 capful liquid soap and 1 cup vinegar. Wipe the floor dry with a soft cloth if you really wish to pick up the loosened dirt.

- Get a shining finish on a no-wax vinyl or linoleum floor by cleaning it with a solution of one cup of white vinegar for every gallon of water.

- Apply full strength vinegar directly to tough linoleum stains. Leave it on for 10 to 15 minutes before wiping it up. If that doesn't work, apply vinegar again and then sprinkle some baking soda over the vinegar. Scrub the area with a brush or sponge. Rinse clean with water.

- Add a cup of vinegar to the rinse water after scrubbing the floor with a floor stripper. This will neutralize chemicals and make the finish adhere better.

- Try this economical and environmentally-friendly solution rather than using expensive floor cleaners for floors that require only light damp cleaning. Add 3 drops dish washing liquid to 1/3 part each of white vinegar, rubbing alcohol and water. Spray sparingly and mop for a fast clean-up. Enjoy having a clean-smelling room.

Carpets

Always test any of these solutions, the first time you try them on an out-of-sight part of the carpet *(especially dark, colored carpet)* to be sure they don't effect the color.

- Some stains can be removed with a paste of vinegar (2 tablespoons) and salt or baking soda (1/4 cup). Rub this into the carpet stain and let it dry. Vacuum up the residue the next day.

- Bring out the color in floor coverings by brushing them with a solution of one cup of vinegar for every gallon of water.

- Remove a non-oily stain as soon as you notice it with a solution of a teaspoon each of vinegar and a mild liquid detergent to a gallon of hot water. Apply and rub in with a soft brush or old toweling piece. Rinse with clean water and blot dry. Repeat if necessary, and give a quick final drying with a hair dryer or fan.

- Use full strength vinegar on food stains, especially oily ones, and rinse and dry as in previous tip.

- Put about 1/4 cup vinegar in a steam cleaner to reduce soap bubbles, and use the same amount in rinse water to remove detergent residue and make carpets stay fresh longer.

- Wash indoor/outdoor carpeting outside using a solution of 1 cup vinegar to one bucket of warm water. Scrub it using a brush or a broom and then hose it off.

Pet Stain Problems

- Clean up pet accidents by first blotting up the area and then adding a vinegar-and-water solution to the area. Blot until it is almost dry. Then sprinkle baking soda over the area and let it dry. Vacuum up the residue the next day.

- Or, for a spot that's been standing for awhile, make up a two-part stain and spot remover that will also help remove odors. Fill one spray bottle with a solution of 1 part white vinegar to 7 parts water and another using the same proportions of water and non-sudsy ammonia. First saturate the spot with the vinegar solution; let it sit for a few minutes, then blot thoroughly with a clean cloth. Repeat the process with the ammonia solution.

- Let full-strength vinegar sit on a pet spot for a few minutes, after testing the colorfastness of the carpet in an inconspicuous place. Blot, rinse and dry.

Shining Windows and Other Glass Surfaces

Remember vinegar when it's window-cleaning time because it adds a "streak-less" quality. Various recommendations exist for optimal solution strengths, from full strength to 1 cup per pail of water, to equal parts vinegar and water, to 2 tablespoons vinegar to 2 pints water. Whatever proportions you choose, apply with a cloth, sponge or pump spray and dry with a soft cloth or paper towels. *(Newsprint is okay but you may wish to use this only when working on large, very dirty areas as the newsprint will also get your hands or rubber gloves dirty.)*

- Consider this favorite homemade window cleaning solution: combine 1/2 cup non-sudsy ammonia, 1 cup white vinegar and 2 tablespoons cornstarch in a gallon of water. Use it in a spray container or wipe it on with a cloth.

- Or combine 1/3 cup vinegar and 1/3 cup cornstarch and apply with a cloth. Let it dry and rub to a shine with a dry clean cloth.

- Stretch any commercial window cleaner (including car window spray) by combining it with water and vinegar. Transfer 2/3 of your commercial cleaner out of its container to another one for now. Fill the original bottle with 1/3 cup water and the last 3rd with white vinegar. *(Of course you can just wait until you're down to 1/3 of the bottle before doing this.)*

- Remove the wax residue left by commercial window-cleaners with a solution of 2 cups water, 1 cup distilled vinegar and 1 teaspoon of liquid soap or detergent.

- Spray full strength vinegar on exterior windows if you live near the ocean. It will remove the salt on windows that sticks from the sea breezes.

- Try using undiluted, hot vinegar to remove paint from windows. Give the solution time to soften the paint and then remove with a razor edge tool.

- Apply full strength vinegar with a clean paint brush when trying to remove paint splatters from windows or when trying to saturate a decal you wish to remove.

TO SPRAY OR NOT TO SPRAY

There are times you should NOT spray your liquid glass cleaner directly on the glass surface. This applies to mirrors with frames, pictures in frames, TVs and computer screens. For these, spray the solution onto your cleaning cloth or towel and *then* wipe the glass surface clean.

Walls and Woodwork

- Get rid of mildew, dust and stale odors by wiping down walls with undiluted vinegar on a cloth or a sponge mop.

- Clean woodwork and walls with a mixture of 1 cup vinegar, 1 cup baking soda, 1/2 cup ammonia and 1 gallon warm water. Wipe on with a sponge or damp—not wet— towel. (Wood finishes differ and this might not be suitable for certain woods—such as on fine furniture. If in doubt, test a small area first.)

- Clean wood paneling with a solution of 1 ounce olive oil, 2 ounces white vinegar and 1 quart warm water. Wipe on with a soft cloth, then remove any yellowing with a clean cloth.

- Or consider a slightly different solution of 1/4 cup olive oil, 1/2 cup vinegar and 2 cups warm water, using the same method.

- Get rid of cloudiness on varnished wood with a solution of 1 tablespoon white vinegar and 1 quart room temperature water. Rub on with a soft, lint-less cloth, then wipe with a clean, dry cloth.

- Remove wallpaper easily by using a paint roller to wet the surface *very* thoroughly with a solution of equal parts vinegar and hot water. Or spray on until saturated.

- Get decals off walls or doors by letting undiluted vinegar soak into them for several minutes before trying to peel them off. Repeat if necessary.

Furniture

- Make a frugal and effective furniture polish with equal parts white vinegar and vegetable oil, or with 1 part vinegar and 3 parts olive oil, always rubbing with the grain of the wood. This same solution will also often remove white water rings from wood.

- Create your own dusting/polishing cloths by first dampening them in a solution of one part vinegar to one part

olive oil. The olive oil gives off a nice aroma and the vinegar smell evaporates.

- Get rid of stains on upholstered furniture by rubbing undiluted white vinegar directly into the stain, then washing according to the manufacturer's directions. (Test first on a hidden area to be sure the fabric does not change color by the application of vinegar.)

Odds and Ends

- Scrub fireplace bricks with undiluted vinegar to remove soot and grime. Use a brush to scrub and a towel to blot up the wetness and dirt.

- Clean fireplace glass doors with a solution of 1 part vinegar to 2 parts water. Spray or wipe on, then wipe clean with a dry cloth.

- Check the growth of mold in a humidifier by rinsing it out thoroughly, then adding about 1/2 cup vinegar when refilling with water.

- Decrease static and dust accumulation on plastic or vinyl surfaces by wiping them down with a cloth dampened with vinegar and water.

- Clean piano keys with a soft cloth barely dampened with a mild solution of 1/2 cup vinegar to 2 cups warm water. Be sure to wring the cloth practically dry before wiping the keys clean.

- Spray full strength vinegar on doorknobs and then wipe them dry. This can be especially helpful during the flu season.

- Remove the smell of a dead mouse or other rodent (after removing all animal remnants) by wiping down the area with either vinegar or bleach—which ever is safe for the particular surface. Then place a fabric softener sheet in the area to remove any lingering odors.

- Scent a room pleasantly by adding a bit of cardamon or another fragrant spice to a small bowl of vinegar and placing the bowl in a warm corner.

- Don't use white vinegar on marble. The acid can adversely affect the surface.

CHAPTER FIVE

LAUNDRY
& CLOTHING

€€€€€€€

Laundry Lore

- Add about 1/4 cup vinegar to the last rinse in just about any kind of laundry. The acid in vinegar is too mild to harm fabrics, yet strong enough to dissolve the alkalies in soaps and detergents. Besides removing soap, vinegar prevents yellowing, acts as a fabric softener and static cling reducer and attacks mold and mildew.

- And add 1/2 cup vinegar to the *wash* cycle to prevent lint from clinging to clothes.

- Add a cup of vinegar to the last rinse when dying fabric to help set the color.

- Wash new clothes with 1/2 cup white vinegar added to the water to eliminate manufacturing chemicals.

- Use vinegar in your final rinse for black washables. It removes soap residue that makes black clothes look dull.

- Use your bleach or fabric softener dispenser to hold vinegar (when it is appropriate) to the wash cycle and when you wish to flush these dispensers clean.

TAKING CARE OF BUSINESS

Vinegar is good for the washing machine itself. Periodically run the machine with only a cup of vinegar in it—nothing else added to the wash cycle. Hoses will be cleaned and soap scum dissolved.

Whitest and Brightest

- Get stained white socks and dingy dishcloths white again with an overnight soak. Add 1 cup vinegar to a large pot of water, bring it to a rolling boil and drop in the articles. The next morning you'll be pleased.

- Use vinegar on mildewed garments that cannot take bleach.

- Scrub a paste of vinegar and baking soda on ring-around-the-collar before shirts go into the washing machine.

- Get rid of the odor bleach leaves, if you've used it in wash water, by adding 1/4 cup vinegar to the rinse water.

- Bring out bright colors by adding 1/2 cup vinegar to the rinse cycle.

- Keep bright colors from bleeding during washing by soaking items in a solution of 1 cup vinegar and 1 gallon water before washing.

Don't use vinegar on silk, acetates or rayons.

Stain Away

- Some stains on clothing and linens can be soaked out using equal parts milk and vinegar.

- Remove grass stains with a solution of water, white vinegar and liquid soap.

- Dab vinegar on mustard stains before washing.

- Attack spaghetti, barbecue or ketchup stains first with a vinegar and water solution.

- Remove cola stains on cotton and cotton-blend fabrics by sponging the area as soon as possible with full strength white vinegar. Launder immediately.

- Sponge fresh beer stains (and their smell) away with a vinegar and water solution. Rinse and wash as usual. Old

beer stains may need to be soaked overnight in a weak
vinegar and water mixture.

Special Care

- Remove perspiration odor and stains on clothing, as well
  as those left by deodorants, by spraying full strength
  vinegar on underarm and collar areas before tossing them
  into the washing machine.

- Fluff up wool or acrylic sweaters (hand- or machine-
  washed) and rid them of soap smell, with 1/2 cup vinegar
  in the last rinse water.

- Add 1 to 2 cups vinegar to the last rinse water for cotton
  or wool blankets to fluff them, too.

- Use vinegar in the rinse water for table linens and bed
  linens to keep them from yellowing in storage.

- Neutralize urine in cloth diapers by adding a cup of
  vinegar to two gallons of water in the diaper pail. Another
  cup in the washing machine rinse water will help too, and
  may well prevent diaper rash.

- Add 1/4 cup vinegar to the rinse water for all baby
  clothes to whiten, brighten and break down uric acid,
  leaving them soft and fresh.

- Cut excess suds when doing hand laundry with a little
  vinegar added to the last rinse. Follow this with another
  plain rinse.

- Make nylon hose look smoother and last longer by adding just a tablespoon of vinegar to the rinse water.

- Loosen dried glue by soaking a clean cloth in white vinegar and saturating the spot until the glue softens. Then launder as usual.

- Use vinegar in the rinse water when washing plastic curtains or tablecloths to cut down on static cling.

- Forget that you left wet laundry in the machine and it now smells moldy? Pour a few cups of white vinegar in the machine and wash the clothes in hot water. Then run a normal cycle with detegerent and your problem is gone!

DE-SKUNK IT

Yes, tomato juice is good for removing skunk odor from clothing, but what if you don't have it on hand when you need it? Reach for your white vinegar and add 1 cup to one gallon of warm water and let the clothing soak for several hours. Repeat as necessary.

- Remove smoky odors from clothes by filling the bathtub with very hot water and 1 cup white vinegar. Hang the garments above the steaming water and shut the door so the steam can penetrate the fibers.

Ironing

- Keep the steam iron clean and in good working order by getting rid of mineral deposits in steam vents and spray nozzles. Fill the water chamber with a solution of equal parts vinegar and distilled water. Set it in an upright position and let it steam for about 5 minutes. When the iron is cool, rinse the tank with water, refill and shake water through the vents onto an old cloth. Test before using.

- Wipe the bottom of your cold iron with a cloth soaked in full strength vinegar to remove any brown residue there. Repeat as needed.

- Remove scorch marks from an iron by rubbing it with a warmed-up solution of equal parts vinegar and salt. If that doesn't work, use a cloth dampened with full strength vinegar.

- Get light scorch marks out of fabric by rubbing gently with vinegar.

- Remove the crease left by the old hem of a wool garment by sponging the line with full-strength vinegar.

- Get rid of the tiny holes left along the hemline when you take out the hem of any garment by moistening a cloth with vinegar, placing it under the fabric and ironing.

- Sharpen a crease in a knitted fabric by sponging it with a cloth dampened with a solution of 1/3 vinegar and 2/3

water, then placing a brown bag over it and ironing it. Be sure there's no printing on the area you're pressing.

- Remove musky smells from cotton clothes by sprinkling them light with vinegar and then pressing them.

Leather or Not

- Get water and salt stains off shoes and boots by wiping them down with a solution of equal parts white vinegar and water. Don't wait too long to do this, especially with salt, because the leather may become permanently damaged. Make the last step a good polishing.

- Remove white water rings on leather by sponging the area with white vinegar.

- Remove wax buildup on leather top tables by wiping them with a cloth dampened in a half vinegar, half water solution. Rub the area dry with a clean soft cloth.

- Clean any leather, (including leather furniture) by rubbing a mixture of white vinegar and linseed oil into the article, then polishing with a soft cloth.

- Give patent leather shoes and bags a better shine by wiping them down with white vinegar.

CHAPTER SIX

BEAUTY
& GROOMING

€€€€€€€

Heads Up

- Condition hair, add shining highlights and fight dandruff by using vinegar as a rinse after shampooing. A solution of 1 cup vinegar to 2 cups water is all you need.

- Create your own scented hair rinse by flavoring white vinegar with herbs or spices of your choice. Let the vinegar sit for 2 weeks before using. Strain and dilute before using. Store in a plastic dispenser to keep in the shower area. Apply to hair and rinse.

- Take extra care, if you wish, by using bottled water with vinegar in that last rinse. It is also a good way to use up

the bottled drinking water that's been opened but not emptied.

- Dealing with head lice? Washing hair with a solution of white vinegar helps to loosen nits from the hair shaft before using a lice-killing shampoo.

- Fight dandruff with regular rinses of white vinegar and water. Or just rub some full strength vinegar into the scalp after shampooing and rinsing, then rinse again. This will also eliminate itchy scalp.

- Give your hairbrush a thorough cleaning. Soak it for a few hours or, better yet, overnight in a sink full of hot water with 1 cup vinegar added. Rinse it well in the morning.

Let's Face It

- Consider this gentlemen: try using undiluted vinegar as an aftershave lotion, especially if commercial aftershaves cause rashes and itching. Your skin will be soft, skin problems will be helped and you'll find that the odor disappears very quickly

- Tone facial skin with a solution of equal parts of vinegar and water.

- Steam clean your face using apple cider vinegar. Lean over a pot of boiling water (carefully—at least 8 inches away from the water) with a towel over your head to trap the steam. After a minute of so, apply apple cider vinegar

with a cotton ball to remove dirt and oil from your skin. After face has cooled, dab more of the cool vinegar on the pores to close them.

Getting to the Bottom of It

- Try vinegar as a relief from athlete's foot, if prescription and over-the-counter methods haven't worked. You can spray it on full strength with the spray bottle you now keep in the bathroom.

- Toes nails fighting a fungus? It is said that soaking in undiluted vinegar will change skin ph, stopping fungus growth.

- Wrap feet in a washcloth dampened with undiluted vinegar to soften skin before a pedicure.

- Treat corns and calluses by taping over them a cloth soaked in vinegar *(an old wives' tale calls for a piece of stale bread)* and leave it overnight.

Allover Body Works

- Reduce age spots, wherever they are, with a daily splash of a mixture of equal parts onion juice and vinegar. Don't expect miracles overnight, but daily use may do the same job expensive products do.

- Lighten body freckles *(not facial freckles)* by rubbing on full strength vinegar.

- Soothe aching muscles and itching skin by soaking in a warm bath to which 1 cup cider vinegar has been added. You can also place some dried herbs or flower petals in a tied square of cheesecloth to float in the bath for extra fragrance.

- Or simmer some vinegar to which herbs, spices or pine needles have been added. Strain these out and pour the heated mixture into your bath before you get in.

- Give yourself a sponge bath when needed using a wash cloth or sponge dampened in a solution of 2 parts water to one part vinegar. It will neutralize body odors and perspiration.

- Use white vinegar as a deodorant. Spray or splash it on with your hand. It will not keep you from perspiring, but it will neutralize odor. The odor vinegar leaves on the skin or clothing evaporates and should be gone within an hour or so.

Tooth Care

- Eliminate bad breath and whiten your teeth by brushing them once or twice a week with white vinegar.

- Soak dentures overnight in hot water with 1/4 cup white vinegar. This will soften tartar so that it can more easily be brushed away with a toothbrush.

Also, with Vinegar You Can. . .

- Keep a small, attractive spray bottle filled with vinegar on your bathroom counter as a convenient dispenser.

- Clean eyeglass lenses (but not coated, non-glare ones, which may scratch) by wiping them clean with a few drops of white vinegar.

- Or dip eyeglasses in a container holding water with a dash of white vinegar. Wipe the lenses dry with a soft lint free cloth.

- Wipe fingernails with cotton balls dipped in vinegar before putting on nail polish—the polish will last longer.

CHAPTER SEVEN

GOOD FOR YOU...
HOME REMEDIES

€€€€€€€

Respiratory Routs

- Mix up a cold reliever you can take by the tablespoon, six or eight times a day. Just stir 1/4 cup cider vinegar and 1/4 cup honey into a cup of warm water.

- Relieve a sore throat by gargling a solution of a teaspoon of vinegar in a glass of warm water, then swallowing.

- Or mix 2 tablespoons honey with 1 tablespoon cider vinegar. Put a small amount on a spoon and slowly suck the mixture off the spoon to soothe a sore throat.

- Cut mucus with a simple mixture of equal amounts of vinegar and honey, taken by the tablespoonful.

- Add 1/4 cup or more vinegar to the water in a vaporizer, when you use one in the bedroom of a cold, sore throat or cough sufferer.

- Try this recipe to soothe a cough: mix 1/2 cup cider vinegar, 1/2 cup water, 1 teaspoon cayenne pepper and 1/4 cup honey. Take a tablespoon at the first sign of a cough and another at bedtime.

- Or just down about 2 tablespoons undiluted cider vinegar. This works for some who cough when sinuses act up.

- Make your own cider cough drops to soothe a sore throat by following the recipe on page 85 and using apple cider vinegar.

Tummy Troubles

- Use a few spoonfuls of peppermint vinegar in a glass of warm water to calm an upset digestive system. Prepare the vinegar by putting a few leaves of peppermint in a small jar of cider vinegar and letting it sit for a few days to infuse. The addition of a few teaspoons of honey will make it easier to drink.

- Dispel gas pains with warm water to which you've added 1 teaspoon of honey and 1 teaspoon of cider vinegar.

- Try to stop a feeling of nausea by sipping on a simple

mixture of a couple of teaspoons of vinegar in a glass of water. Add a little honey for flavor, if you wish. Worth a try if you're experiencing morning sickness.

- Use honey and cider vinegar as a food topping (baked potatoes, cooked cabbage, etc.) if you don't enjoy it as a drink, or just to vary how you ingest it.

HOMEMADE CALCIUM SUPPLEMENT

Wash 3 to 4 raw eggs and then put them in a wide mouth glass jar or bowl and cover them with cider vinegar. Let these stand for 2 days or until the hard shell is dissolved. Remove the eggs (which are raw and can be used in an omelet or for cooking), stir and store the remaining liquid in a jar with a top. Take one tablespoon of the liquid a day with a glass of water as a calcium supplement.

Feet First—and Hands Too

- Get rid of foot odor by washing feet well with antiseptic soap daily, then soaking them in undiluted cider vinegar for 10 minutes or so. Remember that cotton socks aid odor control more effectively than wool ones.

- Try soaking your feet in a solution of equal parts vinegar and warm water to get rid of athlete's foot. Or you can spray it on full strength with the spray bottle you now keep in the bathroom. Over-the-counter medications are more costly and don't always work so this is worth a try.

- Toe nails fighting a fungus? It's said that soaking in undiluted vinegar may change skin ph, stopping a fungus growth.

- Try a vinegar soak *(half and half with water, or undiluted)* to cure a bacteria infection on hands. It's good for cuticles, too, and won't hurt artificial nails.

- Clean out a cut or infection by sprinkling some baking soda on the area, pouring vinegar over the baking soda and waiting until the bubbles subside. Then soak the area in warm water. The bubbles make it fun for kids.

- Dissolve warts, some claim, with a daily application of a solution of equal parts cider vinegar and glycerin.

- Help your hands if they are always moist from perspiration by spraying them for a few days with full strength white vinegar. Rub vinegar in after washing and drying your hands. It will act as an astringent. A scented vinegar can make this more pleasant.

Bugs, Bites and Burns

- Stop itching from insect stings and bites by dabbing them with a cotton ball saturated with undiluted vinegar or, perhaps easier, by using vinegar in a spray bottle.

- Or try a paste made of cornstarch moistened with vinegar.

- Treat stings from contact with ocean jelly fish—whether in the water or on the beach—with a spray of white vinegar.

- Relieve poison ivy itching and other rashes with a mixture of apple cider vinegar and water. Pat it on and let it dry.

- Soothe sunburn with a spray of white vinegar, repeating as often as you like. Ice-cold vinegar will feel even better, and some say it will prevent blistering and peeling.

- Cover severe sunburn with a towel soaked in a vinegar-water mixture.

- Treat jelly fish stings immediately with a dousing of white vinegar. It may inactivate the venom.

Getting Personal

- Try vinegar baths (just a cup or two of vinegar to a tub of water) to clear up sensitive skin that breaks out easily and to cure yeast infections in both women and girls.

- Or use water and vinegar directly on a yeast infection. A tablespoon or more of white vinegar to a quart of warm water used twice daily, may work to cure the problem.

- Splash some vinegar on facial blemishes and acne after washing and let it air dry.

- Consider trying vinegar on hemorrhoids to ease itching and burning. Dab it on with a cotton ball, full-strength or, if it stings, diluted.

- Use warm vinegar on hair when dealing with head lice or an itchy scalp.

- Soak a hairbrush clean in a vinegar solution to get it really clean.

So They Say...

- Drink a solution of a teaspoon of vinegar in a cup of water to stop hiccups.

- Try what some people swear assists weight loss. Mix 1 tablespoon each apple cider vinegar and honey into a glass of unsweetened grapefruit juice, and drink one glass before each meal to help suppress appetite.

- Or use plain water as a mix instead of the grapefruit juice. It's said this gives you an allover feeling of well being and good health.

- Protect your face from windburn and windchill by applying a light layer from a mixture of olive oil thinned with a bit of cider vinegar. Rub it on exposed areas.

- Consider this folk recipe to relieve the pain of arthritis. Three times a day take a mixture of 1 teaspoon each apple cider vinegar and honey. Can't hurt, might help, as some people have said it does.

- To eliminate the "thrush" coating in the mouth that antibiotics sometimes cause, try a solution of 4 tablespoons cider vinegar to a quart of water. Drink at least 4 glasses a day. Or rinse your mouth several times a day with a solution of half cider vinegar and warm water.

- Make a mouthwash to relieve tooth pain, using equal parts vinegar and salt, some say.

- Drinking some cider vinegar and water each day may reduce chances of bladder infections. It may help keep the proper acidity level in your urinary tract.

- Get relief from leg cramps at night, some believe, by drinking a glass of water with a few spoonfuls of cider vinegar before going to bed.

- Prevent "swimmer's ear" by killing bacteria and fungus in the outer ear canals. Mix equal parts of vinegar and rubbing alcohol and put 2 drops in each ear after every swimming session. Let each ear drain after a minute. This can kill the bacteria that maybe present in any water left in the ear.

- Many people use vinegar as an antiseptic for cuts and scrapes.

KEEP IN MIND

If you are sensitive to sulfites, be sure to read the vinegar label on the bottle, especially with specialty vinegars. You'll want to see if your vinegar of choice is sulfite-free.

CHAPTER EIGHT

HANDY DANDY HELP

€€€€€€€

Around the Yard

- Give acid loving plants like azaleas, rhododendrons, hydrangeas and gardenias a little help by watering them with a vinegar solution now and again. A cup of vinegar to a gallon of tap water is a good mixture.

- Neutralize lime used in the garden by washing your hands with vinegar to avoid rough, flaking skin, and to disinfect small cuts and scratches from gardening as well.

- Kill weeds and grass growing in unwanted places by pouring full strength white vinegar on them. This works especially well in crevices and cracks of walkways and driveways.

- Pour vinegar wherever you don't want ants to congregate, around the pool, for example, or on patio furniture.

- And use it to discourage cats from getting into the kids' sandbox.

- Preserve cut flowers and liven droopy ones by adding 2 tablespoons vinegar and 1 teaspoon sugar to a quart of water in the containers.

- Get rid of the water line in a flower vase by filling it with a solution of half water and half vinegar or by soaking a paper towel in vinegar and stuffing it into the vase so that it is in contact with the water line.

- Clean out stains and white mineral crusts in clay, glazed and plastic pots by soaking them for an hour or longer in a sink filled with solution of 1/2 water and 1/2 vinegar.

- Remove those crusty rim deposits on house planters (turn them upside down) or attached saucers by soaking them in an inch of full strength vinegar for several hours.

- Spray or splash some white vinegar on trash bags left outside that don't fit into trash cans. It will keep outdoor critters away from the trash bags.

Auto Ought-to's
- Keep the car windows frost-free overnight in winter by coating them with a solution of 3 parts white vinegar to 1 part water.

- Rid the windshield wipers of road grime by wiping them with a vinegar-soaked cloth.

- Polish car chrome with full-strength vinegar on a soft cloth.

- Remove unwanted decals and bumper stickers by covering them with a cloth soaked in vinegar, or by repeatedly spraying them with full strength vinegar. They should peel off in a couple of hours.

- Remove the left-over odor after a rider has been carsick by closing up the car overnight with a bowl of vinegar on the floor.

- Wipe clean vinyl upholstery with a cloth dampened in a solution of half vinegar and half water.

Decorating Dos

- Remove wallpaper by wetting it thoroughly with a mixture of equal parts vinegar and hot water, either spraying it on or applying it with a well-soaked roller. Let it set for a few minutes, then peel or scrape it off. Finish with a vinegar wipe to remove glue, then rinse well.

- Apply heated vinegar to dried paint on glass. Give it a chance to soften before scraping it off with a razor-edged tool.

- Keep plaster from drying too fast as you work by adding a tablespoon of vinegar to the water as you mix it.

FAUX PAINTING AND GRAINING
WITH VINEGAR PAINT

You can decorate finished or unfinished wooden pieces with a wood grain pattern from boxes to picture frames to furniture using a method a hundred or more years old—*vinegar painting*. First prepare the surface by applying a primer, if necessary. Then paint one or two coats of your base color in an oil-based enamel and let it dry well.

Start your vinegar paint with 1/2 cup white or cider vinegar and 1 teaspoon sugar, being sure the sugar is dissolved. (Some decorators also recommend adding a squeeze of clear liquid detergent to the paint.) Put about 2 tablespoons dry powder tempera paint (*2 parts liquid to 1 part paint pigment*) in a separate, clean container and add the vinegar solution slowly mixing it to a smooth paste and until you have a syrupy consistency.

Now use a texturizing tool to create the finish you desire: a graining comb or roller, a sponge, crumpled rags, paper toweling, a feather, or one of various kinds of special artists' brushes.

This kind of painting is great for the novice because the paint won't dry for 10 to 15 minutes and mistakes can be erased by wiping the surface with a rag moistened with distilled vinegar. Applying coats of different colored vinegar paints, one atop another, and using different patterns for each can offer interesting effects. After the paint is completely dry, apply a top coat of varnish or polyurethane. Step back and admire!

- Be aware that you can correct the ph imbalance of the alkali in plaster (or clay, for that matter) by first washing your hands with soap and water, then rinsing them with a solution of equal parts white vinegar and water.

- Make paint adhere better to a metal surface by cleaning the item well, then wiping it down with full strength vinegar. Let it dry completely before painting.

- Use full strength vinegar on a rag to clean old concrete before painting. Let it air dry.

- Make a great stain for wood by mixing white vinegar with a water-based ink of the desired color, adding ink carefully to get the exact shade you want. Apply with a brush or rag and let dry. You'll find that the wood warps very little, if at all.

- Clean hardened paint brushes by simmering them in a pot with vinegar. Soak them first for an hour before bringing the vinegar to a simmer. Drain and rinse clean. Repeat if necessary, but only for a short time, so hairs won't be loosened from the brushes.

- Minimize paint odors by keeping a few shallow dishes or bowls of vinegar in the painted area. The vinegar will absorb the paint odors.

Handy Odds and Ends

- Get rid of rust on spigots, tools, screws or bolts by soaking the items in undiluted vinegar overnight or even for several days.

- Be aware that vinegar will also soften wood glue. Apply the vinegar in a small oil can or with a sponge or rag and let sit until the bond weakens.

- Tighten the cane in a sagging chair seat by sponging it with a heated solution of half-and-half vinegar and water. Dry the chair in the sun.

- Make inexpensive clear glue for fabrics and leather by first melting on the stove a packet of plain gelatin in 3 or 4 tablespoons water and adding 3 tablespoons white vinegar and 1 teaspoon glycerin. Mix well and apply warm. The mixture can be reheated for future applications.

- Remove mud and stains from plastic, fiberglass or aluminum sports equipment by applying a paste of 1 part vinegar to 3 parts baking soda. Wipe off with soapy water and rinse with clear water.

- Cover up scratches in wood by adding iodine to undiluted vinegar until the desired color is reached and applying it with a small brush.

- Clean up your grill by spritzing white vinegar over wadded-up aluminum foil and scrubbing the grill vigorously with it.

- Deal with mold! Use full strength vinegar on heavy mildew stains or surfaces where you can't—or don't want to—use bleach.

Hint for Hunters
- Wash skinned game (deer, elk, etc.) with a solution of half water, half vinegar. It modifies the gamey taste and helps removes debris often left by water. It also deters insects.

CHAPTER NINE

KID STUFF

€€€€€€€

Cleanups

- Fill glass baby bottles with hot water and vinegar (half and half) for at least an hour. Scrub with a bottle brush. This should remove all film left from formula or milk.

- Add a good-sized splash of white vinegar to soapy water both to clean and to disinfect baby toys.

- Get rid of dirt on plastic dolls by wiping them with full-strength vinegar.

- Spray vinyl baby books or board books with vinegar and wipe clean with a damp sponge or cloth.

- Soak dirty doll clothes in a solution of 1 quart warm water, 2 tablespoons baking soda and 3 tablespoons vinegar. Rinse with plain warm water and spread out or hang to dry.

- Cleanup tricycles, pedal cars and other outside toys with a solution of equal parts water and white vinegar. Sprinkle baking soda on badly soiled spots, let sit for an hour or so and scrub. Rinse with plain water.

- Clean scissors that have become sticky (from cutting tape, for instance) with a cloth dipped in undiluted white vinegar.

- Get crayon stains out of clothing by rubbing them with an old toothbrush dipped in vinegar. Then launder as usual.

- Clean and deodorize urine on a mattress with a vinegar and water solution. Then sprinkle the area with baking soda and let the area dry. Brush or vacuum the residue after it is dry to the touch.

Enhancements

- Shine up pennies to a fare-thee-well by soaking them for a couple of hours or overnight in a glass or ceramic bowl of undiluted vinegar. Bring the vinegar to a boil first to speed up the process, and if pennies are very dirty, let the kids polish them further on a flat surface with an old tooth-brush dipped in the vinegar.

- Get just the colors you want in Easter eggs by dying them

in a solution of 3 cups boiling hot water, 2 tablespoons vinegar and your food coloring. Re-dip to get the depth of color desired.

Quick Tricks

- Make the leg or thigh bone of a chicken bend like rubber. Just soak it in a glass of undiluted vinegar for about three days.

- Astonish others by making a plain, raw egg bounce without breaking. Just let it sit in a bowl of vinegar for two days, rinse it off and bounce away. (The egg is still raw so confine it to "safe" bouncing areas.) Then use the raw egg for cooking.

- Set small, light objects such as buttons or uncooked pasta pieces bouncing in a clear container of a solution of a cup of water, 1/2 cup vinegar and 3 teaspoons baking soda. The items sink at first so be patient. (*Mothballs work beautifully, but use them only if children are old enough not to put them in their mouths. The same is true for buttons and pasta pieces.*) Add a few drops of food coloring to the solution for drama. Renew the solution with vinegar and baking soda as needed.

- Challenge anyone to extinguish the flame on a candle without blowing on it, touching it, covering it or letting it burn out on its own. The trick is to use a spouted glass measuring cup filled with 1/4 cup of white vinegar. Find a small cup or bowl that fits on the top of the measuring cup leaving only the spout exposed. Place a tablespoon of baking soda in the vinegar and cover quickly with the

glass or cup. Now hold the spout of the measuring cup next to the flame, tilting it a bit toward the flame and the flame will be extinguished. The carbon dioxide (CO_2) gas produced by the vinegar and baking soda pushes the oxygen away from the flame. Oxygen is needed for the flame to burn.

For Young Scientists

- Try this magical way of inflating a balloon. First, stretch the balloon a few times to make it more pliable. Then put 2 teaspoons baking soda into an empty soda bottle, using a funnel. Clean the funnel and use it to pour 1/3 cup vinegar into the balloon. Carefully stretch the neck of a balloon over the mouth of the bottle and pull it down an inch. *(The liquid in the balloon hangs to one side.)* While holding the neck of the balloon around the neck of the bottle, lift up the balloon to empty the vinegar into the bottle. The reaction between the vinegar and the baking soda will cause fizzing and produce carbon dioxide gas and inflate the balloon. The balloon will also feel warm from the heat/energy produced by the chemical reaction.

- Make your own "volcano." Fill a small coffee cup, custard cup or empty yogurt container 1/3 to 1/2 full with vinegar. Cut a 4-inch square piece of tissue or paper towel and place 1 teaspoon baking soda in it. Pull the four corners together and twist the "package" shut. Drop it into the vinegar and watch the reaction! *(Hint: the hotter the vinegar, the faster reaction you get.)* Try filling one container with hot vinegar and another with cold, to see different reaction times. The explanation is that particles move faster at higher temperatures.

- Or create a "volcano" in the sandbox. Set a small glass or cup filled with vinegar in a "sand-made" mountain. Add 1 tablespoon baking soda and stand back!

- Make a beautiful crystal garden in a matter of days. Cut a sponge to fit the bottom of a shallow dish or other container. Boil 1 cup water and add 1/4 cup coarse (or kosher) salt to it very slowly, stirring well after each addition. Then add 2 teaspoons vinegar, stirring well. Pour the solution over the sponge (and any undissolved salt on the sponge) and let the liquid just cover the bottom of the dish. Save the extra liquid, adding more to the dish when the liquid evaporates. After a few days, crystals will begin to grow and spread. If you add bluing or food coloring to the solution or pour either on the sponge, the crystals will take on the color.

Make Your Own Hard Candy

Ingredients:

2 tablespoons butter   2 cups sugar
1/2 cup seasoned rice vinegar or any other vinegar

Melt the butter in a medium-size sauce pan on medium to high heat. Add the sugar and vinegar. Stir continuously. Wash down the top inside of the pan with a pastry brush dipped in cold water to keep the mixture from adhering to the side of the pan.

Boil this mixture on high heat for 5 to 10 minutes. It will thicken and may look whitish. Remove from the heat and pour or spoon the mixture on to large pieces of oiled aluminum foil.

As it cools you can pull it as taffy with oiled fingers, or just let it cool and harden. When brittle, break into small pieces and store in small plastic bags.

CHAPTER TEN

BEST FOR PETS

€€€€€€€

Cats and Dogs

- Spray or rub a solution of 1 cup vinegar to 1 quart water on the coat of a dog and be rewarded with a gleaming coat. As a bonus, you save the cost of an expensive shine product used on show animals. *(Works even on a horse!)*

- Try a little stronger solution, 1 part cider vinegar to 3 parts water, as a rinse after your dog's bath, and you may well rid the dog of chronic skin infections or at least control them to a degree.

- Keep a dog from scratching its ears by wiping them out regularly with a soft cloth dipped in undiluted vinegar.

- Treat a real ear infection with 8 to 10 drops of undiluted vinegar from a dropper. Hold the animal's head to the side, letting the vinegar stand in the ear for a few minutes, gently massaging the area around the ear, and drain. If the infection is still present after three daily applications, it's best to see a veterinarian.

- Add a little vinegar to your pet's drinking water. It's said that fleas will be gone and mange will be a problem of the past.

- No tomato juice on hand when your pet and a skunk tangle? Try wiping down the animal with a 50-50 solution of vinegar and water, followed by a plain-water rinse, and the odor should be gone. Repeat if necessary.

- Discourage a cat from sitting on a certain windowsill or other surface, or from scratching upholstery, by spraying vinegar on the item. Of course, check first on an unnoticeable area to be sure there won't be a discoloration.

- Keep a cat out of a garden area by placing paper, a cloth or sponge there that has been soaked in white vinegar.

Pet Cleanups
- Treat animal urine stains on carpeting as soon as possible. Blot up all liquid, then flush the area a few times with plain water, blotting after each. Finally, flush with a solution of equal parts water and vinegar. Rinse and let dry.

- Clean out pets' outdoor water containers and the birdbath by scrubbing them often with straight white vinegar. Rinse well.

- Get rid of the deposits and water lines that form in aquariums and fish bowls by wiping them down with vinegar and following with a good rinse. For stubborn deposits, soak for several hours or overnight.

€€€€€€€

Guidelines for Storing Vinegar

Vinegar lasts a long time. The Vinegar Institute
(www.versatilevinegar.org) believes that the shelf life is almost
indefinite. Because of its acid nature, vinegar is self-preserving
and does not need refrigeration.

Still, the shelf life of a product depends on a number of
factors, such as storage time, temperature, age and the container. Commerical bottles of vinegar often have "use by" or
"best if sold by" dates on them. Take a minute to read bottle
labels. There is good information to be found.

For storing unopened jars of vinegar of H.J. Heinz products,
they suggest these guidelines:

apple cider vinegar	18 months
malt vinegar	24 months
tarragon vinegar	30 months
distilled white vinegar	42 months

To read manufacturing codes on H.J.Heinz bottles:
  old form: if the product code is VF0401
       VF — specifies production location
       040— represents the day (40th) of production (Feb 9)
       1   — represents the year of production (2001)
  new form: if the product code is FR2E06
       FR — specifies production location
       2   — represents the year of production (2002)
       E   — represents the month produced (A=January, etc)
       06 — represents the day of the month

Other books on vinegar:

Antol, Marie Nadine, THE INCREDIBLE SECRETS OF VINEGAR (Avery/Penquin Putnam, 1999)

Chiarella, Michael, FLAVORED VINEGARS: *50 Recipes for Cooking with Infused Vinegars* (Chronicle Books, 1996)

Diggs, Lawrence, VINEGAR: The User-Friendly Standard Text Reference and Guide (iUniverse.com, 1989, 2000)

Halm, Meesha, THE BALSAMIC VINEGAR COOKBOOK (HarperCollins, 1997)

Johns, Pamela Sheldon, BALSAMICO: *A Balsamic Vinegar Cookbook* (Ten Speed Press, 1999)

Johnson, Marsha P., GOURMET VINEGARS: *The How-To's of Making and Cooking with Vinegar* (Sibyl, Publications, 800-240-8566)

Mindell, PH.D., Dr. Earl, AMAZING APPLE CIDER VINEGAR (Contemporary Books, 2002)

Moore, Melodie, VIM & VINEGAR (HarperPerennial, 1997)

Oberbeil, Klaus, LOSE WEIGHT WITH APPLE VINEGAR (Magni Co., 1998)

Orey, Cal, THE HEALING POWERS OF VINEGAR (Kensington Books, 2000)

Oster, Maggie, HERBAL VINEGAR (Storey Books, 1994)

Thacker, Emily, THE VINEGAR BOOK (Tresco Publishers, 1994)

Quillin, Patrick, HONEY, GARLIC & VINEGAR HOME REMEDIES (Leader Company, 1996)

Some producers of consumer vinegar products:

H.J. Heinz Company
357 6th Ave
Pittsburgh, PA 15222
800-255-5750
www.heinz.com

Nakano Foods Inc. *(Nakano, Four Monks, Barengo, Mitsukan, Nature's Intent Organic)*
55 East Euclid Ave #300
Mt. Prospect, IL 60056
800-323-4358
www.nakanovinegar.com

Fleischmann's Vinegar Company, Inc.
(division of Burns Philp Foods)
14722 Anson Ave
Sante Fe Springs, CA 90670
800-443-1067 *(in Canada 800-463-6391)*
www.fleischmannswvinegar.com

Alessi/Vigo Importing *(balsamics from Italy)*
4701 W. Comanche Ave
Tampa, FL 33614
813-884-3491
www.vigoalessi.com

The vinegar trade association:

The Vinegar Institute
Bldg G, Suite 500
5775 Peachtree-Dunwoody Rd
Atlanta, GA 30342
404-252-3663
www.versatilevinegar.org
(post your vinegar tip on their site in the Guest Book)

CONVERSION TABLES

Approximate Equivalents

1 quart	= about 1 liter
1 stick of butter	= 8 tablespoons or 4 oz or 1/2 cup
1 cup sugar	= 7 ounces

3 teaspoons	= 1 tablespoon (15 mL)
4 tablespoons	= 1/4 cup (about 50 mL)
16 tablespoons	= 1 cup (about 250 mL)
2 cups	= 1 pint (about 500 mL)
4 cups *(2 pints)*	= 1 quart (about 1 L)
4 quarts *(liquid)*	= 1 gallon (about 4 L)

Conversion Formulas:

ounces to grams: Multiply the ounce figure by 28.35 to get the number of grams

grams to ounces: Multiply the gram figure by .0353 to get the number of ounces

cups to liters: Multiply the cup figure by .24 to get the number of liters
ounces to milliliters: Multiply ounce figure by 29.57 to get number of milliliters

Fahrenheit to Celsius: Subtract 32 from the Fahrenheit figure, multiply by 5 then divide by 9 to get Celsius
Celsius to Fahrenheit: Multiply the Celsius figure by 9, divide by 5, then add 32 to get Fahrenheit

300 °F	= 128.8 °C
350 °F	= 177 ° C
400 °F	= 204.4 °C

Index